PATTERNS 2020

The Twelfth International Conferences on Pervasive Patterns and Applications

October 25 - 29, 2020

PATTERNS 2020 Editors

Herwig Mannaert, University of Antwerp, Belgium
Ida Pu, Goldsmiths College, University of London, UK
Jacqueline Daykin, Aberystwyth University, UK

Printed from e-media with permission by:

Curran Associates, Inc.
57 Morehouse Lane
Red Hook, NY 12571

Some format issues inherent in the e-media version may also appear in this print version.

Printed with permission by Curran Associates, Inc. (2020)

International Academy, Research, and Industry Association (IARIA)
412 Derby Way
Wilmington, DE 19810

Phone: (408) 893-6407
Fax: (408) 527-6351

petre@iaria.org

Additional copies of this publication are available from:

Curran Associates, Inc.
57 Morehouse Lane
Red Hook, NY 12571 USA
Phone: 845-758-0400
Fax: 845-758-2633
Email: curran@proceedings.com
Web: www.proceedings.com

Table of Contents

PATTERNS 2020

Forward

The Twelfth International Conferences on Pervasive Patterns and Applications (PATTERNS 2020), held on October 25 - 29, 2020, continued a series of events targeting the application of advanced patterns, at-large. In addition to support for patterns and pattern processing, special categories of patterns covering ubiquity, software, security, communications, discovery and decision were considered. It is believed that patterns play an important role on cognition, automation, and service computation and orchestration areas. Antipatterns come as a normal output as needed lessons learned.

The conference had the following tracks:

- Patterns basics
- Patterns at work
- Discovery and decision patterns

Similar to the previous edition, this event attracted excellent contributions and active participation from all over the world. We were very pleased to receive top quality contributions.

We take here the opportunity to warmly thank all the members of the PATTERNS 2020 technical program committee, as well as the numerous reviewers. The creation of such a high quality conference program would not have been possible without their involvement. We also kindly thank all the authors that dedicated much of their time and effort to contribute to PATTERNS 2020. We truly believe that, thanks to all these efforts, the final conference program consisted of top quality contributions.

Also, this event could not have been a reality without the support of many individuals, organizations and sponsors. We also gratefully thank the members of the PATTERNS 2020 organizing committee for their help in handling the logistics and for their work that made this professional meeting a success.

We hope PATTERNS 2020 was a successful international forum for the exchange of ideas and results between academia and industry and to promote further progress in the area of pervasive patterns and applications.

PATTERNS 2020 Steering Committee

Herwig Manaert, University of Antwerp, Belgium
Wladyslaw Homenda, Warsaw University of Technology, Poland
Patrick Siarry, Université Paris-Est Créteil, France
Yuji Iwahori, Chubu University, Japan
Alexander Mirnig, University of Salzburg, Austria
Adel Al-Jumaily, University of Technology, Australia
George A. Papakostas, International Hellenic University – Kavala, Greece

PATTERNS 2020 Publicity Chair

Javier Rocher, Universitat Politecnica de Valencia, Spain

PATTERNS 2020 Industry/Research Advisory Committee

Christian Kohls, TH Köln, Germany

PATTERNS 2020

Committee

PATTERNS 2020 Steering Committee

Herwig Manaert, University of Antwerp, Belgium
Wladyslaw Homenda, Warsaw University of Technology, Poland
Patrick Siarry, Université Paris-Est Créteil, France
Yuji Iwahori, Chubu University, Japan
Alexander Mirnig, University of Salzburg, Austria
Adel Al-Jumaily, University of Technology, Australia
George A. Papakostas, International Hellenic University – Kavala, Greece

PATTERNS 2020 Publicity Chair

Javier Rocher, Universitat Politecnica de Valencia, Spain

PATTERNS 2020 Industry/Research Advisory Committee

Christian Kohls, TH Köln, Germany

PATTERNS 2020 Technical Program Committee

Andrea F. Abate, University of Salerno, Italy
Akshay Agarwal, IIIT Delhi, India
Adel Al-Jumaily, University of Technology, Australia
Ali Reza Alaei, School of Business and Tourism, Australia
Sidnei Alves De Araujo, Nove de Julho University (UNINOVE), Sao Paulo, Brazil
Danilo Avola, Sapienza University of Rome, Italy
Johanna Barzen, University of Stuttgart, Germany
Nadjia Benblidia, Saad Dahlab University - Blida1, Algeria
Anna Berlino, Consultant in Tourism Sciences and Valorization of Cultural and Tourism Systems, Italy
Uwe Breitenbücher, IAAS - University of Stuttgart, Germany
Jean-Christophe Burie, L3i laboratory | La Rochelle University, France
Simone Cammarasana, CNR - IMATI,Genova, Italy
David Cárdenas-Peña, Universidad Tecnológica de Pereira, Colombia
Bidyut B. Chaudhuri, Indian Statistical Institute, India
Sneha Chaudhari, AI Organization | LinkedIn, USA
Diego Collazos, Universidad Nacional de Colombia sede Manizales, Colombia
Sergio Cruces, University of Seville, Spain
Mohamed Daoudi, Institut Mines-Telecom / Telecom Lille, France
Jacqueline Daykin, King's College London, UK / Aberystwyth University, Wales & Mauritius
Moussa Diaf, Mouloud Mammeri University, Algeria

Chawki Djeddi, Université de Tébessa, Algeria
Ole Kristian Ekseth, NTNU & Eltorque, Norway
Carlos Alexandre Ferreira, INESC TEC, Portugal
Markus Goldstein, Ulm University of Applied Sciences, Germany
Geert Haerens, Engie, Belgium
Jean Hennebert, University of Applied Sciences HES-SO, Fribourg, Switzerland
Wladyslaw Homenda, Warsaw University of Technology, Poland
Tzung-Pei Hong, National University of Kaohsiung, Taiwan
Wei-Chiang Hong, School of Computer Science and Technology - Jiangsu Normal University, China
Yuji Iwahori, Chubu University, Japan
Agnieszka Jastrzebska, Warsaw University of Technology, Poland
Maria João Ferreira, Universidade Portucalense, Portugal
Hassan A. Karimi, University of Pittsburgh, USA
Christian Kohls, TH Köln, Germany
Vasileios Komianos, Ionian University, Corfu, Greece
Sylwia Kopczynska, Poznan University of Technology, Poland
Fritz Laux, Reutlingen University, Germany
Reynolds León Guerra, Advanced Technologies Application Center (CENATAV), Havana, Cuba
Frank Leymann, UniversityofStuttgart, Germany
Josep Lladós, Computer Vision Center - Universitat Autònoma de Barcelona, Spain
Himadri Majumder, G. H. Raisoni College of Engineering and Management, Pune, India
Herwig Mannaert, University of Antwerp, Belgium
Ana Maria Mendonça, University of Porto / INESC TEC - INESC Technology and Science, Portugal
Pierre-Francois Marteau, IRISA / Université Bretagne Sud, France
Abdelkrim Meziane, Research Center on Scientific and Technical Information - CERIST, Algeria
Alexander Mirnig, University of Salzburg, Austria
Fernando Moreira, Universidade Portucalense, Portugal
Gyu Myoung Lee, Liverpool John Moores University, UK
Dinh-Luan Nguyen, Michigan State University, USA
Krzysztof Okarma, West Pomeranian University of Technology, Szczecin, Poland
Reynier Ortega Bueno, Center for Pattern Recognition and Data Mining - Universidad de Oriente / Cuban Association for Pattern Recognition, Cuba
Alessandro Ortis, University of Catania, Italy
George A. Papakostas, International Hellenic University - Kavala, Greece
Maria Antonietta Pascali, CNR - Institute of Clinical Physiology, Italy
Giuseppe Patane', CNR-IMATI, Italy
Dietrich Paulus, Universität Koblenz - Landau, Germany
Agostino Poggi, University of Parma, Italy
Vinay Pondenkandath, University of Fribourg, Switzerland
Claudia Raibulet, University of Milano-Bicocca, Italy
Giuliana Ramella, CNR - National Research Council, Italy
Aurora Ramirez, University of Córdoba, Spain
Theresa-Marie Rhyne, Independent Visualization Consultant, USA
Alessandro Rizzi, Università degli Studi di Milano, Italy
Gustavo Rossi, UNLP, Argentina
Sangita Roy, Thapar Institute of Engineering and Technology, India
María-Isabel Sanchez-Segura, Carlos III University of Madrid, Spain
Muhammad Sarfraz, Kuwait University, Kuwait

Friedhelm Schwenker, Ulm University, Germany
Giuseppe Serra, University of Udine, Italy
Isabel Seruca, Portucalense University, Porto, Portugal
Abhishek Sharma, Rush University Medical Center, USA
Kaushik Das Sharma, University of Calcutta, India
Diksha Shukla, University of Wyoming, USA
Patrick Siarry, Université Paris-Est Créteil, France
Shanyu Tang, University of West London, UK
J. A. Tenreiro Machado, Polytechnic of Porto, Portugal
Hiroyasu Usami, Chubu University, Japan
Stella Vetova, Technical University of Sofia, Bulgaria
Panagiotis Vlamos, Ionian University, Greece
Huiling Wang, Tampere University, Finland
Hazem Wannous, UniversityofLille | IMT Lille Douai, France
Ester Zumpano, University of Calabria, Italy

Copyright Information

Diffusion Patterns of Social Network Posts

Alexander Gubanov
Yuliya Mundrievskaya

Center of Applied Big Data Analysis
Tomsk State University
Email: derzhiarbuz@yandex.ru
muo@data.tsu.ru

Ida M. Pu

Department of Computing
Goldsmiths, University of London, UK
Email: idapuone@gmail.com

***Abstract*—Social network posts as an efficient means of communication directly reflect users' interests and engagements. Despite challenges there are strong interests in understanding how social network posts efficiently spread information. In this article some diffusion patterns of social network posts are explored. The information spreading via post chains based on partial data of popular social network is studied to gain insights of the problem of information diffusion. Mathematical models for information cascades are proposed and future research directions are discussed.**

Keywords–information diffusion; posts; reposts; walls; social networks; social media; probability; mathematical modelling

I. Introduction

Social networks are real world systems where people (referred to as *actors*) interact with each other. Actors are represented as nodes of the network, and their interactions are represented as ties between them. Social networks appear in forms of social networking websites (*online platforms*) maintained by serving institutions (*services*), such as Facebook, Twitter, Telegram, etc. In this paper, we focus on diffusion issues of posts of messages based on the data from the on-line social network "Vkontakte".

The "Vkontakte" [1] is one of the largest social networks on the previous-soviet space with 80-100 millions visitors daily. Nodes of the network represent users (individuals or groups), and ties can be a mutual (undirected) link, such as friendship or/and directed link, such as subscribing. Users exchange information by means of private *messages* or/and public *posts*. Posts are publications in texts or/and multimedia (images, sound and videos) on webpages. Recurrent posts are referred to as *reposts* of the original post, and the dedicated display areas for posts are referred to as *walls*. Figure 1 shows a screenshot as an example of the wall and users' posts on the Vkontakte site.

Posts on the wall are also queued in a *newsfeed* (*poster*) and become visible on devices of subscribed users (users for short hereafter). Any post can be reposted by other users, and appears on their walls and in newsfeeds of subscribers (as friends or/and followers). With such iterative processes, multiple chains of posts are formed and information is spread like epidemic.

As a social media website, users can also interact with each other via the platform. They can, for example, leave comments on posts, vote for the favourite, exchange dialogues, etc. At the backend of the website, the notions of walls, posts and newsfeeds are evolved as self-sufficient software agents

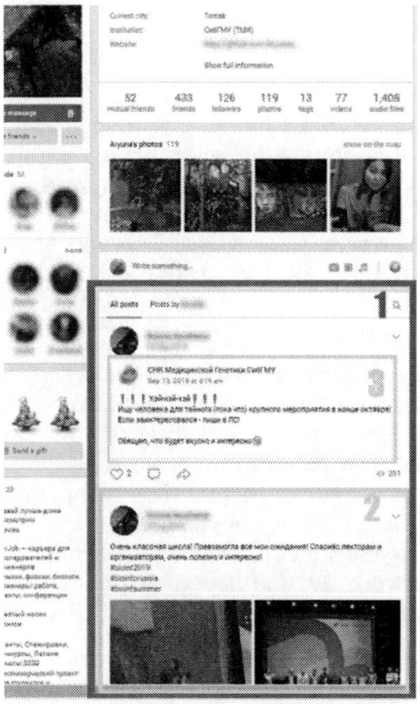

Figure 1. An example of the wall and posts (1:wall, 2:post, and 3:repost)

empowered by technologies allowing communications across different platforms.

Posts, as an efficient means of communication, reflect users' interests and engagements directly. Few businesses do not want to understand them. Despite challenges there are strong interests in understanding how posts spread information. In this article, we model the spread of the posts based on the data of this social network in order to help eventually answer interesting questions, such as the followings:

1) Why do people spread a piece of information? Is it because they like a given piece of news or is it because they just intend to be similar to their social surroundings?
2) How can we classify a piece of information by its spreading behaviour? Can we decouple properties of information from the properties of network?
3) How can we classify people by their contribution in information spreading? For example, how can we find someone whose role in information spreading is significantly different from the average (e.g., opinion leaders, non-conformists, information brokers, etc.)?

To answer these questions, different approaches are considered. The use of network information can vary in existing work. Some approaches discard information about network structure ([2], [3]), some assume that links are unobserved or irrelevant and should be reconstructed ([4], [5]), or is assumed to be correct and fully observable ([6], [7]). Influence of social conformism (or social pressure), is firstly covered by threshold models [8] then accounted in several models [7]. The modelling techniques are also vary: there are machine learning approaches, such as [3], statistical [9], probabilistic ([7], [4]), and game theoretic models [10], etc. Also the roles of different nodes in information spreading (especially opinion leaders) are often studied by analysis of network structure and topic content analysis ([11]–[12]).

Despite efforts, we could not find an approach that can be applied directly to solve our research problems which tend to be more localised in nature, practical and richer in social contexts. Most of the known approaches are useful to predict wide information epidemics on explicit, simple and large networks, such as Twitter, but not readily for Vkontakte. In case of local information (for example, the significant events in a city of average size) the social network can be small (about a hundred of reposts for one post), the number of data can be insufficient and the observed ties in the network can be incomplete or not perfectly relevant.

Known statistical and mean-field approximation approaches, commonly used for prediction of epidemic outbreaks, are not useful here, because the specific of local information can be subjective and exclusive, e.g. interesting only a certain group of people. The assumption that N (number of nodes) is infinite is not applicable for a local cluster. The common assumption of an average infection rate for everyone in the network and the impact of the node depending only on its network characteristics (degree, centrality, etc.) is also wrong in practical settings.

Social contexts are over simplified in models. For example, high degree nodes do not necessarily mean richer information sources. Nodes (users) can be faked by bots and ties (friendships) can be commercialised, biased, or true friendships can be hidden from newsfeeds. Results handled well in some visual approaches may not necessarily be easily obtained in other probabilistic models.

Hence, it would be inappropriate to use a model assuming that the network is known and relevant (IC, SIR and so on). On the other hand, we cannot discard the network information since the amount of data we possess is relatively small. For small datasets, machine learning approaches are not very useful.

Finally, the real local cascade usually has a group of completely isolated nodes (i.e., that are disconnected from any other nodes) in the cascade, and we should assume that they got the information through unobservable ties. Of course, we cannot discard them, neither. As we can see, after all, our small objects are not necessarily simple.

Our goal is to develop a sensitive tool for working with such type of information, that could give us insights to answer the interesting questions above.

The rest of the paper is arranged as follows. Section II briefly describes a model of information cascades. Section III explores the patterns of information spreading using visualisation techniques. Section IV proposes a model of information diffusion. Section V provides the summary and directions of further development.

II. Information Cascade

Information cascade is a phenomenon in which a number of actors make same decisions in a sequential fashion. It is a two-step process in which a Yes-No decision is required by each actor whose decision can be influenced by others. Information cascades occur when the external information from previous participants overrides one's own private judgement.

In our model we assume the followings:

1) Each actor decides what to repost and whether or not to repost.
2) The limited action space is (repost, notrepost).
3) The actions of reposts are sequential in chronological order.
4) Each actor observes the reposts so far.
5) An actor cannot directly observe what other actors are in favour of but (s)he can infer that they like the posts enough if they repost it.

Our modelling is based on two parts: the underlying network of relations (the network) and information cascade (cascade) on this network.

A. Network

The nodes in our network model are identifiers of users and/or groups of users. The links/edges between nodes represent connections/relationships in social network, undirected for "friendship" and directed for "subscribing", corresponding to the model of undirected graph and digraph respectively.

It is impossible to model the entire social network in the real world because of its huge size and data availability. Hence, for a specific post we restrict the network by nodes that have made a repost or liked the post and their friends. Such a network is referred to as the *underlying network* (*network* for short) for specific information cascade.

To build the network we use the Vkontakte public Application Program Interface (API). Due to the privacy policy of Vkontakte that allows users to hide their information, about 30 percents of nodes are actually "hidden". It means that we do not know whether or not they have made a post. Also we do not know all incident links of them (but some links can be reconstructed from other nodes).

The network is modelled as a graph $G = \{U, E\}$, where U is a set of user node identifications (u_i) and E is a set of links (u_i, u_j) between a pair of nodes, where $i = 1, \cdots, N$ and $j = 1, \cdots, N$, and N is the number of nodes in the network. To distinguish a *user* and *group*, u_i can be positive or negative. The positive u_i is used to represent an user, and the negative u_i represents a group of users.

B. Cascade

The information cascade is a sequence of moments when post appeared on user's walls. It is defined as a sequence of the pairs $\{(u_i, t_i)\}_{1 \leq i \leq M}$, where u_i denotes a node from the network and t_i is a timestamp of the moment when repost (or original post) on the wall of this node is appeared. M is the total number of nodes that are "infected" by the information, i.e., that having the post on their wall. This data is also collected using the public Vkontakte API.

It is Vkontakte's policy, however, to forbid general public viewers from accessing any repost chain. Hence, we have no explicit information about information spreading path.

C. Spreading issues

Processes of information spreading are widely studied often using a Twitter social network as the source of experimental data. For every retweet (analog of repost in Vkontakte) it is known exactly, who retweeted whose tweets, so it is possible to build an explicit graph of information propagation. This graph is always a tree. Analysis results of such graphs are used to identify spreading parameters (for example, the intensity of "infection") and important nodes (opinion leaders). But this "exactness" also conceals one significant trait of how people spread the information. Sometimes people choose to manifest something due to its respectable source. Their decision of a repost (or retweet) may not necessarily be purely driven by their inner motives, but also by the apparent positive responses, such as the big number of surroundings who translate the same piece of information. It is a common behaviour involving opinions, social norms, and trusts, etc. [13].

We assume that the fact of repost (retweet) from some node does not mean that it is a merit of only this node. It can be the cumulative contribution of all nodes made the post which was seen by the reposting user before. It can not be substituted by defining individual infection rates or probabilities as ([14], [4]). However, some models [7] takes it into account. We do it also.

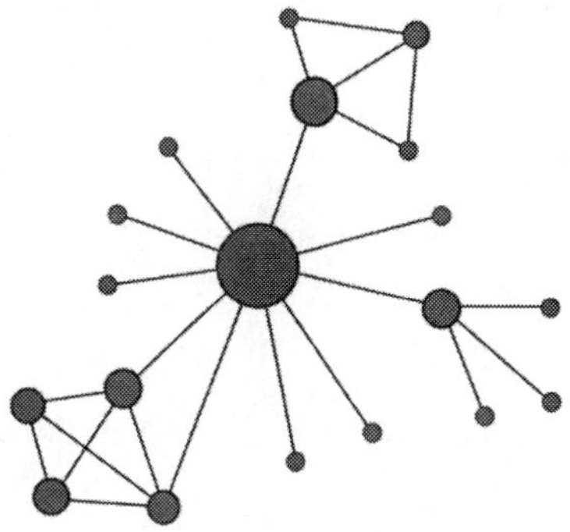

Figure 2. Underlying network

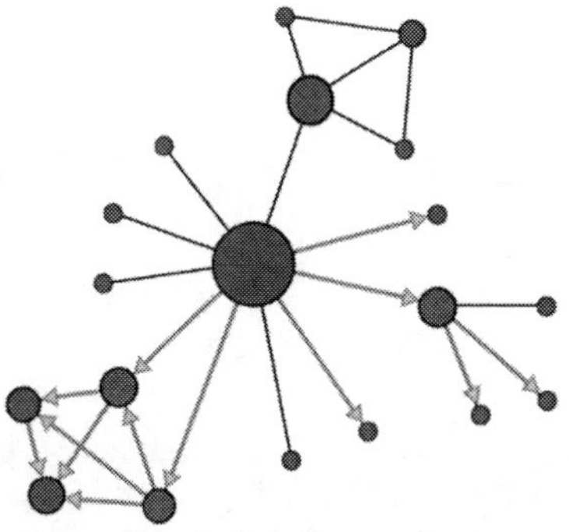

Figure 3. Green is a pattern of spreading

III. Pattern of Spreading

The first step in analysing the spreading of posts is visualisation of the pattern of spreading. This visual technique is useful for practice, also the patterns can be analysed using structural network analysis (measuring centrality, modularity, etc) which is widely covered by appropriate software (for example Gephi). As long as the pattern of spreading is directed aperiodic graph, some bibliometric techniques can also be used, for example main path analysis [Batagelj2014].

The pattern is a way to display the combination of information cascade and underlying network, so the researcher could see key properties of both to be able to make conclusions. It is acyclic oriented graph $G_p = \{U_p, E_p, D_p\}$ with weighted nodes where $U_p \subset U$ is a set of infected nodes (i.e., having a post or repost on their walls). There are M nodes in U_p. $E_p = \{(u_i, u_j) : (u_j, u_i) \in E : u_i \in U_p, u_j \in U_p, t_i < t_j\}$ is a set of ordered pairs of nodes from U_p, representing directed edges such that there is a link between u_j and u_i (in general it means u_j is a friend of or subscribed on u_i) in underlying network and u_i made the repost earlier than u_j. So the edge represents a potential act of information propagation, because u_j is able to see u_i's post in the newsfeed before it decides to make reposts. There is also $D_p = \{d_{u_i}\}_{1 \leq i \leq M}$, a set of weights for nodes, where d_{u_i} is the degree of u_i in underlying network. The example can be seen in Figure 2 and Figure 3.

Figure 4 shows the pattern of spreading of real posts. The size of the node is defined by its degree in underlying network (i.e., the number of neighbours the node could influence). The colour becomes darker as the number of outgoing edges on patterns increases (the darker it is in red, the more neighbours are actually influenced). Note that in this case we use only mutual links for users (Vkontakte is more friendship-style than subscriber-style network and the most of links between users are mutual/undirected). Hence, there is no need to define different in- and out- degrees in the underlying network.

In the figure, we can see the separate cluster of users (1), the nodes that seems to be information brokers or influencer in their cluster (like 2, which has not very high degree, but probably affected a lot of neighbours), the nodes that have no influence at all (3, it has high degree, but infects nobody). Also there is a group of isolated nodes (4) that means that they got the information through inobservable path (private messages or hidden users).

Although the patterns of spreading help researchers make hypotheses and explore intuitive solutions, mathematical models are necessary for rigorous analysis and prediction.

IV. Models of the Information Diffusion

On-line social networks are set up mainly for information diffusion. A number of widely used dynamic models are known as *infection models* (SI, SIR, SIS) [15] of social contagion. They are considered as good for describing diffusion of certain types of information, such as hot news, memos, rumours and in other situations when people become infected regardless his will.

Another type of information spreading model, known as the *threshold model*, describing a situation when each node

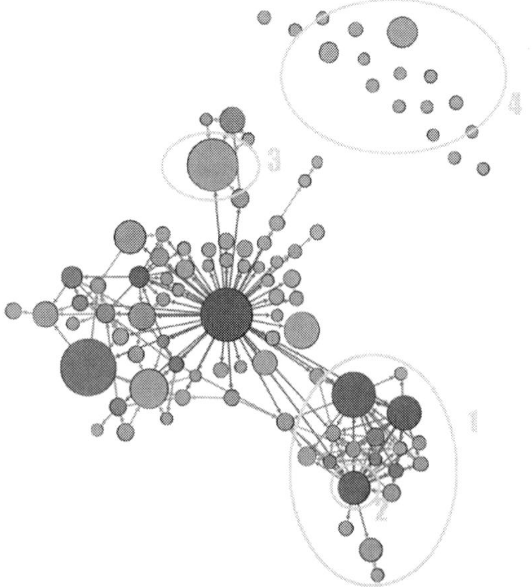

Figure 4. Pattern of spreading

makes a decision to spread the information based on social reinforcement (e.g. social norms or opinions) and susceptibility to information strongly depends on how many neighbours are infected. ([13], [8]).

We build our model as a development of probabilistic SI model for networks. For each edge between an infected and susceptible node, there is a probability of passing the infection during each small time interval Δt that is proportional to $\Delta t + o(\Delta t)$. Our goal is to define this probability.

The SI model is continuous and the time delay in the edge matters. It is interesting that there is a discussion about how important it is to take this delay into account. Some authors [3] insist that in real world social networks this delay is too noisy and it is better to discard it, while other authors [16] think that it is a very important measure and should be taken into consideration.

In our model we took into account the minimum amount of properties of the process that are crucial for its description. On one hand, we consider every data available and try to use the information about known connections between users also. On the other, we respect the fact that the information is not necessarily completely relevant. Some connections are hidden or inobservable.

A. Model parameters

The model has four parameters: namely, observed infection rate θ, *conformism* level (threshold) κ, decay (or obsolence, a kind of recovery rate analogue) δ and unobserved infection rate ρ.

The first is the infection rate θ. In classical network SI model the probability of susceptible $j'th$ node to be infected during small time interval Δt is equal to

$$n_j(t)\theta\Delta t + o(\Delta t) \tag{1}$$

where $n_j(t)$ is a number of infected neighbours at the moment t.

The second is *conformism* κ defining a threshold: a fraction of node's neighbours that should be infected to significantly increase the chance of infection of the node. It is a modifier for infection rate depending on the number of neighbours infected and a total number of neighbours. Thus, the probability of infection during small time interval is

$$n_j(t)\tau_\kappa(j,t)\theta\Delta t + o(\Delta t) \tag{2}$$

where $\tau_\kappa(j,t)$ is threshold function, for example

$$\tau_\kappa(j,t) = \begin{cases} 1, \frac{n_j(t)}{N_j} \geqslant \kappa \\ \epsilon, \frac{n_j(t)}{N_j} < \kappa, \end{cases} \tag{3}$$

where N_j is total number of neighbours that node j has and ϵ is small.

Note $n_j(t)$ and $\tau_\kappa(j,t)$ depend on t and will not write this dependence below. Here can also be used different function which ascends or descends being regulated by κ.

The third is a *background* parameter ρ, which defines the intensity of contagion through unobservable channels. To handle this infection process we take a classical non-network ST/SIR model's assumptions that each node connects to all other nodes. The assumption is that the number of all information sources (observed and unobserved) is proportional to the number of observed sources. The probability of infection should then be

$$(\rho N_I(t) + n_j\tau_\kappa(j)\theta)\,\Delta t + o(\Delta t), \tag{4}$$

where $N_I{}'(t)$ is an overall intensity of contagion ($N_I(t)$ is a number of nodes infected at time t).

The last parameter is a *decay* δ. As the older posts have less chance to be seen in one's newsfeed, the infection rate for each infected node should decrease over time. There can be different types of decay, for the exponential one the probability of contagion during Δt is

$$\left(\sum_{i\in A(t)} \rho e^{-\delta(t-t_i)} + \tau_\kappa(j) \sum_{i\in A_j(t)} \theta e^{-\delta(t-t_i)}\right) \Delta t + o(\Delta t), \tag{5}$$

where $A(t)$ is a set of all infected nodes at time t, $A_j(t)$ is a set of infected neighbours of node j at time t and t_i is the moment at which node i was infected.

Note, that using step decay function (i.e., that equal to 1 until some moment, and 0 after) gives a classic SIR model recover behaviour. In this case setting θ to 0 gives an infection equation for non-network SIR model, and setting ρ and κ to 0 gives an infection equation for network SIR model. However, if step recover function is good for describing biological infections, it is unsuitable for information, so gradual exponential decay is more preferable. Note that if theta, rho and kappa characterise the post, delta is a property of the social network. Thus, we can assume that it is the same for every publication. This assumption is helpful when we start to estimate parameters not just for one information cascade, but for the set of cascades.

As long as our model is a kind of SI, not SIR (as there is no recovery, the post stays on the wall forever, or if it was removed, we have no information about it) the equation (5) defines the model behaviour. The initial condition is a set $A(0)$ of nodes that was infected at the time $t = 0$.

B. Detecting significant nodes

In general every node has its own parameters θ (influence) and κ (conformism). It would be very useful to estimate all of them. Indeed, we cannot identify all individual θ's and κ's for each node because of small amount of data.

The common practical question is "What the most influential node is?". Or "What the less conform node is?". Thus, we should find one or several nodes whose parameters are differ the most from the average. We propose to use greedy algorithms. The algorithms search for the node for which increased θ makes the model better (higher likelihood). Then the second one, etc. The same is for decreased θ's and κ's.

Using such kind of approach should help us to find most "distinctive" nodes without overestimating the model.

V. Conclusion

In this paper we defined an object of study, obtained the data and formulated research questions. We considered several existing approaches and found that they cannot be applied directly to our cases. Patterns of spreading visualisation gave us intuitions on what is the object of research looks like and allows to make some decisions and hypothesis for practical use. The four parameter model of information spreading provides opportunities to answer several questions about an essence of information. The different roles of the nodes, however, still need to be considered. The next step of our studies is to estimate model parameters and then to develop a procedure to detect nodes whose behaviours significantly differs from average.

Acknowledgment

We would like to thank Jacqueline W. Daykin for helpful discussion, the anonymous reviewers for valuable comments, and financial supports for the research, The first author would also like to thank the overseas scholarship that allows his research visit to Goldsmiths, University of London.

References

[1] On-line social network "Vkontakte". [Online]. Available: https://vk.com

[2] A. Najar, L. Denoyer, and P. Gallinari, "Predicting information diffusion on social networks with partial knowledge," in Proceedings of the 21st International Conference on World Wide Web, ser. WWW'12 Companion. New York, NY, USA: Association for Computing Machinery, 2012, pp. 1197–1204. [Online]. Available: https://doi.org/10.1145/2187980.2188261

[3] S. Bourigault, S. Lamprier, and P. Gallinari, "Representation learning for information diffusion through social networks: An embedded cascade model," in Proceedings of the Ninth ACM International Conference on Web Search and Data Mining, ser. WSDM'16. New York, NY, USA: Association for Computing Machinery, 2016, pp. 573–582. [Online]. Available: https://doi.org/10.1145/2835776.2835817

[4] M. Gomez-Rodriguez, L. Song, H. Daneshmand, and B. Schölkopf, "Estimating diffusion networks: Recovery conditions, sample complexity & soft-thresholding algorithm," The Journal of Machine Learning Research, vol. 17, no. 90, 1 2016, pp. 1–29.

[5] M. Rodriguez, D. Balduzzi, and B. Schölkopf, "Uncovering the temporal dynamics of diffusion networks," vol. abs/1105.0697, 05 2011.

[6] M. Kimura and K. Saito, "Tractable models for information diffusion in social networks," in LNCS, 09 2006, pp. 259–271.

[7] C. Lagnier, L. Denoyer, E. Gaussier, and P. Gallinari, "Predicting information diffusion in social networks using content and user's profiles," in Advances in Information Retrieval, P. Serdyukov, P. Braslavski, S. O. Kuznetsov, J. Kamps, S. Rüger, E. Agichtein, I. Segalovich, and E. Yilmaz, Eds. Berlin, Heidelberg: Springer Berlin Heidelberg, 2013, pp. 74–85.

[8] M. Keuschnigg, Granovetter (1978): Threshold Models of Collective Behavior, 01 2019, pp. 239–242.

[9] V. Krishnamurthy, S. Bhatt, and T. Pedersen, "Tracking infection diffusion in social networks: Filtering algorithms and threshold bounds," IEEE Transactions on Signal and Information Processing over Networks, vol. 3, no. 2, June 2017, pp. 298–315.

[10] C. Jiang, Y. Chen, and K. J. R. Liu, "Evolutionary dynamics of information diffusion over social networks," IEEE Transactions on Signal Processing, vol. 62, no. 17, Sep. 2014, pp. 4573–4586.

[11] A. Farzindar and W. Khreich, "A survey of techniques for event detection in twitter," Computational Intelligence, vol. 31, 09 2013.

[12] Q. Li, A. Nourbakhsh, S. Shah, and X. Liu, "Real-time novel event detection from social media," 04 2017, pp. 1129–1139.

[13] C. Kadushin, Understanding social networks: Theories, concepts, and findings. Oxford: Oxford University Press, 2012.

[14] K. Saito, M. Kimura, K. Ohara, and H. Motoda, "Learning continuous-time information diffusion model for social behavioral data analysis," in Advances in Machine Learning, Z.-H. Zhou and T. Washio, Eds. Berlin, Heidelberg: Springer Berlin Heidelberg, 2009, pp. 322–337.

[15] M. E. J. Newman, Networks. Oxford: Oxford University Press, 2010.

[16] A. Guille and H. Hacid, "A predictive model for the temporal dynamics of information diffusion in online social networks," in Proceedings of the 21st International Conference on World Wide Web, ser. WWW'12 Companion. New York, NY, USA: Association for Computing Machinery, 2012, pp. 1145–1152. [Online]. Available: https://doi.org/10.1145/2187980.2188254

Concepts for Computing Patterns in 15th Century Korean Music

Sukhie Moon
Institute of Korean Literature and Arts
Soongsil University, Seoul, Korea
Email: sukhiem@hanmail.net

Jacqueline W. Daykin
Department of Computer Science
Aberystwyth University, UK
Department of Information Science
Stellenbosch University, South Africa
Email: jackie.daykin@gmail.com

Ida M. Pu
Department of Computing
Goldsmiths, University of London, UK
Email: idapuone@gmail.com

***Abstract*—Computational musicology denotes the use of computers for analyzing music. This paper proposes applying techniques from stringology for analyzing classical Korean music. Historically, Sejong, the fourth king of the Joseon Dynasty in Korea, intended to rule the country with courtesy and music following the teaching of Neo-Confucianism. For this, he invented a music score in which music could be written. He made the structure of the music score based on the meaning of Neo-Confucianism, and recorded contemporary music with two notation patterns. In this paper, we first study the patterns in the structure of the music score and then investigate the notation patterns by which contemporary music was recorded in the music score. Finally, we establish links between these musical patterns and computing pattern inference for music via the field of stringology. Future research directions are outlined.**

***Keywords*–Korean music; Lyndon word; Musicology; Notation pattern; Stringology; Structure of music score; V-word.**

I. Introduction

Musicology is the study of music through scholarly analysis and research methodologies. ***Computational musicology*** is the use of computers in order to study music and integrates musicology, computer science and stringology (the study of strings). This interdisciplinary research area includes music information retrieval, pattern matching and music informatics. This paper introduces the computational study of patterns occurring in Korean music and proposes future research directions for this endeavour. We first overview the background for these musical patterns in the structure of the music score and the notation patterns devised for recording Korean music and then describe connections to the field of stringology.

King Sejong (reign 1418–1450) introduced 'yeack' ideology with the goal of ideal Confucian politics. Yeack ideology means ruling the subjects by courtesy and music rather than by punishments. For this he invented a form of music score that has been passed down to this day. This music score is a full score that notates lyric and various musical instruments. Moreover, it is a detailed music score that notates both one-third and one-fourth beats. The music score was improved one step further by his son, King Sejo, and then it has evolved with gradual changes up until now.

King Sejong made the structure of the music score based on the meaning of Neo-Confucianism, and recorded contemporary music with notation patterns fitting to each rhythm. Without understanding the notation patterns, therefore, the music recorded in the music score cannot be interpreted properly. Hence, we first study the structure of the music score and its meaning in Neo-Confucianism. Then, we investigate the notation patterns recorded in the music score and the corresponding rhythms of the 15th century Korean music.

The rest of the paper is arranged as follows. Section II explores the meaningful structure of the music scores of the Joseon Dynastry. Section III identifies the patterns of the music scores. Section IV discusses computational Korean musicology and applications of the stringology in musicology. Section V provides the summary and future directions.

II. The Structure of the Music Score and Its Meaning

A. *Structure of the music score*

The music score of the Joseon Dynasty (the version established by King Sejo) has the structure shown in Figure 1. Small squares form a vertical column, and vertical columns proceed (are read) from right to left. A small square is called a ***jeonggan*** and a vertical column is called a ***haeng***. A vertical column is divided into 6 ***daegangs*** by thick lines. A daegang consists of either three squares or two squares.

Figure 1 shows a full score, and thus five columns make one column set, in which the first column from right represents a string instrument (melody), the second column a wind instrument, the third column percussion instrument 1, the fourth column percussion instrument 2, and the leftmost column the lyric. A note of melody is notated by a pitch name, and percussion is notated by symbols of strokes. The black area at the beginning of the score means that this piece of music has an incomplete bar. This music score is called a ***jeongganbo***.

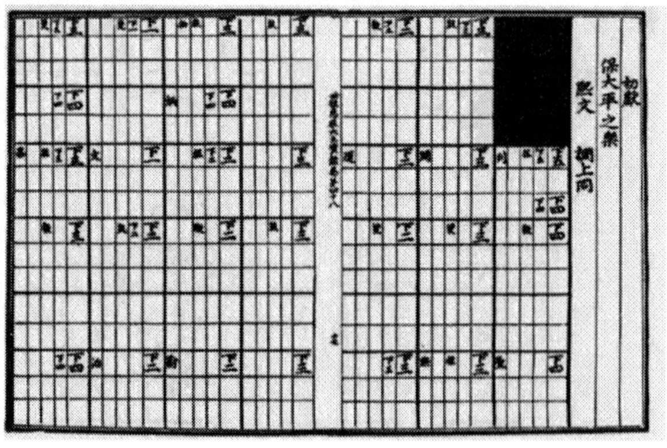

Figure 1. Structure of the music score

If a vertical column in Figure 1 is drawn horizontally, it looks like Figure 2, i.e., a haeng consists of six daegangs, each of which consists of either 3 jeonggans or 2 jeonggans. Therefore, the music score in Figure 1 has the pattern of $(3\ 3\ 2\ 3)^5(3\ 2\ 3\ 3\ 2\ 3)^5(3\ 2\ 3\ 3\ 2\ 3)^5\cdots$, where $(3\ 3\ 2\ 3)$ refers to the 3, 3, 2, and 3 squares in the rightmost column, and $(3\ 3\ 2\ 3)^5$ refers to the column set consisting of the rightmost five columns (under the black box).

Figure 2 shows the names in the structure of the music score.

haeng (column: 行)															
daegang			daegang		daegang			daegang			daegang		daegang		
jg	jg	jg	jg	jg	jg	jg	jg	jg	jg	jg	jg	jg	jg	jg	jg

Figure 2. The names in the structure of the music score

B. The meaning of the structure of the music score

The Neo-Confucian meaning of the music score is embedded in the number of squares. This music score consists of repetitions of 3+2+3=8 squares. In Figure 1, one haeng (i.e., column) consists of 16 squares, but in the original score made by King Sejong one haeng consisted of 32 squares.

Figure 3 shows the meaning of the structure of the music score.

year											
music						music					
8 diagrams spring			8 diagrams summer			8 diagrams fall			8 diagrams winter		
heaven	human	earth	heaven	human	earth	heaven	human	earth	heaven	human	earth
3	2	3	3	2	3	3	2	3	3	2	3

Figure 3. The meaning of the structure of the music score

The Neo-Confucian meanings of the numbers in the music score are shown in Figure 3. The numbers 3, 2, and 3 in a group of 8 squares mean heaven, human, and earth, respectively, and 8 means 8 diagrams from Neo-Confucianism, that is, one season. The number 16 means music, which is a fundamental doctrine of politics. One haeng (i.e., 32 squares) means one year consisting of spring, summer, fall, and winter, and it is repeated like a year [1], [2]. In this way, the structure of the music score was designed based on the meanings of Neo-Confucianism.

There has been research on the rhythm interpretation of this music score since the late 1950s. At first, there was a theory that interprets one square as the unit of beat [3], but it could not be used to play the music because the rhythm of music interpreted by the theory was strange. Later, this theory was slightly generalised to the theory that each square has the same length in rhythm [4], [5], but it had similar problems. Condit [6] and Hong [7] also proposed theories to interpret the rhythm of the music score, but these did not reflect the characteristics of Korean music.

III. Notation Patterns

There were two types of music in the 15th century Joseon: *hyangak* and *dangak*. Dangak is the music that came from China, and its lyric was written in Chinese characters. Hyangak is the indigenous music of Korea, and its lyric was written in the Korean language. The music of the 15th century Joseon was recorded in the music score with the following two notation patterns [8], [9]. Dangak was recorded with notation pattern 1, and hyangak was mostly recorded with notation pattern 2.

- Notation pattern 1: Melody, percussion, and lyric are notated in the unit of 8 squares.
- Notation pattern 2: Melody, percussion, and lyric are notated in the unit of 5 squares and 3 squares.

We will investigate each notation pattern by examining a representative music score of the notation pattern. The music score is a full score that has the column set consisting of 4 columns representing melody, percussion 1, percussion 2, and lyric.

A. Notation pattern 1: Rhythm with binary subdivision of a beat

Notation pattern 1 has the unit of 8 squares, which makes one beat, and one beat is subdivided into two half-beats (i.e., binary subdivision of one beat). But the binary subdivision of the beat is not easy to record in the structure of 3+2+3=8 squares. In notation pattern 1, therefore, 3+2=5 squares represent a half-beat, and the following 3 squares represent the second half-beat. In the first half-beat, the first 3 squares represent a quarter-beat, and the following 2 squares another quarter-beat. In the second half-beat, the first 2 squares represent a quarter-beat, and the following 1 square another quarter-beat. Hence, notation pattern 1 has the rhythm shown in Figure 4. That is, the pattern $(((32)(21))((32)(21)))^n$ in the music score is interpreted as the rhythm $(((aa)(aa))((aa)(aa)))^n$, where 'a' denotes a quarter-beat.

Figure 4 shows Notation Pattern 1.

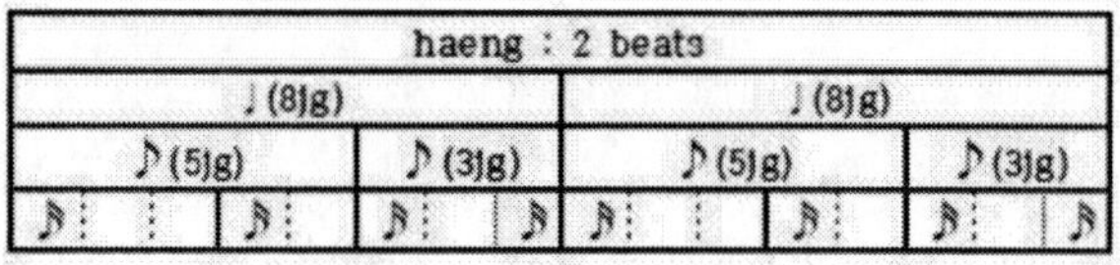

Figure 4. Notation Pattern 1

Gimyeong (基命), an ancient song, which is a representative music passage in notation pattern 1, and its translation into Western stave notation are shown in Figure 5. In this music score, melody, percussions, and lyric are notated in the unit of 8 squares with occasional half-beats in melody. Each Chinese character in lyric lasts two beats. In dangak, each Chinese character has the same length in rhythm in most cases because Chinese characters have almost equal weights in meaning. All pieces of music in dangak were recorded in notation pattern 1, which fits well with Chinese traditional music that favours the binary subdivision of the beat.

B. Notation pattern 2: Rhythm with ternary subdivision of a beat

Notation pattern 2 has the unit of 5 squares and 3 squares, which makes one beat, and one beat is subdivided into 3 one-third beats (i.e., ternary subdivision of one beat). The

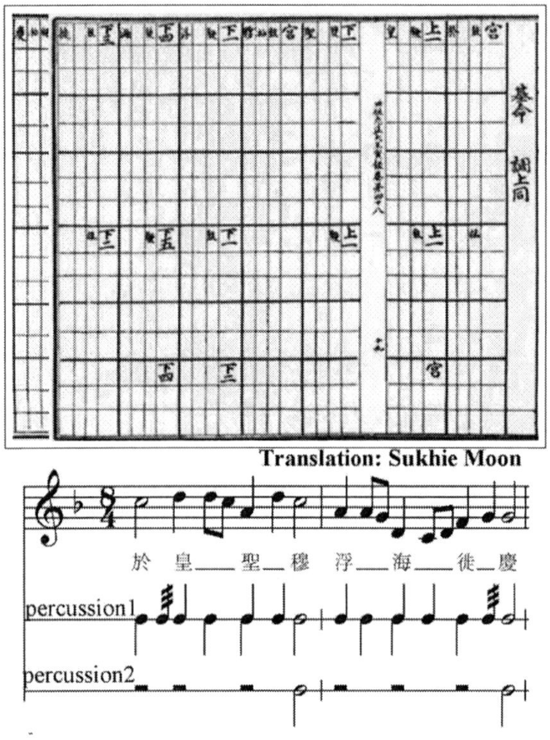

Figure 5. Gimyeong

ternary subdivision of the beat is also not easy to record in the structure of 3+2+3=8 squares. In notation pattern 2, 3+2=5 squares represent one beat, and the following 3 squares represent another beat. In the first beat of 5 squares, each of the first 2 squares, the following 1 square, and the last 2 squares represent a one-third beat. In the second beat of 3 squares, each square represents a one-third beat. Therefore, notation pattern 2 has the rhythm shown in Figure 6, where one beat is denoted by '♩.' for notational convenience. That is, the pattern $((212)(111)(212)(111))^n$ in the music score is interpreted as the rhythm $((bbb)(bbb)(bbb)(bbb))^n$, where 'b' denotes a one-third beat.

Figure 6 shows Notation Pattern 2.

haeng : 4 beats															
♩. (5jg)					♩. (3jg)			♩. (5jg)					♩. (3jg)		
♩			♪		♩			♩			♪		♩.		
♪		♪	♪		♪	♪	♪	♪		♪	♪		♪	♪	♪
𝅘𝅥𝅯	𝅘𝅥𝅯	♪	𝅘𝅥𝅯	𝅘𝅥𝅯	♪	♪	♪	𝅘𝅥𝅯	𝅘𝅥𝅯	♪	𝅘𝅥𝅯	𝅘𝅥𝅯	♪	♪	♪

Figure 6. Notation Pattern 2

Cheongsanbyeolgok (青山別曲), a song of the Goryeo dynasty, which is a representative music passage in notation pattern 2, and its translation into Western stave notation are shown in Figure 7. In this music score, melody, percussions, and lyric are notated in the unit of 5 squares and 3 squares. It can be seen that Korean letters in lyric have different lengths in rhythm. This piece of music is hyangak, descended from the Goryeo dynasty, and was recorded in notation pattern 2, which fits well with indigenous music 'hyangak' that favours the ternary subdivision of the beat.

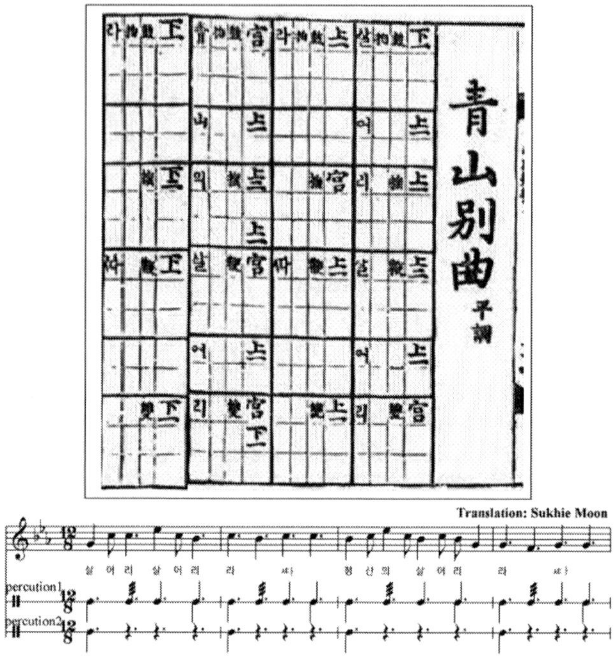

Figure 7. Cheongsanbyeolgok

Following this historical narrative on the creation, development and interpretation of Korean music scores, we proceed to establish a framework suitable for related computational music analysis using techniques from stringology.

IV. Overview of Computational Korean Musicology

A. Stringology notation

Stringology is the mathematical study of strings of data, that is sequences of symbols. Formally, given an integer $n \geq 1$ and a nonempty set of symbols Σ (bounded or unbounded), a ***string of length n***, equivalently ***word***, over Σ takes the form $\boldsymbol{x} = x_1...x_n$ with each $x_i \in \Sigma$. For brevity, we write $\boldsymbol{x} = \boldsymbol{x}[1..n]$ with $\boldsymbol{x}[i] = x_i$. We will assume that Σ is a totally ordered alphabet. The length n of a string $\boldsymbol{x}$ is denoted by $|\boldsymbol{x}|$. The set Σ is called an ***alphabet*** whose members are ***letters*** or ***characters***, and Σ^+ denotes the set of all nonempty finite strings over Σ. The ***empty string*** of length zero is denoted ε; we write $\Sigma^* = \Sigma^+ \cup \{\varepsilon\}$ and let $|\Sigma| = \sigma$. We use exponents to denote repetition, for instance if $\alpha \in \Sigma$ then α^3 means $\alpha\alpha\alpha$. If $\boldsymbol{x} = \boldsymbol{uwv}$ for strings $\boldsymbol{u}, \boldsymbol{w}, \boldsymbol{v} \in \Sigma^*$, then $\boldsymbol{u}$ is a ***prefix***, $\boldsymbol{w}$ is a ***substring*** or ***factor***, and $\boldsymbol{v}$ is a ***suffix*** of $\boldsymbol{x}$; we say $\boldsymbol{u} \neq \boldsymbol{x}$ is a ***proper prefix*** and similarly for the other terms. If $\boldsymbol{x} = \boldsymbol{uv}$, then $\boldsymbol{vu}$ is said to be a ***rotation*** (***cyclic shift*** or ***conjugate***) of $\boldsymbol{x}$. A string $\boldsymbol{x}$ is said to be a ***repetition*** if and only if it has a factorization $\boldsymbol{x} = \boldsymbol{u}^k$ for some integer $k > 1$; otherwise, $\boldsymbol{x}$ is said to be ***primitive***. For a string $\boldsymbol{x}$, the reversed string $\overline{\boldsymbol{x}}$ is defined as $\overline{\boldsymbol{x}} = \boldsymbol{x}[n]\boldsymbol{x}[n{-}1] \cdots \boldsymbol{x}[1]$. A string $\boldsymbol{x}$ is a ***palindrome*** if $\boldsymbol{x} = \overline{\boldsymbol{x}}$. A string which is both a proper prefix and a proper suffix of a string $\boldsymbol{x} \neq \varepsilon$ is called a ***border*** of $\boldsymbol{x}$; a string is ***border-free*** if the only border it has is the empty string ε.

We first illustrate this stringology notation for the patterns in music described in Section II. The pattern 3323 is a string over Σ, where Σ is the naturally ordered non-negative integers, and the string has the border 3 and proper prefixes 3, 33, and 332. The string 3323 is a proper suffix of the string 323323 and $(3323)^5$ is a repetition. The string 1 is a factor of each of the strings 111 and 212. The strings 111, 323323 and 212 are all palindromes.

Clearly a string, a sequence of symbols over an alphabet Σ, is a very fundamental and versatile representation of data. A collection of related or collated strings is often referred to as ***text***. A core stringology task is ***pattern matching***, the computation of patterns in strings, and arises in diverse areas of scientific information and text processing, for instance: retrieving information from a database, bioinformatics software utilies for molecular biology investigations, text editors for the Internet, data compression for Big Data, speech recognition, computer vision, computational geometry, and cryptography. Furthermore, the alphabet letters in Σ can be generalized to sets leading to ***indeterminate***, or equivalently ***degenerate***, strings which consist of sequences of nonempty subsets of letters over Σ. For example, $\boldsymbol{x} = 51877392921115$ is a string of integers whereas $\boldsymbol{x} = \{5,3\}\{1,1,1\}\{8,4\}\{3,9,0,9\}\{2,6,1,6\}\{7\}\{1,3,5,7\}$ is a degenerate string over the integers.

The application of stringology algorithms to measuring musical similarity was considered in [10] where it is also expressed that this similarity is a rather subjective measure. For instance, two otherwise identical musical packages might differ only by being played in a different key or some notes in one might have been recorded incorrectly – different definitions of musical similarity could potentially require distinct algorithmic solutions and both edit and hamming distances have been proposed for these kinds of analyses. Approximate matching methods were developed in [10] which measure the distance between musical passages by looking at the distance between the individual notes. String matching techniques such as approximate matching with gaps (allowing skipping of notes), polyphonic matching (searching for a pattern in a set of sequences of notes), and approximate repetitions have also been considered in computational musicology.

Ordering a set of strings is often used to enhance computational efficiency such as with indexing techniques. If Σ is a totally ordered alphabet then ***lexicographic ordering (lexorder)*** $\boldsymbol{u} < \boldsymbol{v}$ with $\boldsymbol{u}, \boldsymbol{v} \in \Sigma^+$ means that either $\boldsymbol{u}$ is a proper prefix of $\boldsymbol{v}$, or $\boldsymbol{u} = \boldsymbol{r}a\boldsymbol{s}$, $\boldsymbol{v} = \boldsymbol{r}b\boldsymbol{t}$ for some $a, b \in \Sigma$ such that $a < b$ and for some $\boldsymbol{r}, \boldsymbol{s}, \boldsymbol{t} \in \Sigma^*$. We call the ordering $\ll$ based on lexorder of reversed strings ***co-lexicographic ordering (co-lexorder)***. Using the ordered Roman alphabet: $compute < computer < music < musicology < score$ while $music \ll score \ll compute \ll computer \ll musicology$. Ordering techniques can also capture patterns in strings.

B. Application of stringology in musicology

In combinatorics on words, ***Lyndon words*** are (generally) finite words (strings) which are lexicographically least amongst all their cyclic rotations.

Definition 1 (Lyndon word): A string $\boldsymbol{x}$ over an ordered alphabet Σ is said to be a ***Lyndon word*** if it is the unique minimum in lexorder $<$ in the conjugacy class of $\boldsymbol{x}$.

Lyndon words are primitive, have deep connections with algebra, and moreover, any string can be factored or decomposed efficiently into Lyndon words [11] including for degenerate strings [12]. Introduced by Lyndon in 1954 as standard lexicographic sequences, Lyndon words have been studied extensively and are finding an increasing range of applications: string combinatorics and algorithmics including specialized matching scenarios, computing the lexorder of substrings, digital geometry, and bioinformatics. Our interest here is applications of Lyndon words to musicology.

Consider the string 3323, which is part of the pattern of the Korean music score in Figure 1. We will show that 3323 is not a Lyndon word while the conjugate 2333 is a Lyndon word.

TABLE I. CONJUGATES OF 3323

3	3	2	3
3	3	3	2
2	3	3	3
3	2	3	3

TABLE II. THE LEXORDER OF THE CONJUGATES OF 3323

2	3	3	3
3	2	3	3
3	3	2	3
3	3	3	2

Although the string 3323 is not a Lyndon word it can be uniquely factored into Lyndon words as (3)(3)(23).

Interestingly, Lyndon words have been applied in the analysis of music repetition, or looping, which is a fundamental feature of music. When enumerating periodic musical structures (repetitions), the computation is done up to a cyclic shift. In this context, two strings, which are cyclic shifts of one another are considered the same, and primitive Lyndon words, provide a means to capture distinct representatives of the structure. In [13], two examples of traditional African repertoires have been analysed using Lyndon words: harp melodic canons played by Nzakara people from the Central African Republic and also asymmetric rhythmic patterns common to many cultures of Central Africa. This stimulates our interest in potential applications of Lyndon words to analysing Korean music.

We now define a non-lexorder called V-order [14]. Let $\boldsymbol{x} = x_1 x_2 \cdots x_n$ be a string over Σ. Define $h \in \{1, \ldots, n\}$ by $h = 1$ if $x_1 \leq x_2 \leq \cdots \leq x_n$; otherwise, by the unique value such that $x_{h-1} > x_h \leq x_{h+1} \leq x_{h+2} \leq \cdots \leq x_n$. Let $\boldsymbol{x}^* = x_1 x_2 \cdots x_{h-1} x_{h+1} \cdots x_n$, where the star * indicates deletion of x_h. Write $\boldsymbol{x}^{s*} = (...(\boldsymbol{x}^*)^*...)^*$ with $s \geq 0$ stars. Let $g = \max\{x_1, x_2, \ldots, x_n\}$, and let k be the number of occurrences of g in $\boldsymbol{x}$. Then the sequence $\boldsymbol{x}, \boldsymbol{x}^*, \boldsymbol{x}^{2*}, ...$ ends $g^k, ..., g^1, g^0 = \boldsymbol{\varepsilon}$. From all strings $\boldsymbol{x}$ over Σ we form the *star tree*, where each string $\boldsymbol{x}$ labels a vertex and there is a directed edge upward from $\boldsymbol{x}$ to $\boldsymbol{x}^*$, with the empty string $\boldsymbol{\varepsilon}$ as the root.

Definition 2 (V-order): We define V-order $\prec$ between distinct strings $\boldsymbol{x}, \boldsymbol{y}$. First $\boldsymbol{x} \prec \boldsymbol{y}$ if in the star tree $\boldsymbol{x}$ is in the path $\boldsymbol{y}, \boldsymbol{y}^*, \boldsymbol{y}^{2*}, \ldots, \boldsymbol{\varepsilon}$. If $\boldsymbol{x}, \boldsymbol{y}$ are not in a path, there exist smallest s, t such that $\boldsymbol{x}^{(s+1)*} = \boldsymbol{y}^{(t+1)*}$. Let $\boldsymbol{s} = \boldsymbol{x}^{s*}$ and $\boldsymbol{t} = \boldsymbol{y}^{t*}$; then $\boldsymbol{s} \neq \boldsymbol{t}$ but $|\boldsymbol{s}| = |\boldsymbol{t}| = m$ say. Let $j \in [1..m]$ be the greatest integer such that $\boldsymbol{s}[j] \neq \boldsymbol{t}[j]$. If $\boldsymbol{s}[j] < \boldsymbol{t}[j]$ in Σ then $\boldsymbol{x} \prec \boldsymbol{y}$; otherwise, $\boldsymbol{y} \prec \boldsymbol{x}$. Clearly $\prec$ is a total order on all strings in Σ^*.

To illustrate the star tree using ordered integers, if $\boldsymbol{x} = 53638$, then $\boldsymbol{x}^* = 5368$, $\boldsymbol{x}^{2*} = 568$ and $\boldsymbol{x}^{3*} = 68$; then since 68 is in the tree path we have $68 \prec 53638$.

We now introduce the V-order equivalent of the lexorder Lyndon word:

Definition 3 (V-Word): A string $\boldsymbol{x}$ over an ordered alphabet Σ is said to be a ***V*-word** if it is the unique minimum in V-order $\prec$ in the conjugacy class of $\boldsymbol{x}$.

TABLE III. THE V-ORDER OF THE CONJUGATES OF 3323

3	3	3	2
3	3	2	3
3	2	3	3
2	3	3	3

Hence, we see that although 3323 is not a V-word, and is in fact bordered, the conjugate 3332 of 3323 is a V-word. However, note that each of the Korean music score patterns 32, 21 and 3221 are V-words.

Interestingly, the rhythmic pattern 3 2 2 2 2 3 2 2 2 2 2 occurs in Aka Pygmies music [15], and this pattern forms a V-word.

V. Future Research Directions

This introductory paper has stimulated the flow of numerous research questions and directions regarding the application of stringology techniques to the analysis and processing of Korean music:

- apply the analysis of the musical structure to automated Korean music classification
- design and implement pattern matching techniques optimized for Korean music retrieval tasks
- apply indeterminate or degenerate strings to the pattern matching task of finding chords that match with single notes and analyzing chord progressions
- apply factoring techniques for indeterminate strings to music scores for aiding the identification of meaningful musical sequences
- investigate palindromes in the context of analyzing Korean music
- enumerate periodic Korean musical structures using Lyndon words
- apply V-words to music pattern inference and discovery

VI. Conclusion: From Ideology to Practice

King Sejong invented a form of a music score based on Neo-Confucian ideology. This music score has the structure, which is a repetition of 3+2+3=8 squares, and this structure embeds the meanings of heaven, human, earth, and four seasons in a year. He recorded contemporary music of the 15th century into the music score using two notation patterns. Notation pattern 1 records music with the binary subdivision of one beat, and notation pattern 2 records music with the ternary subdivision of one beat. In the late 16th century, these music scores, which were originally used only in the palaces, were handed down to aristocrats. From this time on the music score gradually lost Neo-Confucian meanings and has been transformed into notation patterns expressing the rhythm of music more directly. In the 20th century the music score 'jeongganbo' finally abandoned Neo-Confucian meanings and became a music score that reflected the rhythm of music exactly.

This paper addresses computational musicology and has initiated the application of stringology techniques for analysing classical Korean musical patterns exhibited in both the structure and notation in the associated music scores. Lyndon words and V-words are mathematical structures with interesting combinatorial properties. By citing examples of patterns in African music which form Lyndon words we raise the question of using Lyndon words to analyse classical Korean music. Further, examples have been given of V-words arising in the structure of a Korean music score which indicate promising directions for further study. The proposed line of research impacts on the digital conservation of Korean culture and heritage.

Acknowledgment

1) The images in this article predate copyright laws and practice. We thank the National Gugak Center (government institute for Korean music) for use of the music score images and the sources Figures 1 and 5 [16], and Figure 7 [17].
2) The second author was part-funded by the European Regional Development Fund through the Welsh Government, Grant Number 80761-AU-137 (West):

Cronfa Datblygu Rhanbarthol Ewrop
European Regional Development Fund

References

[1] H. John, An Attempt to Interpret Early Jeongganbo focused on Yixue, 1995, pp. 221–262.

[2] J. Lee, A Study on the Structure and Numerical System of 'Siyong Mubo 時用舞譜' focused on the numerical principle of I-Ching, 2002, pp. 277–316.

[3] H. Lee, Jeonggan, Daegang and Jangdan of Jeongganbo. Segwangeumak, 1987.

[4] J. Hwang, Diachronic Consideration on the time Value of Jeongganbo of Joseon Dynasty. Research on Jeongganbo of Joseon Dynasty. Seoul National University Press, 2009, pp. 1–42.

[5] J. Lee, Interpretation of the Time Value of Chongganbo Notation - Focusing on Scores and Literature of the Early Choson Period -. Korean Historico-Musicology 50. Society for Korean History Musicology, 2013, no. 50, pp. 251–294.

[6] J. Condit, A fifteenth-century Korean score in mensural notation. Oxford University, 1979, pp. 2–22.

[7] J. Hong, An Interpretation of Deciphering. Society for Korean History Musicology, 1993, ch. Korean Historico-Musicology 11, pp. 19–80.

[8] S. Moon, A Study on the Interpretation of the Rhythm of Jeongganbo of Old Manuscripts. Society for Korean History Musicology, 2010, ch. Korean Historico-Musicology 45, pp. 293–330.

[9] ——, The Original Form and Restoration of Jongmyo Jeryeak. Hakgobang, 2011.

[10] R. Clifford and C. Iliopoulos, "Approximate string matching for music analysis," Soft Computing 8 (2004) 597–603 Ó Springer-Verlag, no. 8, 2004, pp. 597–603.

[11] J. Duval, "Factorizing words over an ordered alphabet," J. Algorithms, vol. 4, no. 4, 1983, pp. 363–381. [Online]. Available: https://doi.org/10.1016/0196-6774(83)90017-2

[12] J. W. Daykin and B. W. Watson, "Indeterminate string factorizations and degenerate text transformations," Math. Comput. Sci., vol. 11, no. 2, 2017, pp. 209–218. [Online]. Available: https://doi.org/10.1007/s11786-016-0285-x

[13] M. Chemillier, "Periodic musical sequences and lyndon words," Soft Computing. Springer-Verlag, no. 8, 2004, pp. 1–6.

[14] D. E. Daykin, J. W. Daykin, and W. F. Smyth, "A linear partitioning algorithm for hybrid lyndons using V-order," Theor. Comput. Sci., vol. 483, 2013, pp. 149–161. [Online]. Available: https://doi.org/10.1016/j.tcs.2012.02.001

[15] M. Chemillier and C. Truchet, "Computation of words satisfying the "rhythmic oddity property" (after simha arom's works)," Information Processing Letters, no. 86, 2003, pp. 255–261.

[16] The National Gugak Centre (government institute for Korean music), https://www.gugak.go.kr/site/program/board/basicboard/view?currentpage=5&menuid=001003002003&pagesize=10&boardtypeid=18&boardid=1360.

[17] The National Gugak Centre (government institute for Korean music), https://www.gugak.go.kr/site/program/board/basicboard/view?currentpage=5&menuid=001003002003&pagesize=10&boardtypeid=18&boardid=1362.

Spambots: Creative Deception

Hayam Alamro

Department of Informatics
King's College London, UK
Department of Information Systems
Princess Nourah bint Abdulrahman University
Riyadh, KSA
email: hayam.alamro@kcl.ac.uk

Costas S. Iliopoulos

Department of Informatics
King's College London, UK
email: costas.iliopoulos@kcl.ac.uk

***Abstract*—In this paper, we present our spambot overview on the creativity of the spammers, and the most important techniques that the spammer might use to deceive current spambot detection tools to bypass detection. These techniques include performing a series of malicious actions with variable time delays, repeating the same series of malicious actions multiple times, and interleaving legitimate and malicious actions. In response, we define our problems to detect the aforementioned techniques in addition to disguised and "don't cares" actions. Our proposed algorithms to solve those problems are based on advanced data structures that are able to detect malicious actions efficiently in linear time, and in an innovative way.**

Keywords–Spambot; Temporally annotated sequence; Creative; Deception.

I. INTRODUCTION

A *bot* is a software application that is designed to do certain tasks. Bots usually consume network resources by accomplishing tasks that are either beneficial or harmful. According to Distil Networks' published report '2020 Bad Bot Report', prepared by data from Imperva's Threat Research Lab, the bots make up 40% of all online traffic, while the human driven traffic makes up to 60%. The report shows that the bad bots traffic has risen to 24.1% (A rise of 18.1% from 2019), while good bots traffic decreased to 13.1% (A 25.1% decrease from 2018) [1]. The good bots, for example, are essential in indexing the contents of search engines for users' search, and recently have been used by some companies and business owners to improve customer services and communications in a faster way by employing the use of Artificial Intelligence (AI). These bots are useful in large businesses or businesses with limited resources through the use of *chatbots*, which can benefit the organization in automating customer services like replying to questions and conducting short conversations just like a human. However, bots can be harmful in what is known as a *spambot*. A spambot is a computer program designed to do repetitive actions on websites, servers, or social media communities. These actions can be harmful by carrying out certain attacks on websites/ servers or may be used to deceive users such as involving irrelevant links to increase a website ranking in the search engine results. Spambots can take different forms which are designed according to a spammer's desire. They can take the form of web crawlers to plant unsolicited material or to collect email addresses from different sources like websites, discussion groups, or news groups with the intent of building mailing lists to send unsolicited or phishing emails. Furthermore, spammers can create fake accounts to target specific websites or domain specific users and start sending predefined designed actions which are known as scripts. Moreover, spammers can work on spreading malwares to steal other accounts or scan the web to obtain customers contact information to carry out *credential stuffing* attacks, which is mainly used to login to another unrelated service. In addition, spambots can be designed to participate in deceiving users on online social networks through the spread of fake news, for example, to influence the poll results of a political candidate. Therefore, websites administrators are looking for automated tools to curtail the actions of web spambots. Although there are attempts to prevent spamming using anti-spambots tools, the spammers try to adopt new forms of creative spambots by manipulating spambots actions' behaviour to appear as it was coming from a legitimate user to bypass the existing spam-filter tools.

This work falls under the name of digital creativity where the *http* requests at the user log can be represented as temporally annotated sequences of actions. This representation helps explore repeated patterns of malicious actions with different variations of interleaving legitimate actions and malicious actions with variable time delays that the spammer might resort to deceive and bypass the existing spam detection tools. Consequently, our proposed algorithms for tackling the creative deception techniques are based on advanced data structures and methods to keep the performance and efficiency of detecting creative deception sequences at first priority. Here, we are going to provide a summary of the creativity of the spambot programmers, and the most important creative techniques that the spammer might use to deceive current spambot detection tools. Then, we are going to present our proposed solutions at this field to tackle those problems based on employing the AI approach to monitor the behaviour of the stream of actions using advanced data structures for pattern matching and to uncover places of the spambot attacks.

In Section II, we detail the related works in the literature review. In Section III, we introduce notations, background concepts, and formally define the problems we address. In Section IV, we present our solution for detecting deception with errors. In Section V, we present our solution for detecting deception with disguised actions and errors. In Section VI, we present our solution for detecting deception with don't cares actions. In Section VII, we conclude.

II. LITERATURE REVIEW

Spamming is the use of automated scripts to send unsolicited content to large members of recipients for commercial advertising purposes or fraudulent purposes like phishing emails. Webspam refers to a host of techniques to manipulate the ranking of web search engines and cause them to rank search results higher than the others [2]. Examples of such techniques include *content-based* which is the most popular type of web spam, where the spammer tries to increase term frequencies on the target page to increase the score of the page. Another popular technique is through using *link-based*, where the spammer tries to add lots of links on the target page to manipulate the search engine results [3] [4]. There are several works for preventing the use of content-based or link-based techniques by web spambots [5]–[10]. However, these works focus on identifying the content or links added by spambots, rather than detecting the spambot based on their actions. For example, Ghiam et al. in [4] classified spamming techniques to link-based, hiding, and content-based, and they discussed the methods used for web spam detection for each classified technique. Roul et al. in [3] proposed a method to detect web spam by using either content-based, link-based techniques or a combination of both. Gyongyi et al. in [11] proposed techniques to semi-automatically differ the good from spam page with the assistance of human expert, whose his role is examining small seed set of pages, to tell the algorithm which are 'good pages' and 'bad pages' roughly based on their connectivity to the seed ones. Also, Gyongyi et al. in [12] introduced the concept of spam mass and proposed a method for identifying pages that benefit from link spamming. Egele et al. [13] developed a classifier to distinguish spam sites from legitimate ones by inferring the main web page features as essential results, and based on those results, the classifier can remove spam links from search engine results. Furthermore, Ahmed et al. [14] presented a statistical approach to detect spam profiles on Online Social Networks (OSNs). The work in [14] presented a generic statistical approach to identify spam profiles on OSNs. For that, they identified 14 generic statistical features that are common to both Facebook and Twitter, then they used three classification algorithms (naive Bayes, Jrip and J48) to evaluate those features on both individual and combined data sets crawled from Facebook and Twitter networks. Prieto et al. [15] proposed a new spam detection system called Spam Analyzer And Detector (SAAD) after analyzing a set of existing web spam detection heuristics and limitations to come up with new heuristics. They tested their techniques using Webb Spam Corpus(2011) and WEBSPAM-UK2006/7, and they claimed that the performance of their proposed techniques is better than others system presented in their literature. There are also techniques that analyze *spambot behaviour* [9] [16]. These techniques utilize Supervised Machine Learning (SML) to identify the source of the spambot, rather than detecting the spambot. In this regard, Dai et al. [17] used SML techniques to combine historical features from archival copies of the web, and use them to train classifiers with features extracted from current page content to improve spam classification. Araujo et al. [18] presented a classifier to detect web spam based on qualified link (QL) analysis and language model (ML) features. The classifier in [18] is evaluated using the public WEBSPAM-UK 2006 and 2007 data sets. The baseline of their experiments was using the precomputed content and link features in a combined way to detect web spam pages, then they combined the baseline with QL and ML-based features which contributed to improving the detecting performance. Algur et al. [19] proposed a system which gives spamicity score of a web page based on mixed features of content and link-based. The proposed system in [19] adopts an unsupervised approach, unlike traditional supervised classifiers, and a threshold is determined by empirical analysis to act as an indicator for a web page to be spam or non-spam. Luckner et al. [20] created a web spam detector using features based on lexical items. For that, they created three web spam detectors and proposed new lexical-based features that are trained and tested using WEBSPAM-UK data sets of 2006 and 2007 separately, then they trained the classifiers using WEBSPAM-UK 2006 data set but they use WEBSPAM-UK 2007 for testing. Then, the authors based on the results of the first and second detectors as a reference for the third detector, where they showed that the data from WEBSPAM-UK 2006 can be used to create classifiers that work stably both on the WEBSPAM-UK 2006 and 2007 data sets. Moreover, Goh et al. [21] exploited web weight properties to enhance the web spam detection performance on a web spam data set WEBSPAM-UK 2007. The overall performance in [21] outperformed the benchmark algorithms up to 30.5% improvement at the host level, and $6-11\%$ improvement at the page level. At the level of OSNs, the use of social media can be exploited negatively as the impact of OSNs has increased recently and has a major impact on public opinion. For example, one of the common ways to achieve media blackout is to employ large groups of automated accounts (bots) to influence the results of the political elections campaigns or spamming other users' accounts. Cresci et al. [22] proposed an online user behavior model which represents a sequence of string characters corresponding to the user's online actions on Twitter. The authors in [22] adapt biological Deoxyribonucleic Acid (DNA) techniques to online user behavioral actions, which are represented using digital DNA to distinguish between genuine and spambot accounts. They make use of the assumption of the digital DNA fingerprinting techniques to detect social spambots by mining similar sequences, and for each account, they extract a DNA string that encodes its behavioral information from created data set of spambots and genuine accounts. Thereafter, Cresci et al. [23] investigate the major characteristics among group of users in OSNs. The study in [23] is an analysis of the results obtained in DNA-inspired online behavioral modeling in [22] to measure the level of similarities between the real behavioral sequences of Twitter user accounts and synthetic accounts. The results in [23] show that the heterogeneity among legitimate behaviors is high and not random. Later, Cresci et al. in [24] envisage a change in the spambot detection approach from reaction to proaction to grasp the characteristics of the evolved spambots in OSNs using the logical DNA behavioral modeling technique, and they make use of digital DNA representation as a sequence of characters. The proactive scheme begins with modeling known spambot accounts with digital DNA, applying genetic algorithms to extract new generation of synthetic accounts, comparing the current state-of-art detection techniques to the new spambots, then design novel detection techniques.

More relevant to our work are string pattern matching-based techniques that detect spambots based on their actions (i.e., based on how they interact with the website these spambots attack) [25] [26]. These techniques model the user's log as a large string (sequence of elements corresponding to actions of users or spambots) and common/previous web spambot actions as a dictionary of strings. Then, they perform pattern matching of the strings from the dictionary to the large string. If a match is found, then they state that a web spambot has been detected. For example, the work by Hayati et.al [25] proposes a rule-based, on-the-fly web spambot classifier technique, which identifies web spambots by performing exact string pattern matching using tries. They introduce the idea of web usage behavior to inspect spambots behavior on the web. For that, they introduce an action string concept, which is a representation of the series of web usage actions in terms of index keys to model user behavior on the web. The main assumptions of Hayati et.al proposed method are: web sites spambots mainly to spread spam content rather than consume the content, and the spambot sessions last for some seconds unlike the human sessions that last normally for a couple of minutes. The trie data structure is built based on the action strings for both human and spambots where each node contains the probability of a specific action being either human or spambot. Each incoming string through the trie is validated, and the result falls into two categories: match and not match. Hayati et.al used Matthews Correlation Coefficient (MCC) of binary classification to measure the performance of their proposed framework. The work of [26] improves upon [25] by considering spambots that utilize decoy actions (i.e., injecting legitimate actions, typically performed by users, within their spam actions, to make spam detection difficult), and using approximate pattern matching based on the Fast computation using Prefix Table *FPT* algorithm [27] under Hamming distance model to identify spambot action strings in the presence of decoy actions. However, both [25] and [26] are limited in that they consider consecutive spambot actions. This makes them inapplicable in real settings where a spambot begins to take on sophisticated forms of creative deception and needs to be detected from a log representing actions of both users and spambots, as well as settings where a spambot injects legitimate actions in some random fashion within a time window to deceive detection techniques. Also, both [25] and [26] do not address the issue of time (the spambot can pause and speed up) or errors (deceptive or unimportant actions). The algorithms presented here are not comparable to [25] and [26] as they address different issues.

III. Background and Problems Definitions

In this section, we introduce the main concepts and definitions of the key terms used throughout this paper. Then, we state the main problems that the paper will address.

A. Background

Let $T = a_0a_2 \dots a_{n-1}$ be a string of length $|T| = n$, over an alphabet Σ, of size $|\Sigma| = \sigma$. The empty string ε is the string of length 0. For $1 \leq i \leq j \leq n$, $T[i]$ denotes the ith symbol of T, and $T[i, j]$ the contiguous sequence of symbols (called *factor* or *substring*) $T[i]T[i+1] \dots T[j]$. A substring $T[i, j]$ is a suffix of T if $j = n$ and it is a prefix of T if $i = 1$. A string p is a *repeat* of T, iff p has at least two occurrences in T. In addition p is said to be *right-maximal* in T, iff there exist two positions $i < j$ such that $T[i, i+|p|-1] = T[j, j+|p|-1] = p$ and either $j + |p| = n + 1$ or $T[i, i + |p|] \neq T[j, j + |p|]$ [28], [29]. For convenience, we will assume each T ends in a special character \$, where \$ does not appear in other positions and it is less than a for all $a \in \Sigma$.

A *degenerate or indeterminate string* , is defined as a sequence $\tilde{X} = \tilde{x}_0\tilde{x}_1 \dots \tilde{x_{n-1}}$, where $\tilde{x}_i \subseteq \Sigma$ for all $0 \leq i \leq n-1$ and the alphabet Σ is a non-empty finite set of symbols of size $|\Sigma|$. A *degenerate symbol* $\tilde{x}$ over an alphabet Σ is a non-empty subset of Σ, i.e. $\tilde{x} \subseteq \Sigma$ and $\tilde{x} \neq \emptyset$. $|\tilde{x}|$ denotes the size of $\tilde{x}$ and we have $1 \leq \tilde{x} \leq |\Sigma|$. A degenerate string is built over the potential $2^{|\Sigma|} - 1$ non-empty subsets of letters belonging to Σ. If $|\tilde{x}| = 1$, that is $|\tilde{x}|$ repeats a single symbol of Σ, we say that $\tilde{x}_i$ is a *solid symbol* and i is a *solid position*. Otherwise, $\tilde{x}_i$ and i are said to be a *non-solid symbol* and *non-solid position* respectively. For example, $\tilde{X} = ab[ac]a[bcd]bac$ is a degenerate string of length 8 over the alphabet $\Sigma = \{a, b, c, d\}$. A string containing only solid symbols will be called a solid string. A *conservative degenerate string* is a degenerate string where its number of non-solid symbols is upper-bounded by a fixed position constant c [30] [31]. The previous example is a conservative degenerate string with $c = 2$.

A *suffix array* of T is the lexicographical sorted array of the suffixes of the string T i.e., the suffix array of T is an array $SA[1 \dots n]$ in which $SA[i]$ is the ith suffix of T in ascending order [32]–[34]. The major advantage of *suffix arrays* over *suffix trees* is space. The space needed using suffix trees increases with alphabet size. Thus, suffix arrays are more useful in computing the frequency and location of a substring in a long sequence, when the alphabet is large [33]. $LCP(T_1, T_2)$ is the length of the longest common prefix between strings T_1 and T_2 and it is usually used with SA such that $LCP[i] = lcp(T_{SA[i]}, T_{SA[i-1]})$ for all $i \in [1..n]$ [29] [32].

The *suffix tree T* for a string *S* of length n over the alphabet Σ is a rooted directed compacted trie built on the set of suffixes of S. The suffix tree has n leaves and its internal nodes have at least two children, while its edges are labelled with substrings of S. The labels of all outgoing edges from a given node start with a different character. All leaves of the suffix tree are labelled with an integer i, where $i \in \{1 \dots n\}$ and the concatenation of the labels on the edges from the root to the leaf gives us the suffix of *S* which starts at position i. The nodes of the (non-compacted) trie, which have branching nodes and leaves of the tree are called *explicit nodes*, while the others are called *implicit nodes*. The occurrence of a substring P in S is represented on T by either an explicit node or implicit node and called the *locus* of P. The *suffix tree T* can be constructed in $O(n)$ time and space. In order to have one-to-one correspondence between the suffixes of *S* and the leaves of *T*, a character $\$ \notin \Sigma$ is added to the end of the label edge for each suffix i to ensure that no suffix is a prefix of another suffix. To each node α in T is also associated an interval of leaves $[i..j]$, where $[i..j]$ is the set of labels of the leaves that have α as an ancestor (or the interval $[i..i]$ if α is a leaf labelled by i). The intervals associated with the children of α (if α is an internal node) form a partition of the interval associated with α (the intervals are disjoints sub-intervals of $[i..j]$ and their union equals $[i..j]$). For any internal node α in the *suffix tree T*, the concatenation of all edge labels in the path from the root to the node α is denoted by $\bar{\alpha}$ and the string depth of a node α is denoted by $|\bar{\alpha}|$ [28].

Definition 1. A TEMPORALLY ANNOTATED ACTION SEQUENCE is a sequence $T = (a_0, t_0), (a_1, t_1)...(a_n, t_n)$, where $a_i \in A$, with A set of actions, and t_i represents the time that action a_i took place. Note that $t_i < t_{i+1} \;, \forall\, i \in [0, n]$ see (Figure 1).

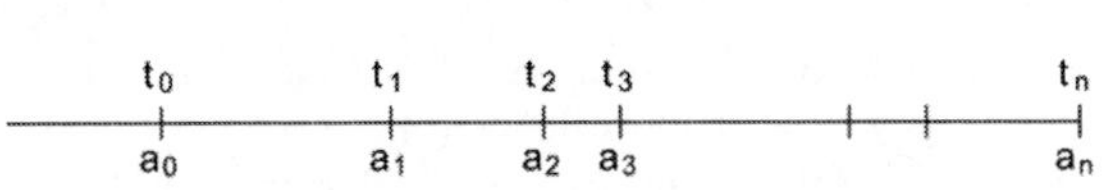

Figure 1. Temporally annotated action sequence T.

Definition 2. AN ACTION SEQUENCE is a sequence: $s_1...s_m$, where $s_i \in A$, with A is the set of all possible actions.

Definition 3. A DICTIONARY $\hat{S}$ is a collection of tuples $\langle S_i, W_i \rangle$, where S_i is a temporally annotated sequence corresponding to a spambot and W_i is a time window (total estimated time for all set of actions performed by the spambot).

Definition 4. The *Enhanced Suffix Array (ESA)* is a data structure consisting of a suffix array and additional tables which can be constructed in linear time and considered as an alternative way to construct a *suffix tree* which can solve pattern matching problems in optimal time and space [35] [36].

Definition 5. The *Generalized Enhanced Suffix Array (GESA)* is simply an enhanced suffix array for a set of strings, each one ending with a special character and usually is built to find the *Longest Common Sequence* (LCS) of two strings or more. *GESA* is indexed as a pair of identifiers (i_1, i_2), one identifying the string number, and the other is the lexicographical order of the string suffix in the original concatenation strings [37].

B. Problems definitions

Web spambots are becoming more advanced, utilizing techniques that can defeat existing spam detection algorithms. These techniques include performing a series of malicious actions with variable time delays, repeating the same series of malicious actions multiple times, and interleaving legitimate actions with malicious and unnecessary actions. In response, we define our problems in the following sections and give a summary on our algorithms which we use to detect spambots utilizing the aforementioned techniques. Our algorithms take into account the temporal information, because it considers time annotated sequences and requires a match to occur within a time window.

Problem 1: DECEPTION WITH ERRORS*:* Given a temporally annotated action sequence $T\ (a_j, t_j)$, a dictionary $\hat{S}$ containing sequences S_i each associated with a time window W_i, a minimum frequency threshold f, and a maximum Hamming distance threshold k, find all occurrences of each $S_i \in \hat{S}$ in T, such that each S_i occurs: (I) at least f times within its associated time window W_i, and (II) with at most k mismatches according to Hamming distance.

Problem 2: DECEPTION WITH DISGUISED ACTIONS AND ERRORS*:* Given a temporally annotated action sequence $T\ (a_j, t_j)$, a dictionary $\overline{S}$ containing sequences $\hat{S}_i$ each has a c non-solid symbol (represented by '#'), associated with a time window W_i, a minimum frequency threshold f, and a maximum Hamming distance threshold k, find all occurrences of each $\hat{S}_i \in \overline{S}$ in T, such that each $\hat{S}_i$ occurs: (I) at least f times within its associated time window W_i, and (II) with at most k mismatches according to Hamming distance.

Problem 3: DECEPTION WITH DON'T CARES ACTIONS*:* Given a temporally annotated action sequence $T\ (a_j, t_j)$, a dictionary $\hat{S}$ containing sequences S_i over the alphabet $\Sigma \cup \{*\}$, each associated with a time window W_i, a minimum frequency threshold f, and a maximum Hamming distance threshold k, find all occurrences of each $S_i \in \hat{S}$ in T, such that each S_i occurs: (I) at least f times within its associated time window W_i, and (II) with at most k mismatches according to Hamming distance.

In the following sections, we present a summary on our algorithms which we use to tackle the aforementioned problems. It is worth noting that the algorithms require a preprocessing stage before including the main algorithm. This includes input sequences temporally annotated actions T where these temporally annotated sequences are produced from the user's logs consisting of a collection of *http* requests. Specifically, each request in a user log is mapped to a predefined index key in the sequence and the date-time stamp for the request in the user log is mapped to a time point in the sequence. Then, the algorithm extracts the actions of the temporally annotated action sequence T into a sequence T_a that contains only the actions $a_0 \ldots a_n$ from T.

IV. DECEPTION WITH ERRORS

Current spambot countermeasure tools are mainly based on the analysis of the spambot content features which can help in distinguishing the legitimate account from the fake account. Furthermore, there are tools that work on the network level by tracking the excessive number of different IP addresses over a network path for a period of time that might indicate the presence of a spambot network. However, these techniques do not effectively identify the behavioural change of the spambot where most of them did not come up with satisfactory results. At this regard, the spammer is constantly trying to change the spambot actions behaviour to make it appear like human actions, either by replacing specific actions by others or changing the order of actions which ultimately leads to the primary goal of creating the spambot to evade the detection. This type of manipulation falls under the umbrella of creative deception which intentionally causes errors in order to bypass the existing detection tools. For example, suppose a spambot designed to promote the selling of products to the largest number of websites as a sequence of actions: *{User Registration, View Home Page, Start New Topic, Post a Comment on Products, View Topics, Reply to Posted Topic "with Buy Link"}* can be redesigned by replacing a few actions with others such that it does not affect the goal of the spambot as following: *{User Registration, View Home Page, Update a Topic, Post a Comment on Products, Preview Topic, Reply to Posted Comment "with Buy Link"}*. To solve this type of problems, the solution should take into account the occurrence of spambot actions with mismatches. For that, our contribution to solve PROBLEM 1 supposes that the spambot performs the same sequence of malicious actions multiple times. Thus, we require a sequence to appear at least f times to attribute it as a spambot. In addition, we take into account the fact that spambots perform their actions within a time window. We consider mismatches, and we assume that the spambots dictionary and parameters are specified on domain knowledge (e.g. from external sources or past experience).

Uncover Deception with errors

Our algorithm for solving (PROBLEM 1) needs to perform pattern matching with k errors where each sequence S_i in $\hat{S}$ should occur in T at least f times within its associated time window W_i. For that, we employ an advanced data structure *Generalized Enhanced Suffix Array* (GESA) with the help of *Kangaroo* method [38]. First, our algorithm constructs GESA for a collection of texts to compute the *Longest Common Sequence* LCS between the sequence of actions T_a and the dictionary $\hat{S}$ in linear time and space. The algorithm concatenates sequences (T_a and spambots dictionary $\hat{S}$) separated by a special delimiter at the end of each sequence to build our GESA, using *almost pure Induced-Sorting* suffix array [39] as follows:

$$GESA(T_a, \hat{S_{S_i}}) = T_a\$_0 S_1\$_1 S_2\$_2 \dots S_r\$_r$$

such that, $S_1 \dots S_r$ are sets of spambot sequences that belong to dictionary $\hat{S_{S_i}}$, and $\$_0, \dots, \$_r$ are special symbols not in Σ and smaller than any letter in T_a with respect to the alphabetical order. Then, the algorithm constructs GESA^R, a table which retains all the lexicographical ranks of the suffixes of GESA. Our algorithm uses the collection of tables (GESA, GESA^R, LCS, T, $\hat{S}$) to detect each sequence $S_i = s_1 \dots s_m$ in $T = (a_0, t_0), (a_1, t_1) \dots (a_n, t_n)$ that occurs with a maximum number of mismatches k in the spambot time window W_i. To do that, for each spambot sequence S_i in the spambot dictionary $\hat{S}$, the algorithm calculates the *longest common sequence* LCS between S_i and T_a starting at position 0 in sequence S_i and position j in sequence T_a such that the common substring starting at these positions is maximal as follows:

$$LCS(S_i, T_a) = max(LCP(GESA(i_1, i_2), GESA(j_1, j_2)) = l_0,$$

Where l_0 is the maximum length of the *longest common prefix* matching characters between $GESA(i_1, i_2)$ and $GESA(j_1, j_2)$ until the first mismatch occurs (or one of the sequences terminates). Next, we find the length of the longest common subsequence starting at the previous mismatch position l_0 which can be achieved using the *Kangaroo* method as follows:

$$max(LCP(GESA(i_1, i_2 + l_0 + 1), GESA(j_1, j_2 + l_0 + 1)) = l_1$$

The algorithm will continue to use the *Kangaroo* method to find the other number of mismatches, until the number of errors is greater than k or one of the sequences terminates. Finally, in each occurrence of S_i in T_a, the algorithm will check its time window W_i using the dictionary $\hat{S}$ and T such that it sums up each time t_i associated with its action a_i in T starting at the position j_2 in $GESA(j_1, j_2)$ until the length of the spambot is $|S_i|$, and compares it to its time window W_i. If the resultant time is less than or equal to W_i, the algorithm considers that the pattern sequence corresponds to a spambot.

V. DECEPTION WITH DISGUISED ACTIONS AND ERRORS

Spammers might attempt to deceive detection tools by creating more sophisticated sequences of actions in a creative way as their attempt to disguise their actions is by varying certain actions and making some errors. For example, a spambot takes the actions $AFCDBE$, then $AGCDBE$, then $AGDDBE$ etc. This can be described as $A[FG][CD]DBE$. They try to deceive by changing the second and third action. The action $[FG]$ and $[CD]$ are variations of the same sequence. We will call the symbols A, D, B, E solid, the symbols $[FG]$ and $[CD]$ indeterminate or non-solid and the string $A[FG][CD]DBE$ degenerate string which is denoted by $\tilde{S}$. At this case, we are not concerned which actions will be disguised, but we assume that the number of attempts to disguise is limited by a constant c and the number of errors is bounded by k.

Uncover Deception with Disguised Actions and Errors

Our algorithm for solving (PROBLEM 2) uses the following three steps which make the pattern matching with disguised actions fast and efficient:

Step 1: For each *non-solid* s_j occurring in a degenerate pattern $\tilde{P} = s_1 \dots s_m$, we substitute each s_j with '$\#$' symbol, where '$\#$' is not in Σ. Let $\hat{P}$ be the resulting pattern from the substitution process and will be considered as a *solid* pattern, see (Table I).

TABLE I. CONVERTING $\tilde{P}$ TO $\hat{P}$

$\tilde{P}$	A	[FG]	[CD]	D	B	E
$\hat{P}$	A	$\#_1$	$\#_2$	D	B	E

Step 2: This step is similar to the algorithm being used in PROBLEM 1, which constructs GESA to concatenate a collection of texts (T_a and set of action sequences $\overline{S_{\hat{S}_i}}$) separated by a special delimiter at the end of each sequence as follows:

$$GESA(T_a, \overline{S_{\hat{S}_i}}) = T_a!_0\hat{S}_1!_1\hat{S}_2!_2 \dots \hat{S}_r!_r$$

Such that, $\hat{S}_1 \dots \hat{S}_r$ are set of spambots sequences that belong to dictionary $\overline{S_{\hat{S}_i}}$, and $!_0, \dots, !_r$ are special symbols not in Σ and smaller than any alphabetical letter in T_a and smaller than '#' with respect to the alphabetical order. The algorithm works similarly to the algorithm described in the previous section with the help of the *Kangaroo* method in addition to *hashMatchTable* (Table II) to do *bit masking*. At any time, the algorithm encounters '#' at the matching pattern, it will get into the *Verification process*.

Step 3 (Verification process): At this step, the algorithm considers each '#' as an allowed mismatch and does *bit masking* operation using *hashMatchTable*, to find whether the current comparing action a_i in T_a has a match with one of the actions in '$\#_l$'. The columns of *hashMatchTable* are indexed by the (*ascii code*) of each alphabets in Σ by either using the capital letters or small letters to make the pattern matching testing fast and efficient.

TABLE II. HASHMATCHTABLE OF THE PATTERN $\tilde{P}_1 = A[FG][CD]DBE$ WHERE ITS CONVERSION IS $\hat{P}_1 = A\#_1\#_2DBE$

asscii(a_i) a_i	65 A	66 B	67 C	68 D	69 E	70 F	71 G	… …	88 X	89 Y	90 Z
$\hat{P}_1\#_1$	0	0	0	0	0	1	1	0	…	0	0
$\hat{P}_1\#_2$	0	0	1	1	0	0	0	0	…	0	0
…	…	…	…	…	…	…	…	…	…	…	…
$\hat{P}_r\#_l$	…	…	…	…	…	…	…	…	…	…	…

VI. DECEPTION WITH DON'T CARES ACTIONS

This type of creative deception can be used when we do not care about the type of some actions, which appear between important actions in a sequence of actions. This is important when we want to examine a sequence of actions where some of the actions should be included in the same order to be carried out regardless of the type of other actions in between. For example, travel booking websites which are specialized in selling products and services such as booking flights, hotels, and rental cars through the company itself or through an online travel agency are the most vulnerable businesses to spambots. More accurately, spambots are commonly used at those traveling portals to transfer customers from a specific traveling portal to a competitive one in seconds. This can be done by using an automated script called *price scraping*, which helps steal real-time pricing data automatically from a targeted traveling website to the competitor one. This can help in the decision making of the competitor's products prices, which will be adjusted to a lower price to attract more customers. The competitors also can use *web scrapping* which helps steal the content of the entire traveling website or some parts, with the intent to have the same offers with some modifications that will give them a competitive advantage. For that, we should employ the AI approach using clever algorithms, to detect the most threatened actions in a sequence of actions. For example, suppose a bot script designed to steal some parts of the targeted website (such as pages, posts, etc.), and make a click fraud on selected advertisements as follows: *(Login website:A, Web admin section:B, Select pages:C, Export:D, Save to file:E, Get element:F, Get "ad1":G, Click():H)*. Note that, we give an index key for each action, for it to be easy to create a sequence of actions, like that: $ABCDEFGH$. As we see, there are some actions that can be replaced with others such as action (Select pages:C) which can be any other select (posts, images, etc.), and the same thing for the actions (EFG). Those type of actions are the ones we "don't care" about, and thus, we can formulate the bot as follows: $AB * D * * * H$.

Uncover Deception with Don't Cares Actions

Our algorithm for solving (PROBLEM 3) uses a fast and efficient algorithm which can locate all sequences of actions P with "don't cares" of length m in text of actions S of length n in linear time, using *suffix tree* of S and *Kangaroo* method. Suppose we have this sequence ($P = AB * D * * * H$), and we want to locate all occurrences of pattern P in log of actions S. Our algorithm will solve it using the following steps:

- Build the *suffix tree* of S
- Divide P into sub-patterns P_k: $P_1P_2P_3 = (AB*)(D * **)(H)$
- Using the *suffix tree* of S and the *Kangaroo* method which can be applied to selected suffixes of the suffix tree of S by the use of a predefined computational method to answer subsequent queries in $O(k)$ time. This will find all occurrences of pattern P with "don't cares" in text S such that each query tests the explicit actions of each sub-pattern without caring of "don't cares" actions which are represented by '*'.

VII. CONCLUSION AND FUTURE WORK

We have presented our proposed algorithms that can detect a series of malicious actions which occur with variable time delays, repeated multiple times, and interleave legitimate and malicious actions in a creative way. Our proposed solutions tackled different types of creative deception that spammers might use to defeat existing spam detection techniques such as using errors, disguised, and "don't cares" actions. Our algorithms took into account the temporal information because they considered time annotated sequences and required a match to occur within a time window. The algorithms solved the problems exactly in linear time and space, and they employed advanced data structures to deal with problems efficiently. We are planning to extend this work by designing new methods for different variations of uncertain sequences, e.g., introducing probabilities (calculating whether it is false positive or false negative), statistics (frequency of symbols), and weights (penalty matrices for the errors).

REFERENCES

[1] E. Roberts, "Bad bot report 2020: Bad bots strike back," 2020. [Online]. Available: https://www.imperva.com/blog/bad-bot-report-2020-bad-bots-strike-back/

[2] M. Najork, "Web spam detection." Encyclopedia of Database Systems, vol. 1, 2009, pp. 3520–3523.

[3] R. K. Roul, S. R. Asthana, M. Shah, and D. Parikh, "Detecting spam web pages using content and link-based techniques," Sadhana, vol. 41, no. 2, 2016, pp. 193–202.

[4] S. Ghiam and A. N. Pour, "A survey on web spam detection methods: taxonomy," arXiv preprint arXiv:1210.3131, 2012.

[5] J. Yan and A. S. El Ahmad, "A low-cost attack on a microsoft captcha," in CCS. ACM, 2008, pp. 543–554.

[6] A. Zinman and J. S. Donath, "Is britney spears spam?" in CEAS 2007 - The Fourth Conference on Email and Anti-Spam, 2-3 August 2007, Mountain View, California, USA, 2007. [Online]. Available: http://www.ceas.cc/2007/accepted.html#Paper-82

[7] S. Webb, J. Caverlee, and C. Pu, "Social honeypots: Making friends with a spammer near you." in CEAS, 2008, pp. 1–10.

[8] P. Heymann, G. Koutrika, and H. Garcia-Molina, "Fighting spam on social web sites: A survey of approaches and future challenges," IEEE Internet Computing, vol. 11, no. 6, 2007, pp. 36–45.

[9] P. Hayati, K. Chai, V. Potdar, and A. Talevski, "Behaviour-based web spambot detection by utilising action time and action frequency," in International Conference on Computational Science and Its Applications, 2010, pp. 351–360.

[10] F. Benevenuto, T. Rodrigues, V. Almeida, J. Almeida, C. Zhang, and K. Ross, "Identifying video spammers in online social networks," in International workshop on Adversarial information retrieval on the web. ACM, 2008, pp. 45–52.

[11] Z. Gyongyi, H. Garcia-Molina, and J. Pedersen, "Combating web spam with trustrank," in Proceedings of the 30th international conference on very large data bases (VLDB), 2004.

[12] Z. Gyongyi, P. Berkhin, H. Garcia-Molina, and J. Pedersen, "Link spam detection based on mass estimation," in Proceedings of the 32nd international conference on Very large data bases. VLDB Endowment, 2006, pp. 439–450.

[13] M. Egele, C. Kolbitsch, and C. Platzer, "Removing web spam links from search engine results," Journal in Computer Virology, vol. 7, no. 1, 2011, pp. 51–62.

[14] F. Ahmed and M. Abulaish, "A generic statistical approach for spam detection in online social networks," Computer Communications, vol. 36, no. 10-11, 2013, pp. 1120–1129.

[15] V. M. Prieto, M. Álvarez, and F. Cacheda, "Saad, a content based web spam analyzer and detector," Journal of Systems and Software, vol. 86, no. 11, 2013, pp. 2906–2918.

[16] A. H. Wang, "Detecting spam bots in online social networking sites: a machine learning approach," in CODASPY, 2010, pp. 335–342.

[17] N. Dai, B. D. Davison, and X. Qi, "Looking into the past to better classify web spam," in Proceedings of the 5th international workshop on adversarial information retrieval on the web, 2009, pp. 1–8.

[18] L. Araujo and J. Martinez-Romo, "Web spam detection: new classification features based on qualified link analysis and language models," IEEE Transactions on Information Forensics and Security, vol. 5, no. 3, 2010, pp. 581–590.

[19] S. P. Algur and N. T. Pendari, "Hybrid spamicity score approach to web spam detection," in International Conference on Pattern Recognition, Informatics and Medical Engineering (PRIME-2012). IEEE, 2012, pp. 36–40.

[20] M. Luckner, M. Gad, and P. Sobkowiak, "Stable web spam detection using features based on lexical items," Computers & Security, vol. 46, 2014, pp. 79–93.

[21] K. L. Goh, R. K. Patchmuthu, and A. K. Singh, "Link-based web spam detection using weight properties," Journal of Intelligent Information Systems, vol. 43, no. 1, 2014, pp. 129–145.

[22] S. Cresci, R. Di Pietro, M. Petrocchi, A. Spognardi, and M. Tesconi, "Dna-inspired online behavioral modeling and its application to spambot detection," IEEE Intelligent Systems, vol. 31, no. 5, 2016, pp. 58–64.

[23] ——, "Exploiting digital dna for the analysis of similarities in twitter behaviours," in 2017 IEEE International Conference on Data Science and Advanced Analytics (DSAA). IEEE, 2017, pp. 686–695.

[24] S. Cresci, M. Petrocchi, A. Spognardi, and S. Tognazzi, "From reaction to proaction: Unexplored ways to the detection of evolving spambots," in Companion Proceedings of the The Web Conference 2018, 2018, pp. 1469–1470.

[25] P. Hayati, V. Potdar, A. Talevski, and W. Smyth, "Rule-based on-the-fly web spambot detection using action strings," in CEAS, 2010.

[26] V. Ghanaei, C. S. Iliopoulos, and S. P. Pissis, "Detection of web spambot in the presence of decoy actions," in IEEE International Conference on Big Data and Cloud Computing, 2014, pp. 277–279.

[27] C. Barton, C. S. Iliopoulos, S. P. Pissis, and W. F. Smyth, "Fast and simple computations using prefix tables under hamming and edit distance," in International Workshop on Combinatorial Algorithms. Springer, 2014, pp. 49–61.

[28] H. Alamro, G. Badkobeh, D. Belazzougui, C. S. Iliopoulos, and S. J. Puglisi, "Computing the Antiperiod(s) of a String," in CPM, pp. 32:1–32:11.

[29] T. Kasai, G. Lee, H. Arimura, S. Arikawa, and K. Park, "Linear-time longest-common-prefix computation in suffix arrays and its applications," in CPM, 2001, pp. 181–192.

[30] C. Iliopoulos, R. Kundu, and S. Pissis, "Efficient pattern matching in elastic-degenerate strings," arXiv preprint arXiv:1610.08111, 2016.

[31] M. Crochemore, C. S. Iliopoulos, R. Kundu, M. Mohamed, and F. Vayani, "Linear algorithm for conservative degenerate pattern matching," Engineering Applications of Artificial Intelligence, vol. 51, 2016, pp. 109–114.

[32] S. J. Puglisi, W. F. Smyth, and A. H. Turpin, "A taxonomy of suffix array construction algorithms," ACM Comput. Surv., vol. 39, no. 2, Jul. 2007.

[33] M. Yamamoto and K. W. Church, "Using suffix arrays to compute term frequency and document frequency for all substrings in a corpus," Comput. Linguist., vol. 27, no. 1, Mar. 2001, pp. 1–30.

[34] J. Kärkkäinen, P. Sanders, and S. Burkhardt, "Linear work suffix array construction," JACM, vol. 53, no. 6, 2006, pp. 918–936.

[35] M. I. Abouelhoda, S. Kurtz, and E. Ohlebusch, "Replacing suffix trees with enhanced suffix arrays," J. Discrete Algorithms, vol. 2, 2004, pp. 53–86.

[36] M. Abouelhoda, S. Kurtz, and E. Ohlebusch, Enhanced Suffix Arrays and Applications, 12 2005, pp. 7–1.

[37] F. A. Louza, G. P. Telles, S. Hoffmann, and C. D. Ciferri, "Generalized enhanced suffix array construction in external memory," AMB, vol. 12, no. 1, 2017, p. 26.

[38] N. Ziviani and R. Baeza-Yates, String Processing and Information Retrieval: 14th International Symposium, SPIRE 2007 Santiago, Chile, October 29-31, 2007 Proceedings. Springer, 2007, vol. 4726.

[39] G. Nong, S. Zhang, and W. H. Chan, "Linear suffix array construction by almost pure induced-sorting," in DCC, 2009, pp. 193–202.

Evolvability Analysis of Multiple Inheritance and Method Resolution Order in Python

Marek Suchánek and Robert Pergl

Faculty of Information Technology
Czech Technical University in Prague
Prague, Czech Republic
Email: marek.suchanek, robert.pergl@fit.cvut.cz

***Abstract*—Inheritance as a relation for expressing generalisations and specialisations or taxonomies is natural for conceptual modelling, but causes evolvability problems in software implementations. Each inheritance relation represents a tight coupling between a superclass and a subclass. Coupling in this case leads to a combinatorial effect or even combinatorial explosion in case of complex hierarchies. This paper analyses how multiple inheritance and method resolution order affect these problems in the Python programming language. The analysis is based on the design of inheritance implementation patterns from our previous work. Thanks to the flexibility of Python, it shows that inheritance can be implemented with minimisation of combinatorial effect using the patterns. Nevertheless, it is crucial to generate helper constructs related to the patterns from the model automatically for the sake of evolvability, including potential future in the patterns themselves.**

Keywords–Multiple Inheritance; Python 3; Evolvability; Method Resolution Order; Composition Over Inheritance.

I. Introduction

Inheritance in software engineering is a widely used term and technique in both system analysis and software development. During analysis, where we want to capture a specific domain, inheritance serves for refining more generic entities into more specific ones, e.g., an employee as a specialisation of a person. It is natural to have multiple inheritance, e.g., a wooden chair is a seatable physical object and is also a flammable object. On the other hand, in Object-Oriented Programming (OOP), inheritance can be used or even misused for various purposes, including re-use of methods and attributes. In OOP, it causes so-called ripple effects violating evolvability of software [1]–[3].

The Python programming language is (according to [4]) the most popular multi-paradigm and general-purpose programming language. It is dynamically typed, but allows multiple inheritance and also type hints [5]. Sometimes, Python is also referred as "executable pseudocode" thanks to its easy-to-read syntax and versatility [6]. For the implementation of conceptual-level inheritance in OOP, there are several patterns suggested in [2]. Although the patterns are compared and evaluated, implementation examples and empirical proofs are missing.

In this paper, we want to design implementation of the conceptual-level inheritance patterns in Python using its specific constructs to allow easy use of the patterns instead of traditional OOP inheritance that causes ripple effects. The prototype implementation is design to serve for comparison and demonstration of complexity added in terms of additional constructs versus complexity caused by combinatorial effects. First, Section II acquaints the reader with terminology and the overall context. Then in Section III, we analyse how traditional inheritance work in Python and then describe the design and implementation of each pattern. Finally, Section IV evaluates the implementations, as well as the traditional Python inheritance and suggests possible future research.

II. Related Work and Terminology

In this section, we briefly introduce the related research and terminology required for our approach. It refers to vital sources related to software evolvability, both conceptual-level and OOP inheritance, and Python programming languages.

A. Normalized Systems Theory

Normalized Systems Theory [1] (NST) explains how to design systems that are evolvable using the fine-grained modular structure and elimination of combinatorial effects, i.e., size of change impact is proportional to the size of the system. The book [1] also describes how to build such software systems based on four elementary principles: Separation of Concerns, Data Version Transparency, Action Version Transparency, and Separation of States. Violation of any of these principles leads to combinatorial effects. A code generation techniques producing skeletons from the NS model and custom code fragments are applied to make the development of evolvable information systems possible and efficient.

The theory [1] states that the traditional OOP inheritance inherently causes combinatorial effects. Without multiple inheritance, it even leads to the so-called "combinatorial explosion", as you need a new class for each and every combination of all related classes to make an instance that inherits different things from multiple classes, e.g., a class `JuniorBelgianEmployeeInsuredPerson`. But even with multiple inheritance, the generalisation/specialisation relation is special and carries potential obstacles to evolvability. First, the coupling between subclasses and superclasses with the propagation of non-private attributes and methods is evident. Also, persisting the objects in traditional databases is challenging [1] [2] [7].

B. Conceptual-Level Inheritance

Inheritance in terms of generalisation and specialisation relation is ontologically aligned with real-world modelling. It is tightly related to ontological refinements, where some concept is further specified in higher detail. It forms a taxonomy – a classification of things or concepts. For example, an employee is a special type of a person, or every bird is an animal. In conceptual modelling, inheritance is widely used to capture taxonomies and refine concepts under certain conditions. Although it is named differently in various languages, e.g., is-a hierarchy, generalisation, inheritance, all usually work with the ontological refinements. As shown in [8] different views on inheritance can be made with respect to implementation, where it can be (mis)used for reuse of classes without a relevant conceptual sense [2] [9].

C. Object-Oriented Programming and Inheritance

When talking about inheritance in OOP, it is crucial to distinguish between class-based and prototype-based style. In prototype-based languages, objects inherit directly from other objects through a prototype property. Basically, it is based on cloning and refining objects using specially prepared objects called prototypes [10]. On the other hand, a more traditional and widespread class-based programming creates a new object through a class's constructor function that reserves memory for the object and eventually initialises its attributes. In both cases, inheritance is used for polymorphism by substituting superclass instance by subclass instance with eventually different behaviour [8] [11].

Both single and multiple inheritance can be used for reuse of source code. In [8], a clear explanation between essential and accidental (i.e., purely for reuse) use of inheritance is made. Moreover, [12] shows how multiple inheritance leverages reuse of code in OOP, including its consequences. According to [13], Python programs use widely (multiple) inheritance and it is comparable to use of inheritance in Java programs of the similar sample set.

D. The Python Programming Language

Python is a high-level and general-purpose programming language that supports (among others) the object-oriented paradigm with multiple inheritance. It allows redefinition of almost all language constructs including operators, implicit conversions, class declarations, or descriptors for accessing and changing attributes of objects and classes. Both methods and constants for such redefinitions start and end with a double underscore and are commonly called "magic", e.g., magic method __add__ for addition operator. The syntax is clean as it uses indentation for code blocks and limits the use of brackets. Python can be used for all kinds of application from simple utilities and microservices to complex web application and data analysis [5] [13].

Often, Python is used for prototyping, and then the production-ready system is built in different technologies such as Java EE or .NET for enterprise applications and C/C++ or Rust for space/time optimisation. Another essential aspect that makes Python a suitable language for prototyping is its dynamic type system that allows duck typing [14], however static typing is supported using annotations since version 3.5. A Python application can be then checked using type checkers or linters similarly to compilers, while preserving a flexibility of dynamic typing [5] [15].

"The diamond problem" related to multiple inheritance is solved using "Method Resolution Order" (MRO) that is based on the C3 superclass linearisation algorithm. Normally, a class in Python has method `mro` that lists the linearised superclasses. It can also be redefined using metaclasses, i.e., classes that have classes as its instances. By default, a class is a subclass of class `object` and an instance of metaclass `type`. Class `object` has no superclass and it is an instance of `type`. Class `type` is a subclass of `object` and is an instance of itself [5] [11].

III. Python Inheritance Analysis

In this section, we analyse how conceptual-level inheritance implementation patterns proposed in [2] can be used in Python. We discuss the implementation options with respect to evolvability and ease of use, i.e., the impact of the pattern on the potential code base.

For demonstration, we use a conceptual model depicted in Figure 1 using OntoUML [9]. We use monospaced names of class and object names in the following text, e.g., `Person`. We strive to design the implementation of such a model where object `marek` is an instance of multiple classes with minimal development effort but also minimal combinatorial effects. Our model also contains the potential diamond problem, i.e., class `AlivePerson` inherits from `Locatable` via `Insurable` but also via `LivingBeing` and `Person`. Overriding is also included using derived attributes, as we avoid methods for the sake of clarity; however, it would work equivalently.

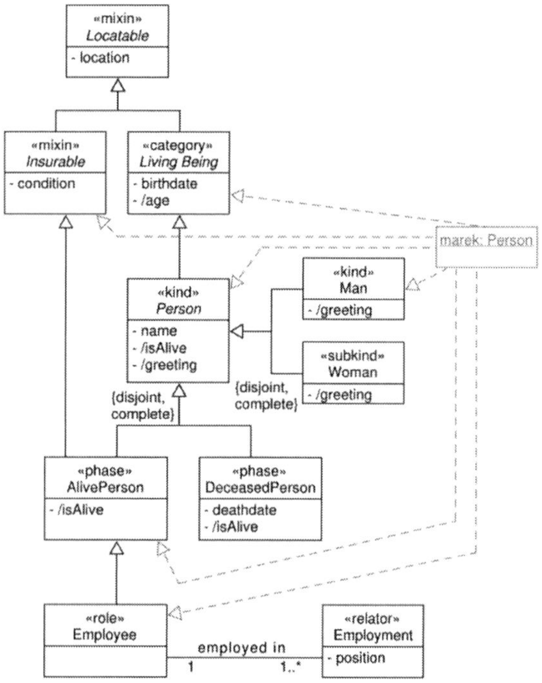

Figure 1. Diagram of OntoUML example model with instance

A. Traditional OOP Inheritance

The first of the patterns uses a default implementation of inheritance in the underlying programming language. In case of Python, multiple inheritance with MRO allows creating subclasses for combinations given by the conceptual model. We immediately run into the combinatorial effect. First, we need to implement classes according to the model with inheritance and call the initializer of superclass(es) in the initializer (i.e. `__init__` method). In case of single inheritance, it can be easily resolved using the built-in `super` function, but in case of multiple inheritance, all superclasses must be named again as call of the function `super` returns only the first matching according to MRO as shown in Section III-A. Also notice that all arguments of the initializer must be propagated and repeated. A possible optimization would be to use variadic `*args` and `**kwargs`, but in exchange for readability and checks with respect to number (and type) of arguments passed. Another interesting fact in our example is that `EmployeeMan` does not need to define the initializer, as it inherits the one from `Employee` and `Man` inherits it from `Person`. If `Man` has its own attributes, then `EmployeeMan` would have the initializer similarly to `AlivePerson`.

```
class LivingBeing(Locatable):

    def __init__(self, birthdate, location):
        super().__init__(location)
        self.birthdate = birthdate

    @property
    def age(self):
        # computation of age
        return result

class Man(Person):

    @property
    def greeting(self):
        return f'Mr. {self.name}'

class AlivePerson(Person, Insurable):

    def __init__(self, name, birthdate, location,
    ↪   condition):
        Person.__init__(self, name, birthdate,
        ↪   location)
        Insurable.__init__(self, condition)

    @property
    def is_alive(self):
        return True

class EmployeeMan(Employee, Man):
    pass  # Employee __init__ inherited


marek = EmployeeMan("Marek", ...)
```

Figure 2. Part of the traditional inheritance implementation

After having the model classes implemented, extra classes must be generated as an object can be instance of only one class. For example, `marek` is instance of such class `EmployeeMan`. For our simple case, number of extra classes is six – `Man` and `Woman` combined with `AlivePerson`, `DeceasedPerson`, and `Employee`. Adding a single new subclass of `Person`, e.g., `DisabledPerson`, would result in doubling the number and therefore a combinatorial explosion. The second point where a combinatorial effect resides is the order of superclasses (*bases* or *base classes* in Python), which influences MRO. For instance, if `Person` and `Insurable` define the same method – in our case the one from `Person` – it would be resolved for execution according to order in list `EmployeeMan.mro()`. On the attribute level, each change propagates to all subclasses, i.e., it is again a combinatorial effect. This can be avoided using the mentioned `**kwargs` and their enforcing, as shown in Section III-A. Knowledge of superclasses for initialization can be then used to automatically call the initializer of all the superclasses. We implement this in helper function `init_bases`, where superclasses are iterated a initialized in the reverse order to follow the MRO, i.e., the initializer of first listed superclass is used as the last one to eventually override effects of others.

With implementation shown in Section III-A, all classes with initializers can be easily generated automatically from the model with a single exception. The order of classes – i.e., if `AlivePerson` should be a subclass of `Person` and then `Insurable` or vice versa – is not captured in the model, but it is crucial for MRO. The order of superclasses has to be encoded in the model, or alternatively all permutations must be generated, which would result in a significantly higher number of classes that are not necessarily needed. Navigation is done naturally thanks to MRO and Python itself, for example, `marek.greeting` or `marek.location`.

```
def init_bases(obj, cls, **kwargs):
    for base in reversed(cls.__bases__):
        if base is not object:
            base.__init__(obj, **kwargs)

class Person(LivingBeing):

    def __init__(self, *, name, **kwargs):
        init_bases(self, Person, **kwargs)
        self.name = name

class AlivePerson(Person, Insurable):

    def __init__(self, **kwargs):
        init_bases(self, AlivePerson, **kwargs)

    ...

class EmployeeMan(Employee, Man):

    def __init__(self, **kwargs):
        init_bases(self, EmployeeMan, **kwargs)


marek = EmployeeMan(name="Marek", ...)
```

Figure 3. Implementation of initializers and extra classes with use of keyword arguments and helper function for model-driven development

B. The Union Pattern

The Union pattern basically merges an inheritance hierarchy into a single class. In our case, the "core" class of hierarchy can be naturally selected as `Person`. All subclasses are uniquely merged into `Person` and `Person` merges also all superclasses as shown in Section III-B. For example, if there is another subclass of `Insurable`, it would not be merged into `Person`. On the other hand, for example, a new subclass of `Man` would be merged. This pattern is inspired closely by the "single-table inheritance" used in relational databases, but it immediately runs into problems once behaviour should be implemented.

According to the pattern, each decision on generalisation set of subclasses must be captured in the class that unions the hierarchy. In our case, we need three discriminators – for `Man` and `Woman`, for `AlivePerson` and `DeceasedPerson`, and for `Employee`. Value of each discriminator described what subclass(es) are "virtually" instantiated. All of these generalisation sets are disjoint and complete with the exception of the one with `Employee` that is not complete (i.e., not all alive persons must be employees). If there is a non-disjoint generalisation set, it would be solved using enumeration of all possibilities for the discriminator. For example, if `Man/Woman` is not disjoint nor complete, there would be four possible options (no, just man, just woman, both) instead of current two (just man or woman).

To allow polymorphism without branching and checking the discriminator value and taking a decision on behaviour with combinatorial effect, we use directly classes for delegation as values for discriminators, similarly to the well-known "State pattern". With this implementation, it incorporates separation of concerns and improves re-usability. It is crucial that all attributes, i.e., data, are encapsulated in the single object that is passed during the calls. Section III-B shows `Delegation` descriptor for secure delegation of behaviour to separate classes that even do not need to be instantiated; therefore, static methods are used, and an instance of the union class is passed.

```
class Man:

    @staticmethod
    def greeting(person):
        return f'Mr. {person.name}'

class Delegation:

    def __init__(self, discriminator, attr):
        self.discriminator = discriminator
        self.attr = attr

    def __get__(self, instance, owner):
        d = getattr(instance, self.discriminator)
        a = getattr(d, self.attr) if d else None
        return a(instance) if callable(a) else a

class Person:

    greeting = Delegation('_d_man_woman',
    ↪   'greeting')
    is_alive = Delegation('_d_alive_deceased',
    ↪   'is_alive')
    age = Delegation('_x_living_being', 'age')

    def __init__(self, name, birthdate, location,
    ↪   condition):
        self.location = location
        self.condition = condition
        self.birthdate = birthdate
        self.name = name
        # optional-subclass attributes
        self.employment = None
        self.deathdate = None
        # discriminators
        self._d_man_woman = None
        self._d_alive_deceased = None
        self._d_employee = None
        # superclasses with behaviour
        self._x_living_being = LivingBeing

    def d_set_man(self):
        self._d_man_woman = Man

    def d_set_employee(self, employment):
        self._d_employee = Employee
        self.employment = employment

    ...
```

Figure 4. Part of union pattern implementation

It is essential to point out that this solution may reduce the number of classes, but only of purely data classes without behaviour. Union classes can be then easily generated from a conceptual model. The detection of the "core" class is a matter of the model – if OntoUML is used, naturally all identity providers (e.g., with stereotype `Kind`) are suitable. In modelling languages that have no such explicit indication, a special flag has to be encoded in the model. Classes encapsulating behaviour can also be easily generated from the model and related to data class using the explained `Delegation` descriptor. There is one problem with this pattern implementation – it does not support `isinstance` checks. When avoiding inheritance, the only possible solution lies in special metaclass that would override `__instancecheck__`. This would also require to forbid instantiation of behaviour classes, so it is unambiguous if the object is an instance of a data or a behaviour class.

C. Composition Pattern

The composition pattern follows the well-known precept from OOP – "composition over inheritance". Similarly to union pattern, a "core" class per hierarchy in the model must be identified. Classes are then connected using association *is-a* instead of inheritance. The Union pattern basically merges an inheritance hierarchy into a single class. For the original subclass, it is required to have a link to its superclass(es), but the other direction is optional unless the generalization set is complete or the superclass is abstract.

The final implementation of this pattern is based on the improved traditional OOP inheritance. Instead of inheritance, i.e., specification of superclasses, all superclasses from the conceptual model are instantiated during the object initialization. During this step, a bidirectional link must be made to allow navigation from both superclass and subclass instances. The "core" class must be again chosen to allow creation of composed object using multiple subclasses, e.g., an instance of `Person` that is also an `Employee` and a `Man`.

```
class Delegation:

    def __init__(self, p_name, a_name):
        self.p_name = p_name
        self.a_name = a_name

    def __get__(self, instance, owner):
        p = getattr(instance, f'{self.p_name}')
        a = getattr(p, self.a_name) if p else None
        return a(instance) if callable(a) else a

    def __set__(self, instance, value):
        p = getattr(instance, f'{self.p_name}')
        setattr(p, self.a_name, value)

class LivingBeing:

    location = Delegation('_p_locatable',
    ↪   'location')

    def __init__(self, *, birthdate, _c_person=None,
    ↪   _p_locatable=None, **kwargs):
        self._p_locatable = _p_locatable or
        ↪   Locatable(_c_living_being=self,
        ↪   **kwargs)
        self._c_person = _c_person
        self.birthdate = birthdate

    ...
```

Figure 5. Part of composition pattern implementation

The example in Section III-C shows that we also incorporated a *Delegation* descriptor. Although it results in repetition when defining where to delegate, it clearly describes the origin of a method or an attribute, and it can be generated easily. With the fact that these parts can be generated, combinatorial effects related to renaming or other changes of methods and attributes used for delegation are mitigated. The diamond problem is solved directly by passing child and parent class objects as optional arguments during initialisations. It could also be solved using metaclasses, but as this code can be generated, it allows higher flexibility and eventual overriding.

As the built-in MRO is not used, the resolution must be made manually on the model level similarly to the Union pattern, i.e., to decide what overrides and what is overridden. By replacing inheritance with bidirectional links, we managed to significantly limit combinatorial effects, but in exchange for the price in requiring additional logic and moving the MRO into the model itself. Unfortunately, this implementation needs also to incorporate model-consistency checks, as we do not enforce multiplicity in child-parent links according to the pattern design.

D. *Generalisation Set Pattern*

This pattern enhances the Composition pattern by adding particular constructs that encapsulate logic regarding generalisation sets. Inheritance relation is not transformed into *is-a* association but into connection via a special entity that handles related rules, such as complete or disjoint constraints and cardinality. As we present in Section III-D this helps to remove shortcomings of the Composition pattern and its difficult links and composed-object instantiation. Instead of multiple child links, there is just one per Generalisation Set (GS), and parent links are changed accordingly. An object of `GS` class maintains the inheritance and ensures the bi-directionality of links.

```
class Delegation:

    ...

    def __get__(self, instance, owner):
        gs = getattr(instance, f'{self.gs_name}')
        p = getattr(gs, f'{self.p_name}')
        a = getattr(p, self.a_name) if p else None
        return a(instance) if callable(a) else a

    ...


class GS_ManWoman:

    _gs_name = '_gs_man_woman'

    disjoint = True
    complete = True

    def __init__(self, person, man=None,
    ↪   woman=None):
        self.person = person
        self.man = man
        self.woman = woman
        self.update_links()

    def update_links(self):
        setattr(self.person, self._gs_name, self)
        if self.man is not None:
            setattr(self.man, self._gs_name, self)
        if self.woman is not None:
            setattr(self.woman, self._gs_name, self)

    ...
```

Figure 6. Generalisation Set implementation example

Introduction of an intermediate object to encapsulate inheritance and related constraints adds complexity in two aspects. First, the diamond problems must be still treated by sharing superclass objects in the hierarchy for eventual reuse. Second, the delegation must operate with the intermediary object when accessing the target child (or parent) object. However, solutions to these issues can be also generated directly from the model and in principle – despite their complexity – they do not hinder evolvability.

Finally, this solution (if entirely generated from a model) is the most suitable, since it limits combinatorial effects and allows to efficiently check consistency with the model in terms of inheritance and generalisation set constraints. Although in some cases, the `GS` object is not adding any value (e.g., a single child and a single parent case), implementing a combination of a generalisation set and composition patterns would make the software code harder to understand. Unity in implementation of conceptual-level inheritance is crucial here.

IV. Implementation Summary and Future Research

In this section, we summarize and evaluate achievements of our research. Based on our observations and implementation of inheritance using patterns, we evaluate inheritance in Python. The patterns and its key aspects are compared in Table I. Then, we also describe the future steps that we plan to do as follow-up research and projects based on outputs described in this paper.

A. *Resulting Prototype Implementation*

We demonstrated our implementation of all four previously designed patterns. Mostly, results and related usability options are consistent with the design. The more we minimize or constrain combinatorial effect, the more complex and hard-to-use (in terms of working with final objects) the implementation gets. We were able to simplify use of objects for the price of repetition and use of special constructs for delegation. Contrary to the original patterns design, we were not able to efficiently combine multiple patterns together based on various types of inheritance used in the model. As a result, our implementation of the most complex generalisation set pattern is suggested as a prototype of how inheritance may be implemented if one wants to avoid combinatorial effects while still needing to capture inheritance in a generic way for models of any size and complexity.

B. *Evolvability of Python Inheritance*

During the implementation of the patterns, it became obvious that even high flexibility of programming language and allowed multiple inheritance do not help in terms of coupling and combinatorial effects caused by using class-based inheritance. With a simple real-world conceptual model, we were able to show how the combinatorial explosion endangers the evolvability of software implementation. MRO algorithm used in Python does not help with limiting combinatorial effects. Rather it is the opposite since order in which superclasses are enumerated significantly influences implementation behaviour. Also, it makes harder to combine overriding from two superclasses, for example, both class `A` and `B` implement methods `foo` and `bar` but subclass `C` cannot inherit one from `A` and other from `B` (solution is to override both and call it from subclass manually).

TABLE I. COMPARISON OF THE INHERITANCE IMPLEMENTATION PROTOTYPES

Implementation	Classes*	Extra constructs	CE-handling	Issues
Traditional	$N + 2^N$	0	none	initialization, order of superclasses, uncontrolled change propagation
Traditional + init_bases	$N + 2^N$	init_bases function	shared initialization	shared attributes across hierarchy, order of superclasses, uncontrolled change propagation
Union pattern	2	Delegation class	shared class (merged)	Separation of Concerns violated, maintainability, discriminators
Composition pattern	N	Delegation class	shared initialization, delegation	manual handling of GS constraints, added complexity (for humans)
GS pattern	$N + 1$	Delegation class, GS helpers	shared initialization, delegation	added complexity (for humans)

(*) per single hierarchy of N classes, worst case (all combinations needed)

On the other hand, the flexibility of Python proved to be useful while we were implementing the patterns. Thanks to magic methods, descriptors, and metaclasses, the final implementations allow creating easy-to-use and inheritance-free objects even though underlying complex relations with constraints are needed as shown in the examples. Notwithstanding, such possibilities of Python are similar to constructs and methods in other languages (e.g., reflection). While trying to implement the patterns efficiently, we concluded that generating implementation from a model is crucial for evolvability regardless of what technologies are used, as a lot of repetition is needed.

C. *Production-Ready Technology Stack*

The goal of the paper was to use Python to show reference patterns implementation prototypes. The next step may be to leverage the lessons learned to formulate a single transformation description using production-ready technology stack, e.g., Java EE. This final transformation of conceptual-level inheritance should allow simple extensibility and customizations. Moreover, it should cover all possibilities with respect to the underlying modelling language. This language does not have to be OntoUML used in this paper; however, it must be expressive enough to capture all the necessary details for a correct implementation – for instance, hierarchy "core" classes.

D. *Model-Driven Development*

Having a final, production-ready, and well-described transformation of conceptual-level inheritance into implementation, it is not expected that it will be used to manually write source code. An essential part would be generation of a source code directly from the model capturing the inheritance together with domain knowledge. Normalized Systems (NS) theory [1] and related tooling can provide a way here using the so-called expanders. The challenge here would be to encode inheritance in the NS models directly or propose its extension, on the other hand we can expect flexibility and guarantees in terms of software evolvability.

V. CONCLUSIONS

In this paper, we analysed and demonstrated the evolvability of inheritance in Python using already-designed implementation patterns. Although Python offers multiple inheritance based on the method resolution order algorithm, software written in Python that uses inheritance suffers from coupling and related combinatorial effects similarly to software in other languages. Nevertheless, thanks to the Python's flexibility and ability to redefine core constructs, we managed to implement the conceptual-level inheritance implementation patterns easily with minimisation of combinatorial effects, while maintaining code readability. The suggestions for future development go mostly in direction of generating a production-ready software systems from conceptual models, where inheritance is used as a natural construct used to reflect real-world domains.

ACKNOWLEDGEMENTS

This research was supported by the grant of Czech Technical University in Prague No. SGS20/209/OHK3/3T/18.

REFERENCES

[1] Herwig Mannaert, Jan Verelst, and Peter De Bruyn, Normalized Systems Theory: From Foundations for Evolvable Software Toward a General Theory for Evolvable Design. Kermt (Belgium): Koppa, 2016.

[2] Marek Suchánek and Robert Pergl, "Evolvability Evaluation of Conceptual-Level Inheritance Implementation Patterns," in PATTERNS 2019, The Eleventh International Conference on Pervasive Patterns and Applications, vol. 2019. Venice, Italy: IARIA, May 2019, pp. 1–6, [retrieved: Aug, 2020]. [Online]. Available: https://www.thinkmind.org/index.php?view=article&articleid=patterns_2019_1_10_78001

[3] Antero Taivalsaari, "On the Notion of Inheritance," ACM Computing Surveys, vol. 28, no. 3, September 1996, pp. 438–479.

[4] Pierre Carbonnelle, "PYPL: PopularitY of Programming Language," Feb 2020, [retrieved: Aug, 2020]. [Online]. Available: http://pypl.github.io/PYPL.html

[5] Python Software Foundation, "Python 3.8.0 Documentation," 2019, [retrieved: Aug, 2020]. [Online]. Available: https://docs.python.org/3.8/#

[6] David Hilley, "Python: Executable Pseudocode," [retrieved: Aug, 2020]. [Online]. Available: http://citeseerx.ist.psu.edu/viewdoc/download?doi=10.1.1.211.7674&rep=rep1&type=pdf

[7] Andrei Alexandrescu, Modern C++ Design: Generic Programming and Design Patterns Applied, ser. C++ in-depth series. Addison-Wesley, 2001.

[8] Antero Taivalsaari, "On the Notion of Inheritance," ACM Computing Surveys, vol. 28, no. 3, September 1996, pp. 438–479.

[9] Giancarlo Guizzardi, Ontological Foundations for Structural Conceptual Models. Centre for Telematics and Information Technology, 2005.

[10] Alan Borning, "Classes versus prototypes in object-oriented languages." in FJCC, 1986, pp. 36–40.

[11] John Hunt, "Class Inheritance," in A Beginners Guide to Python 3 Programming. Springer, 2019, pp. 211–232.

[12] Fawzi Albalooshi and Amjad Mahmood, "A Comparative Study on the Effect of Multiple Inheritance Mechanism in Java, C++, and Python on Complexity and Reusability of Code," International Joutnal of Advanced Computer Science and Applications, vol. 8, no. 6, 2017, pp. 109–116.

[13] Matteo Orru et al., "How Do Python Programs Use Inheritance? A Replication Study," in 2015 Asia-Pacific Software Engineering Conference (APSEC). IEEE, 2015, pp. 309–315.

[14] Ravi Chugh, Patrick M Rondon, and Ranjit Jhala, "Nested refinements: a logic for duck typing," ACM SIGPLAN Notices, vol. 47, no. 1, 2012, pp. 231–244.

[15] John Hunt, Advanced Guide to Python 3 Programming, ser. Undergraduate Topics in Computer Science. Springer International Publishing, 2019.

On Evolvability Issues of Robotic Process Automation (RPA)

Geert Haerens

Department of Management Information Systems
Faculty of Business and Economics
University of Antwerp, Belgium
Engie IT — Digital & IT Consulting
Email: geert.haerens@engie.be

Herwig Mannaert

Department of Management Information Systems
Faculty of Business and Economics
University of Antwerp, Belgium
Email: herwig.mannaert@uantwerp.be

***Abstract*—Robotic Process Automation (RPA) receives a lot of publication attention in business and academic publications. RPA has also become big business, as it offers a cheap, fast and non-intrusive solution for businesses who want to improve their process performance while not having to re-engineer their processes and/or overhaul their IT landscape. Current literature points out some limitations for RPA but does not go much further than some rules of thumb. Using the Normalized Systems (NS) theory - a theory to study modular structures' behavior under change - we can surface that RPA has serious evolvability issues. These evolvability issues have been observed as well by RPA practitioners. This paper contributes to both the value of NS to study evolvability and to point out the evolvability limitations of RPA, which are currently underrepresented in related research.**

Keywords–RPA; Normalized Systems; Evolvability

I. INTRODUCTION

RPA is popular in the landscape of business process optimization methods. While executing a business process, multiple applications may be used. In an ideal and fully digital world, each process step can be handled by an IT system. The IT systems can exchange information and trigger each other, without the need for human intervention during to execution of the business process. Most companies have not reached this level of digitalization. They may lack applications to handle a part of the process or have existing applications that are not suited for application interaction and triggering. In those cases, a human will bridge the gap between applications to keep the process going. The idea behind RPA is to replace a human, who is performing tedious and repetitive tasks within or between applications, by a software robot - also known as a bot. Like the human, the bot - a software program operating on the user interface of a computer system [1] - only acts via the user interface of the application(s) to manipulate information stored in one or more applications. Manipulations happen via mouse-clicks and keyboard-strokes, just like humans would. RPA is a kind of outsourcing of repetitive tasks to the computer. The bots are our new "Co-workers" [2]. They are part of the future digital workforce [3]. A bot does not replace the human. A bot takes the "robot" out of the human [4], meaning that repetitive/robotic tasks are no longer done by the human, allowing human resources to focus on more value-added activities.

RPA is realized by a client-based piece of software and includes both a design- and a runtime aspect. The design-time part of RPA is typically a low code environment that allows to define what the bot needs to do. The run bot is running on a client-based machine, performing activities according to the scenarios outlined during design time.

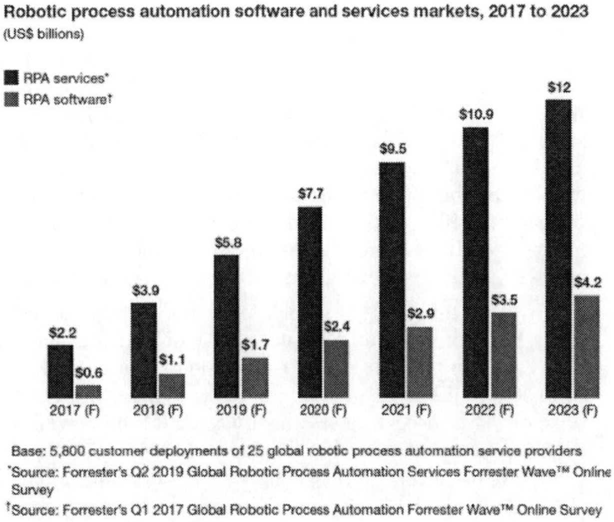

Figure 1. RPA market predictions according to Forrester - from [5]

RPA works well on cases where structured data is available as input and a clear, stable and standardized set of action rules exist, such that the outcome of the performed actions is unambiguous [4]. Typical targets for RPA are shared-service-center activities, which are highly standardized, such as financial, procurement, and HR Backoffice processes.

Process automation is widely accepted as a first step to the digital transformation of a company. Techniques, such as Business Process Management and Automation (BPM/A), have been around for some time. While those focus on fundamentally changing and continuously improving the process, RPA keeps the existing process and application landscape intact. RPA takes the valuable human resources out of the loop and replaces it by a bot. RPA promises faster, cheaper, and better execution of specific processes in a non-intrusive way. The RPA business is booming, both in terms of tooling which allow the design and run of bots, as in the services (consultancy) related to RPA, that include the selection of the right process for RPA, creation of the business case, setup of centers of excellence and operational maintenance of bots.

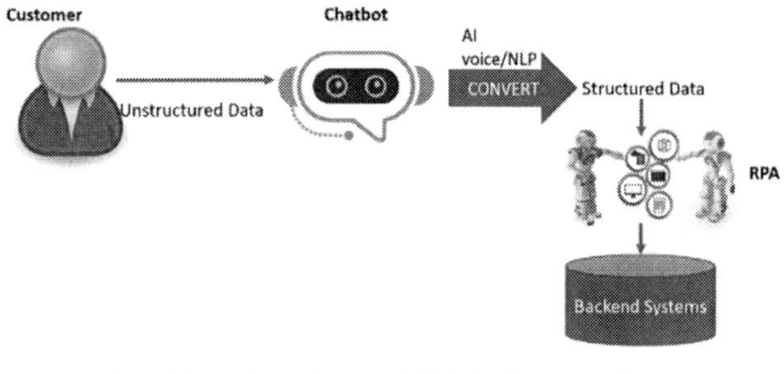

Figure 2. Combining AI (chatbots) and RPA for Customer Communications - from [8]

Figure 1 shows the predictions Forrester [5] is making with regards to the RPA market, both in tooling and services.

A great future is being projected for RPA, and that future becomes even more ambitious if RPA would be combined with Artificial Intelligence (AI) [6]. RPA can only work with structured data. AI holds the promise to convert unstructured data into structured data and continuously learn and improve in this. By combining both AI and RPA, processes previously out of reach for RPA become feasible candidates for automation. Figure 2 outlines a process that includes both AI at the front and RPA at the backend to interact with the customer [7].

Bright as this future may look, choosing the right process to apply RPA to, is the critical success factor. Existing literature limits itself to providing some rules of thumb. A critical aspect of choosing the right process for RPA, is the stability of the process. This aspect raises the question of how well RPA performs under a set of anticipated changes. The Normalized Systems theory [9]-[10] studies the effect of anticipated changes on modular systems. The theory uses concepts of classic engineering, such as system stability – Bounded Input = Bounded Output - and statistical entropy - possible microstates for a given macrostate - to determine the necessary conditions a modular system must adhere to, in order for the system to be stable under a set of anticipated changes. In this paper, NS will be used to study the impact of change on RPA [11].

The remainder of this paper is structured as follows. In Section II, RPA is being elaborated, including an overview of existing and related work. The Section also includes a basic introduction to NS. In Section III, the evolvability of RPA will be investigated using a simple but realistic process related to expense notes. In Section IV, two companies testify with regards to their RPA initiative. In Section V, the theoretical findings of Section III and the practical feedback from Section IV will be discussed. Finally, Section VI concludes and provides suggestions for further research.

II. Literature Study and Related Work

This paper focusses on the ability of RPA to cope with change and uses NS [11] theory as an analysis instrument. The next paragraphs will provide an overview of known RPA issues and a short introduction to NS.

A. *Literature on RPA issues*

In [12] it is stated that multiple publication can be found about the various benefits of RPA, based on real-life implementations - 68% of publications - but less on academic research

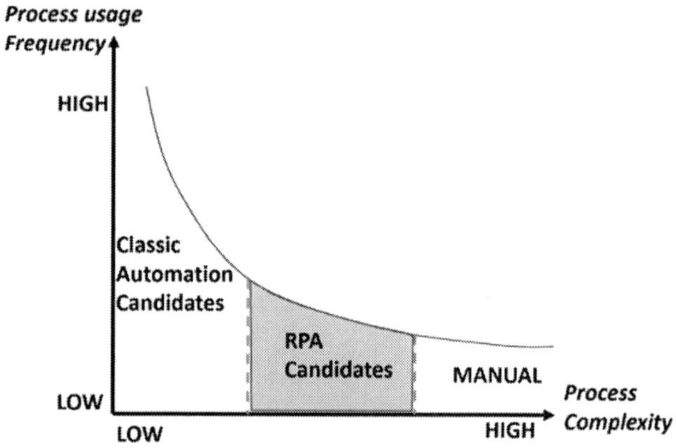

Figure 3. RPA processe candidates by process frequency and complexity - from [4]

on the topic -15% of publications). The remaining 18% are literature studies. The literature study [12] focused on publications that could provide insight to the following research questions: "RQ1: What is the current state and progress of RPA?", "RQ2: How is RPA defined and how does it relate to BPMS", and "RQ3: How is RPA used in practice according to the scientific literature".

RPA is taking up a good part of the current process management industry and is frequently a subject of analysis reports by Forrester and Gartner. Forrester analyst Craig Le Clain has made multiple reports on RPA, including observed limitations. The "Rule of five" [8] is an RPA design criteria that comes back a few times in his reports. The rule states that an RPA solution should limit itself of max five decisions, access to 5 applications, and should not contain more than 500 clicks. The main motivation for this rule of thumb, the limited rule capabilities, the static nature of the code, and vulnerability to application changes are given. According to Le Clain[6] [7][8], AI can help to overcome some of those issues. AI will reduce robot maintenance (auto-adjust to application changes), externalize decisions from the bot scripts, use unstructured data as input, and team-up with chatbots for data input. Some scenario's for auto-correction include AI as well. Changes to the application images/screens are to be detected by AI, and will adjust the bot script automatically. AI can be fed with information from outside of the RPA digital world, to understand and interpret the context of changes and sending alerts to bot control for issue that cannot be corrected with a high degree of certainty.

In [4], Jovanović et all point out the benefit of the non-intrusive nature of RPA. Business Process Management and Automation can only work if the applications used in a process have some integration points, like APIs, which allows the manipulation of data elements and execution of tasks. Those kind of integrations are more complicated and require higher programming skills compared to the low-code environment RPA often provides. With RPA, no adjustments of the existing applications are required, which is a compelling fact for businesses to choose RPA over BPM/A. Jovanovic et all [4] sum up properties of processes suitable for RPA:

- Low cognitive requirements

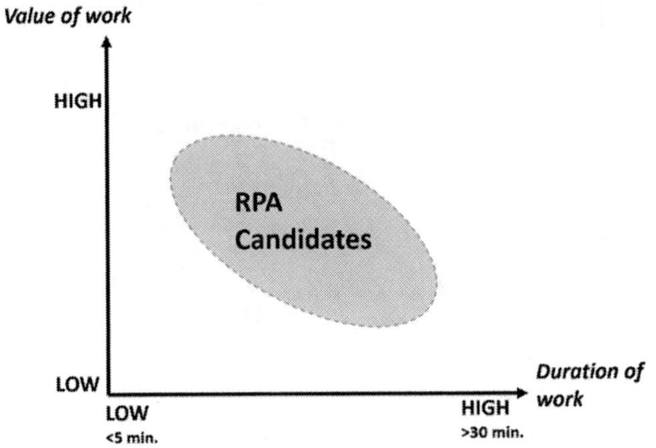

Figure 4. RPA processe candidates by value of work and duration of work - from [4]

- Access to multiple systems not required
- High Volume
- High probability of human error
- Limited exception handling

One may notice those are stricter compared to the "Rule of 5" of Forrester. Previous studies [2] show that supporting processing, such as those handled in shared service centers, are better candidates for RPA than the core (key) business processes. Supporting processes are more standardized and fall into the RPA candidates regions outlined in Figure 3 and 4. The paper of Jovanovic et all [4] concludes with a quote from Bill Gates [13]: 'The first rule of any technology used in a business is that automation applied to an efficient operation will magnify the efficiency. The second is that automation applied to an inefficient operation will magnify the Inefficiency'.

In [2], Osmundsen et all refers to work of Bygstad [14], which discusses the position of RPA in the IT organization. RPA can be seen as a personal productivity tool for business people, allowing them to automate parts of a process without having to go via the IT department. Such an approach is related to the setup of lightweight IT or Bimodal IT, as Gartner calls it. Business is able to self automate without having to startup big, lengthy, expensive, and sometimes frustrating IT projects. Classic IT departments (heavyweight IT) are of course, not happy with lightweight IT and often have a deep aversion against bots. They see bots as a poor man's integration tool, not even worthy of the name IT solution. Bygstad [14] argues RPA should be part of lightweight IT. The business knows best its processes and will thus be more successful in configuring the bot. Lightweight IT should be loosely coupled to heavyweight IT. This does introduce additional challenges, such as the lack of control mechanisms around RPA, leading to spaghetti-solutions and automating the wrong processes. The lack of end-to-end process views leading to local optimization, not necessarily global optimization, is listed as a second challenge. To overcome those challenges, one can see RPA in lightweight IT as a way to foster innovation and build enthusiasm for digitalization, while tightening the relationship with heavyweight IT at a later point in time.

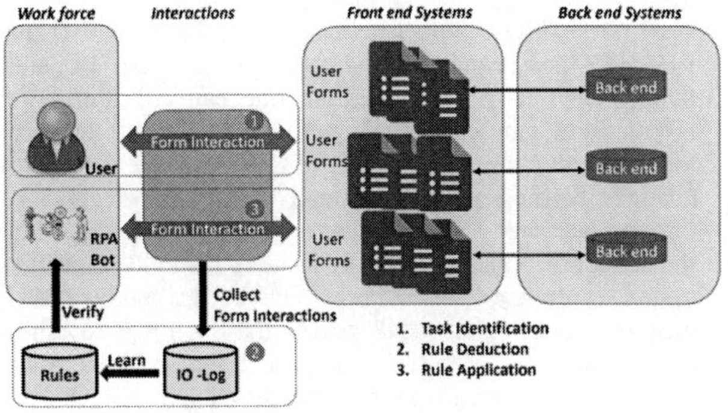

Figure 5. Method followed to deduce rule base, based on learing from human application interaction - from [15]

Goa et all [15] focus on the configuration of the bot. Instead of consciously creating the rule base the bot must use, they propose to learn the rule base from a human. An artifact is being proposed (see Figure 5) , which will deduce the rule base based on the interaction the human has with the application. After a while, the artifact will have sufficiently learned about the usage of the system to take over from the human. In their current approach, nothing is mentioned about re-training the bot in case of application changes and thus the impact of change on the bot.

In [16] the risks associated with RPA are divided into three categories: governance risks, technical risks, and process risks. The governance risks are related to the operating model associated with RPA: centralized, federated, or decentralized. Each operating model has different characteristics, which influence RPA maturity. The technical risks are about the impact of IT availability on RPA. If the technical side is not working, the process is directly impacted. The process risks are about the selection of the correct process to apply RPA to and the development steps to come to a working solution. RPA can execute repetitive work faster and with higher quality. However, if the process is not properly reflected or if it gets erroneous data as input, it will make mistakes more swiftly and with certainty [1]. Hence the need to select only processes that are well known and have stable and reliable input data.

To best of the authors efforts, no papers were been found that explicitly address the evolvability issues of RPA (main contribution of this paper). The literature that discusses the technical risks are the closets match. They describe the effects of change, not the root cause of these effects.

B. Introduction to NS

NS originates from the field of software development [9] [17] [10] . There is a widespread belief in the software engineering community that using software modules decrease complexity and increases evolvability. It is also well known that one should strive towards "low coupling and high cohesion". The problem is that the community does not seem to agree on how exactly "low coupling and high cohesion" needs to be achieved and what the size of a module should be, to achieve low complexity and high evolvability. NS takes the concept of system theoretic stability from the domain of classic engineering to determine the necessary conditions a modular structure of a system must adhere to in order for the system to exhibit stability under change. Stability is defined as Bounded Input equals Bounded Output (BIBO). Transferring this concept to software design, one can consider bounded input as a certain amount of functional changes to the software and the bounded output as the number of effective software changes. If the amount of effective software changes is not only proportional to the amount of functional changes but also the size of the existing software system, then NS states that the system exhibits a Combinatorial Effect (CE) and is considered unstable under change. NS proves that, in order to eliminate CE, the software system must have a certain modular structure, where each module respects four design theorems. Those rules are:

- Separation of Concern (SoC): A module should only address one concern or change driver
- Separation of State (SoS): A module should have a state which is observable by other modules.
- Action Version Transparency (AVT): A module, performing an action should be changeable without impacting modules calling this action.
- Data Version Transparency (DVT): A module performing a certain action on a data structure, should be able to continue doing this action, even is the data structures has undergone change (add/remove attributes)

Only by respecting those rules, the system can infinitly grow and still be able to incorporate new requirements. While the four theorems mentioned above are used during design time, NS has additional theorems usable for run time as well. Making use of the concept of statistical entropy, NS derives the necessary condition for a system to be diagnosable, being the ability to determine the actual microstate of a system, given a certain macrostate. Formulated differently, the software is not working (macrostate) because module x is not working (a microstate). The necessary condition for this is summarized in the following theorem:

- Instance Traceability: The ability to know the state of an instance of a module at run time.

Although NS originates in software design, the applicability of the NS principles in other disciplines, such as process design, organizational design, accounting, document management, and physical artifacts. The theory can be used to study evolvability in any system, which can be seen as a modular system and drive design criteria for the evolvability of the system.

The environment in which RPA is applied can be split into three layers: process, application, and infrastructure. Each of those layers can incure change. Making use of the NS theorems, it can be determined whether those changes will have an effect on RPA proportional to the change, or to the change AND the system itself (a combination of process, application, application, and RPA). In the former case, the introduction of RPA should be declared stable under change; in the latter case, RPA should be declared unstable under change.

III. Investigating Evolvability of RPA

In the next paragraph, a simple process step in an expense note process will be presented, followed by the introduction of RPA to automate this process step. This section is continued with a paragraph on the general impact of change in the process environment and concludes with the specific impact of those changes to RPA, to evaluate the degree of stability of RPA with respect to anticipated changes.

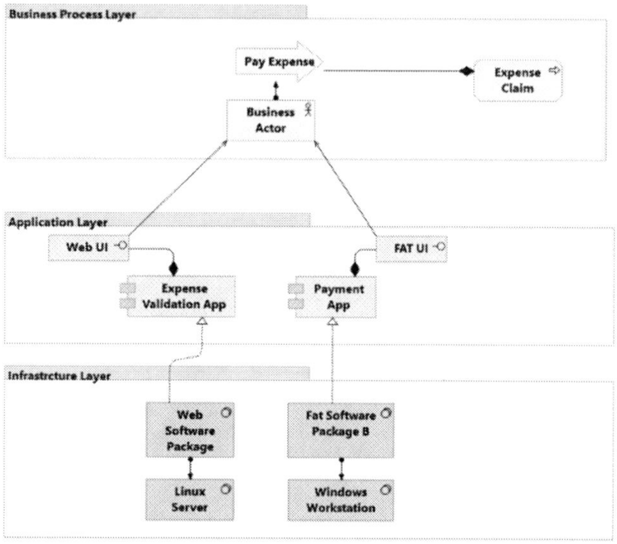

Figure 6. Refund process without RPA

A. Description of the process

Consider an expense note process. The process consists of an employee declaring his expenses, approval by the manager, and finally, reimbursement of the expense. Assume that a company has no IT system available, that has the possibility to detect the approval of an expense note by the manager, and a system that automatically performs the refund (money transfer). The company has an "Expense Validation" application and a "Payment" Application. A human (business actor) will connect to the "Expense Validation" application to see which expenses are currently flagged as "validated" and then use the "Payment" application to perform the actual money transfer to the expense claimer. The "Expense Validation" application is realized by a web application installed on a Linux host. The "Payment" application consists of a fat client application realized by a software package running on a Windows workstation. The UIs (Web and fat client) of both applications are used by the human business actor to perform the "Pay Expense" process step. A visual representation of the layered architecture, using ArchiMate [18], can be found in Figure 6.

B. Introducing RPA

The described process step would be a good candidate for RPA as the process step is simple, and all information required for deciding and launching the "Pay Expense" process step, is available in the "Expense Validation" and "Payment" application. The human Business Actor is being replaced by a bot, which will use the UI of both applications to perform the process step. The bot itself is a "bot Player" application, which is realized by RPA system software, which is being installed on a Windows workstation. A visual representation

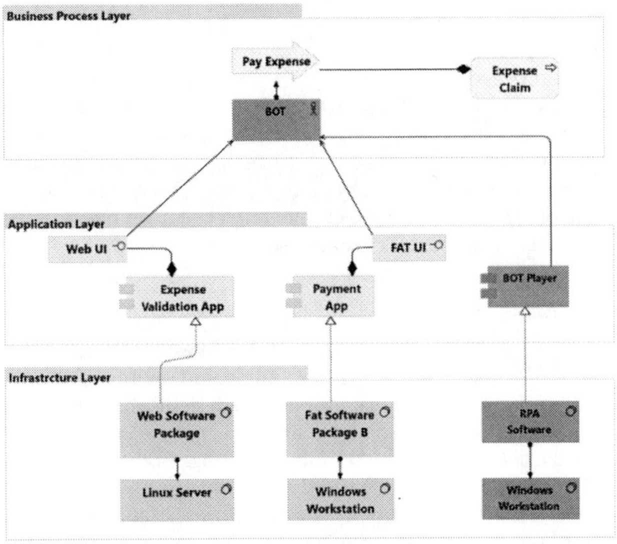

Figure 7. Refund process with RPA

of the layered architecture, including the bot, can be found in Figure 7.

C. Changes in the process environment

A lot of businesses struggle with change in general. Putting cultural change aside, making changes to a company often has unforeseen side effects, coined as ripple effects in NS, due to hidden couplings in the organization. Those couplings can be found in and between the organizational structure of the business, the processes inside the organization, the applications supporting the processes and the infrastructure supporting the applications. NS has studied the effects of change at the business process layer [19], the application layer [9] [17] [10], and the infrastructure layer [20]. In each of those layers, CE are present. They can be eliminated or mitigated by applying the NS principles by careful and conscious design of processes, applications, and infrastructure.

RPA is part of the process environment. It is part of an environment in which changes can ripple in all directions and with varying intensity. It should come as no surprise that a system as RPA, which works at the edge of the environment via the UI, will be impacted by changes to the process, application, and infrastructure layer.

D. Changes in the RPA environment

The environment in which the bot is working can be subject to the following changes:

- At the Business Process Layer, changes to the process can happen, such as the addition of an extra process step and the introduction of a new business actor. In the example process, an extra validation step could be added for expenses higher than a certain amount.
- At the Application Layer, changes to the application can happen due to changes in the process or changes to the software (the addition/removal of data objects, data object attributes, new process steps, new UI components). In the example process, expense claims higher than a certain amount needs to be explicitly selected and a particular transaction with this selection needs to be launched
- At the Infrastructure Layer, changes to hosts and system software can happen due to the scaling of the application, new system software releases, the usage of different compute resources. In the example process, changes to the OS version may lead to a higher screen resolution, resulting in a repositioning of UI elements on the screen.

The above changes can be anticipated over the life cycle of the Business Process. The changes will ultimately become visible to the Business Actor via the UI:

- New clicks and stokes to be performed in the UI of the application due to changes in the process.
- New clicks and stokes to be performed in the UI of the application due to addition, removal or relocation of information and action items in the UI.
- New location and/or size of action and information items due to new UI elements, UI look and feel and UI behavior.

The UI of the application is literally the only window on the process in the digital world. Human actors can act according to information available in the real world and the digital world. For instance, a change in the process could be explained via a communication letter, and the human actor would be able to understand and act on the corresponding application changes due to information provided outside of the digital world. A bot cannot do this and will require reprogramming to cope with the changing scenario. As the UI is the only window on the process in the digital world, the UI will reflect the aggregation of all change drivers possible in the environment. This is a clear violation of the Separation of Concerns principle of NS. Behind one UI element, multiple concerns may be hidden. Changes to the UI element can be due to several reasons. Without additional information outside of the digital world, the reason for the change and the appropriate action to take, cannot be determined. The fact that the UI is the aggregation of all change drivers also makes the diagnosability of RPA an issue. A change visible in the UI cannot be traced back to its origin (process, application, infrastructure) by only looking at the UI. The full-stack needs to be investigated. This is a violation of the Instance Traceability principle, leading to a CE.

From the above, the conclusion can be drawn that the environment in which RPA operates, being an environment in which the only interaction point with the process is through application UI's, is inherently unstable under change, as it violates both the Separation of Concerns and Instance Traceability design principles of NS. Although the impact of change to the RPA solution itself has not been studied, one can expect evolvability issues there as well. A new version of the bot software, run time, or design time could affect the previous behavior of the bot. The design of the bot behavior could also include CE, as a change to the behavior of the bot (adding an additional click in the workflow) could be proportional to the size of the program/configuration expressing that behavior.

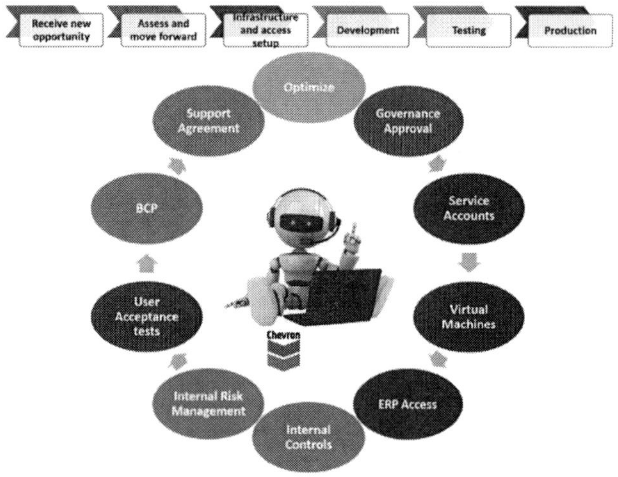

Figure 8. RPA path @ Chevron - from [21]

IV. RPA CASES

In this section, 2 international companies in the energy sector, Chevron and Engie, testify about thier experience with RPA.

A. Chevron

During Oracle Open World 2019 [21] , Carolina Barcos and Enrique Barrantes of Chevron shared their experience with RPA during the session "Robotic Process Automation: Lessons Learned". Chevron (a worldwide utilities company) has defined an RPA path (see Figure 8), which consists of six steps. During the "Process intake" step, the candidate process is being investigated for suitability for RPA. During the "Assess and move forward" step, the business case for applying RPA on the process is being presented to get governance approval. During the "Infrastructure and access setup" step, application accounts, application access, the compute resources, and service accounts are being collected. In the "Development" step, the bot rule base is developed, and the necessary internal controls are put in place to feed internal risk management. During the "Testing" step, the bot undergoes user acceptance tests. In the final "Production" step, the Business Continuity plan is set up (what if the bot fails?), and the support agreement with the business is drawn.

Chevron quickly learned that there is no such thing as a "simple process". Business typically oversimplifies their process description, and at the beginning of the RPA initiative, only a part of the actual process is known. Because of the popularity of RPA, the business is sometimes too eager to use RPA, while there may be other quick wins and low hanging fruit available to optimize the process. An essential enabler of the RPA setup process is to get risk management, internal control, and business continuity on board asap and to get their approval before go-live. In terms of development approach, Chevron goes for agile: fail fast – improve – do it again. Chevron identifies the collection of all accesses to all required systems and applications, as an attention point.

At Chevron, RPA is not seen as a local and personal productivity tool. A lot of effort goes into setting up the right RPA environment, running on virtual machines, having development, acceptance, and production bot and using scheduling and orchestration between bots. The impact of infrastructure changes, such as Windows patching, is recognized. The last but not least lessons learned is the need to be in the loop of "unexpected changes in systems," ...which seems like a contradiction. The experience certainly comes from often encountered bot failure or incorrect behavior due to change the RPA team was not aware of.

B. Engie IT

Engie IT is part of Global Business Services at Engie (Utilities and Energy Services company). Within Engie IT, a particular group has been set up which helps the business with the setup of RPA solution and the operational maintenance of the RPA solutions. During a meeting, both the results and reflection of Section III and the Chevron case where presented. The team wholeheartedly agreed with the conclusions from Section III and has similar experiences as Chevron. Engie IT has the advantage of being part of a lot of IT initiatives within the group. When they receive a request to use RPA, the process and applications are also checked against known ongoing efforts, like consolidation or improvements at group level. This can help in the decision to go for RPA (process suited or new initiatives related to process optimization are too far away), or not (process not suited or process/application will undergo major change soon). The RPA team admits that it's sometimes hard to properly evaluate a process/application for RPA suitability. The team was seeking additional guidance. It was those remarks which triggered the creation of this paper. They mentioned one compelling use case, which was not mentioned in the studied literature. Within Engie here as some strategic initiatives regarding consolidations and moves towards SAP4HANA. They found RPA to be an excellent solution to migrate data from the current systems to the new ones. The creation and testing of special application used for the transfer of data from the current application to the new application, can be more cumbersome and expensive compared to a simple re-keying all information from the as-is application into the to-be application, by a short-lived, straight forward, never tiering bot.

V. DISCUSSION

Not every process is suitable for RPA, but still, a lot of processes, especially supporting processes, are a good candidate for RPA. Sufficient cases exist where RPA turns out to be quite profitable (just Google "RPA success stories" and/or see [22] [23] [24] for some examples). Based on the analysis done in Section III, the conclusion can be drawn that RPA is inherently unstable under change. By only looking at the UI, the origin of change and reason for change cannot be deducted. Both Chevron and Engie IT confirm that protection against unplanned change is not possible. The only kind of reasonable protection is proper logging of the bot steps and detection of which action caused failure. As shown in Section III, that may tell when a crash occurred but not to why it occurred.

The "Rule of 5" of Forrester [8] is a mechanism to make sure that the complete system does not become too big. Although not presented or described this way, the rule recognizes the CE in the system. If the system is not too big, you can still handle the CE. But as the system grows, the effect becomes larger up to the point where it no longer manageable.

RPA tool vendors already mention today the usage AI in bots, allowing them to autocorrect and thus compensate for the inherent instabilities of RPA due to change. One must be skeptical about those kind statements for multiple reasons. First, if a bot would make use of programming techniques where all screen elements are represented by concepts that are independent of the actual screen layout or usage of relevant positions, a bot could indeed be protected from cosmetic changes on the screen. Although a smart move, it has nothing to do with AI. Second, as the UI is the aggregation of all concerns, in the UI there is no data available on which a Machine Learning Algorithm could perform any kind of learning. The "cause" data is not available; only the "effect" data (not working) is. Third, even if data about the origin of the change is available, where would the training data for the AI come from? For a Machine Learning Algorithm, large quantities of data on all kinds of changes at the process, application, and infrastructure layer, plus their effect and remediation, need to be available to have a decent set of training data. Where would this data come from? For a Deep Learning Algorithm, the same restriction holds.

AI could work if it is fed by data external to the RPA digital world. But if that is the case, then it must mean that AI is able to use data from within an application and thus have access to internal data and function of the application. In those cases, one can ask the question of what would be the point of still using RPA, as all elements could be on the table to have a real application integrate with existing applications and thus perform automation via programming, even via low code programming, without having to change the existing IT landscape as well. This paper does not have the ambition to prove the statements around AI formally. What it does want to do is to provide a critical note using a reductio ad absurdum approach. The subject should be further investigated.

One of the Engie IT RPA support engineers is seeing RPA tool vendors moving toward API based interaction between applications instead of UI based interaction. This means that those vendors are moving more into the realm of BPM/A.

Besides the potential stability issues of RPA, some other perverse side effects may arise. An Enterprise Architect of a Belgium Banking and Assurance company, sees RPA becoming a blocking factor for system evolution and innovation. As the business has invested a lot of money in RPA, changes to their existing landscape directly impact their RPA investments. The business becomes reluctant to improve and innovate on their current landscape and chooses a status quo to protect their RPA investments.

VI. CONCLUSION

RPA is popular, certainly within the business, as it offers a fast, cheap, and non-intrusive way to boost the performance of business processes. Although some rules of thumb exist regarding which processes to choose, current studies go past the inherently unstable nature of RPA. The impact of change is reported, not the root cause. Using NS, the reasons for the impact become clear: violation of the minimum requirements for evolvability.

AI is often mentioned as a mechanism to compensate for the instabilities of RPA due to change, but additional research on this topic is required. The stability of the RPA configuring and programming methods with regards to change – add new clicks, strokes – has been left out of scope but merits additional research as well.

ACKNOWLEDGMENT

The authors wishe to express their gratitude to Engie IT and Chevron for sharing their experiences, and to Frederik Leemans, Bertrand Perardelle and Stefan Thys for reviewing and commenting on the paper.

REFERENCES

[1] M. Kirchmer, "Robotic process automation - pragmatic solution or dangerous illusion?" 2017, URL: https://www.researchgate.net/publication/317730848 Robotic¡ _Process_Automation_-_Pragmatic_Solution_or_Dangerous_Illusion, [accessed: 2020-08-01].

[2] K. Osmundsen, J. Iden, and B. Bygstad, "Organizing Robotic Process Automation: Balancing Loose and Tight Coupling," in Proceedings of the 52nd Hawaii International Conference on System Science, Jan 8-11, 2019,Grand Wailea, Maui, Hawaii, Januari 2019, pp. 6918–6926, URL: https://scholarspace.manoa.hawaii.edu/handle/10125/60128?mode=full, ISBN: 978-0-9981331-2-6, [accessed: 2020-08-01].

[3] S. Madakam, R. M. Holmukhe, and D. K. Jaiswal, "The future digital work force: Robotic process automation (rpa)," JISTEM-Journal of Information Systems and Technology Management, vol. 16, 2019, URL: https://www.scielo.br/scielo.php?script=sci_arttext&pid= S1807-17752019000100300, [accessed: 2020-08-01].

[4] S. Jovanović, J. Đurić, and T. Šibalija, "Robotic process automation: overview and opportunities," International Journal "Advanced Quality", vol. 46, no. 3-4, 2018, pp. 34–39, URL: http://journal.jusk.rs/index.php/ijaq/issue/view/12, [accessed: 2020-08-01].

[5] C. LeClain, "Use The Rule Of Five To Find The Right RPA Process," Forrester, September 2018.

[6] B. Evelson and C. LeClain, "Look To Four Use Case Categories To Push RPA And AI Convergence," Forrester, August 2018.

[7] C. Craig, "RPA, DPA, BPM, And DCM Platforms: The Differences You Need To Know," Forrester, March 2019.

[8] C. LeClain, "Attended-Mode RPA: The Differences You Need To Know," Forrester, August 2019.

[9] H. Mannaert, J. Verelst, and K. Ven, "The transformation of requirements into software primitives: Studying evolvability based on systems theoretic stability," Science of Computer Programming, vol. 76, no. 12, 2011, pp. 1210–1222, URL:https://www.sciencedirect.com/journal/science-of-computer-programming/vol/76/issue/12, [accessed: 2020-08-01].

[10] ——, "Towards evolvable software architectures based on systems theoretic stability," Software: Practice and Experience, vol. 42, no. 1, 2012, pp. 89–116, URL:https://onlinelibrary.wiley.com/toc/1097024x/2012/42/1,[accessed: 2020-08-01].

[11] P. Huysmans, G. Oorts, D. Bruyn, H. P., Mannaert, and J. Verelst, "Positioning the normalized systems theory in a design theory framework," in Second International Symposium, BMSD 2012, July 4-6, 2012,Geneva, Switzerland. Springer, 2012, pp. 43–63, URLhttps://link.springer.com/book/10.1007/978-3-642-37478-4, [accessed: 2020-08-01].

[12] L. Ivančić, D. S. Vugec, and V. B. Vukšić, "Robotic process automation: Systematic literature review," in Proceedings of Business Process Management: Blockchain and Central and Eastern Europe Forum, Sept 1-6, 2019, Vienna. Springer, 2019, pp. 280–295, URL: https://link.springer.com/book/10.1007/978-3-030-30429-4, [accessed: 2020-08-01.

[13] "Quote Bill Gates on automation," 2015, URL: https://www.capgemini.com/2015/01/tempted-to-rewrite-bill-gates-rules-on-automation/, [accessed: 2020-08-01].

[14] B. Bygstad, "Generative innovation: a comparison of lightweight and heavyweight it," Journal of Information Technology, vol. 32, no. 2, 2017, pp. 180–193, URL: https://link.springer.com/journal/41265/32/2, ISSN: 0268-3962 (Print) 1466-4437 (Online), [accessed: 2020-08-01].

[15] J. Gao, S. J. van Zelst, X. Lu, and W. M. van der Aalst, "Automated robotic process automation: A self-learning approach," in Proceedings of "OTM Confederated International Conferences" On the Move to Meaningful Internet Systems, Confederated International Conferences: CoopIS, ODBASE, C&TC 2019, October 21–25, 2019, Rhodes, Greece, ". Springer, October 2019, pp. 95–112, URL: https://link.springer.com/book/10.1007/978-3-030-33246-4), [accessed: 2020-08-01].

[16] M. Lacity and L. P. Willcocks, Robotic process automation and risk mitigation: The definitive guide. SB Publishing, 2017, ISBN:978-09-95-68-20-30.

[17] H. Mannaert, J. Verelst, and P. De Bruyn, Normalized systems theory: from foundations for evolvable software toward a general theory for evolvable design. Koppa, 2016, ISBN: 978-90-77160-09-1.

[18] "ArchiMate 3.1 Specifications," 2019, An Open Group Standard URL: https://pubs.opengroup.org/architecture/archimate3-doc/, [accessed: 2020-08-01].

[19] D. Van Nuffel, H. Mannaert, C. De Backer, and J. Verelst, "Towards a deterministic business process modelling method based on normalized systems theory," International Journal on Advances in Software, vol. 3, no. 1-2, 2010, URL:http://www.iariajournals.org/software/tocv3n12.html, [accessed: 2020-08-01].

[20] G. Haerens, "Investigating the applicability of the normalized systems theory on it infrastructure systemst," in Workshop on Enterprise and Organizational Modeling and Simulation (EOMAS), 2018, Jun 11-12, Talinn, Estonia. Springer, June 2018, pp. 123–137, URL: https://link.springer.com/book/10.1007/978-3-030-00787-4, [accessed: 2020-08-01].

[21] "Robotic Process Automation: Lessons Learned," 2014, Presentation Oracle Open World 2019, URL: https://events.rainfocus.com/widget/oracle/oow19/catalogow19?search=Chevron, [accessed: 2020-08-01].

[22] A. Asatiani and E. Penttinen, "Turning robotic process automation into commercial success–case opuscapita," Journal of Information Technology Teaching Cases, vol. 6, no. 2, 2016, pp. 67–74, URL: https://link.springer.com/journal/41266/6/2, ISSN: 2043-8869 (Online), [accessed: 2020-08-01].

[23] S. Balasundaram, , and S. Venkatagiri, "A structured approach to implementing robotic process automation in hr," in Proceedings of the Third National Conference on Computational Intelligence NCCI 2019, 2019 Dec 6-7, Bangalore, India, vol. 1427, no. 1. IOP Publishing, 2019, p. 012006, URL: https://iopscience.iop.org/issue/1742-6596/1427/1, [accessed: 2020-08-01.

[24] W. A. Ansari, P. Diya, S. Patil, and S. Patil, "A review on robotic process automation-the future of business organizations," 2019, URL: https://papers.ssrn.com/sol3/papers.cfm?abstract_id=3370211, [accessed: 2020-08-01].

Exploring the Application of Ontologies in Organizations for Data Harmonization

Carlos Tubbax

Faculty of Business and Economics
University of Antwerp
Antwerp, Belgium
Email: carlos.tubbax@uantwerpen.be

Jan Verelst

Faculty of Business and Economics
University of Antwerp
Antwerp, Belgium
Email: jan.verelst@uantwerpen.be

***Abstract*—In this contribution, it is explained how ontologies could be used by business organizations to integrate data from heterogenous sources in a systematic process called *data harmonization*. In order to add academic rigor, Normalized Systems Theory (NST) has been used as a rationale to study the modularity concerns of this data harmonization project. Data harmonization consists in this contribution of three steps and offers certain advantages compared to other data integration approaches such as data-warehousing. The first are its simplicity and flexibility. The second is that the mapping costs of such an approach will just increase linearly and no longer exponentially. Additionally, the author illustrates how data harmonization can be conducted through a use case in which several datasets on US stock exchanges are mapped to the Financial Industry Business Ontology (FIBO) before being integrated for information retrieval through predefined SPARQL queries. The main contribution of this work is that it shows step-by-step how data harmonization can be conducted with costs that no longer increase exponentially but linearly as the number of data sources and destinations increases by means of a numeraire topology.**

Keywords*–Ontology; Data Harmonization; Financial Industry Business Ontology; Numeraire Typology; Graph

I. Introduction

Data management issues might have significantly contributed to the unfolding of the 2008-2009 financial crisis [1]. As a response to this, several news regulatory efforts have appeared to tackle this issues, such as *BCBS239* [2]. However, financial institutions and banks still have problems when integrating data from different sources due to several causes. The first set of causes consists namely of the heterogeneity of data sources in terms of granularity, formats, technologies and schemas [3]. Another cause is the large amounts of data that emerge every day (i.e., Big Data) that are still troublesome for most financial organizations. The last cause is the rigidity of traditional relational and data-warehousing systems making them not scalable and flexible enough to cope with Big Data. That being said, all these problems combined hamper financial organizations to comply with new regulatory efforts, to act upon new challenges and to reap new business models [4] [5].

This work aims at illustrating how that can be done in a rather systematic and simple way in the context of business organizations. In section 2, a literature review will cover the different theories and technologies used in this work. Section 3 dives deeper into the data harmonization methodology used in this work. In section 4, a use case has been chosen to illustrate the implementation of this data harmonization methodology. Finally, section 5 describes the execution of such a use case and its results.

II. Literature Review

This section will give an introduction of the different technologies and theories used in this work.

A. The Semantic Web

The current World Wide Web lacks the ability to represent meaning in a way that not only humans can understand but also computers. As means to tackle this problem, the Semantic Web is equipped with languages that express inference rules that allow computers to do reasoning on data [6]. Additionally, the Semantic Web is aimed at enabling *smart* behavior across the web consisting of different applications where data in each application are kept up-to-date, synchronized and connected to changes in other applications. This is done by assigning a Unique Resource Identifier (URI) to each individual piece of data about a *resource*, such as a person, an object or a date in order to refer to them at the level of data rather than at the level of representation in the form of excel-sheets or websites as in the case of the current World Wide Web. That being said, the Semantic Web might be a web of data instead of a web of only applications [7].

B. Data storage paradigms

Relational databases may neglect the semantic of the relationships. Additionally, as the number of rows within a table increases, the number of joins and query time may increase, such as in the case of transitive queries (e.g., 'Who-are-the-friends-of-all-my-friends?'). Another problem is the lack of rigidity of relational databases making them particularly difficult to adapt to new business requirements or to scale them up. They may not be fit to integrate data from different sources due to their rigid nature either. Finally, changes in their schemas (i.e., deleting a foreign key) may have pervasive ripple effects across the entire database [5] [8] [9].

Concerning the second paradigm, the construction of a data-warehouse is a rather complex and arduous process in which several trade-offs and decisions have to be made in advance. Some of them are the up-front selection of a certain architecture, defining the right level of data granularity, the design of Extract-Transform-Load (ETL) capabilities and the design of an access layer with OLAP capabilities. Additionally, data-warehouses do not update data to changes in sources or other systems. Therefore, they are not suited as data repositories in the context of the *smart web* [7].

The last main paradigm is graph databases. Graph databases have a number of advantages compared to the previous paradigms. The first is stable performance by just performing queries over a portion of the total graph. The second is that no formal model is needed upfront making it more flexible to changes in business requirements, etc. The third is no longer having the need of a schema before ingesting data, such as in the case of ETL in traditional data-warehousing. The last advantage is the ability to increase the database's capacity by adding new servers (i.e., scale out) whereas relational databases scale up by adding more memory to a monolithic server. That means that the database is divided in several servers and only the servers containing the data needed to answer a certain query are accessed rather than the whole monolithic server. There are two types of graph databases, namely Property Graphs and RDF stores [5] [9]. This work only studies the latter.

C. Semantic Modelling

As previously mentioned, the Semantic Web is equipped with languages that allow users to define models of the domain of discourse in terms of taxonomies and inference rules. These models are called *ontologies* [6]. The more detailed a model is, the more expressive it is considered to be. The Semantic Web offers different modeling languages that offer different expressivity levels and are listed below [7].

- The Resource Description Framework (RDF)
- The RDF Schema Languages (RDFS)
- RDFS-plus
- The Ontology Web Language (OWL)

D. SPARQL

The 'S' Protocol and RDF query language or SPARQL is the query language of the Semantic Web. Every SPARQL query follows the pattern of the graph that is being queried. Although sharing many characteristics with SQL, such as the SELECT and WHERE commands, it has the unique feature of retrieving a graph as query output by using the CONSTRUCT command [10].

E. Financial Industry Business Ontology

The Financial Industry Business Ontology (FIBO) is a modular ontology aimed at representing the business logical of financial organizations in a standardized and unambiguous way that is readable by computers and humans. FIBO is jointly developed by the Enterprise Data Management (EDM) council and the Object Management Group (OMG) [11].

F. Normalized Systems theory

NST offers a set principles to build modular structures in software, organizations, etc. Such principles are based on systems stability and thermodynamics theory to reduce the number of ripple effects and increase the traceability of problems within a system. Although following such principles does not imply that all ripple effects will be eliminated, not following them will certainly lead to more ripple effects than otherwise. NST also depart from the notion of *Bounded Input Bounded Output* which implies that a bounded number of changes in a systems should always lead to a bounded number of impacts (i.e., ripple effects). In order to achieve this, NST offers four principles which are listed as follows [12].

- Separation of Concerns
- Data version transparency
- Action version transparency
- Separation of states

G. Data Harmonization

In spite of the abundance of data harmonization works, no formal definition is provided. Therefore, a definition for data harmonization will be provided. Since *semantic harmonization* should be separated from *technical harmonization*, both will be considered as separate dimensions [13]. In top of that, *data quality harmonization* will be considered the third dimension as follows:

- **Technical harmonization:** it entails converting data contained in heterogenous datasets and databases to be merged into a singular format that can be stored and queried by the same technical implementation (e.g., transforming data contained as XML-files, .csv-files and in other formats into triples that can be stored in the same RDF store and queried by the same SPARQL engine). These are rather cross-cutting concerns that should be separated from other aspects of the data harmonization process as suggested by NST [13].
- **Semantic Harmonization:** this entails mapping the different concepts and data fields in the heterogeneous sources to a representation of the domain of discourse needed and agreed on by domain experts and business users [13].
- **Data quality harmonization:** heterogeneity of data sources and datasets also brings heterogeneity in terms of data quality which needs to be handled properly to create a singular view in the form of a federated database consisting of high quality data. Therefore, data quality must be brought to a level that complies with business requirements [13].

In addition to these dimensions of data harmonization, a data harmonization architecture will be needed to integrate different systems [14]. Two possible architectures are described in further detail below (see Figure 1).

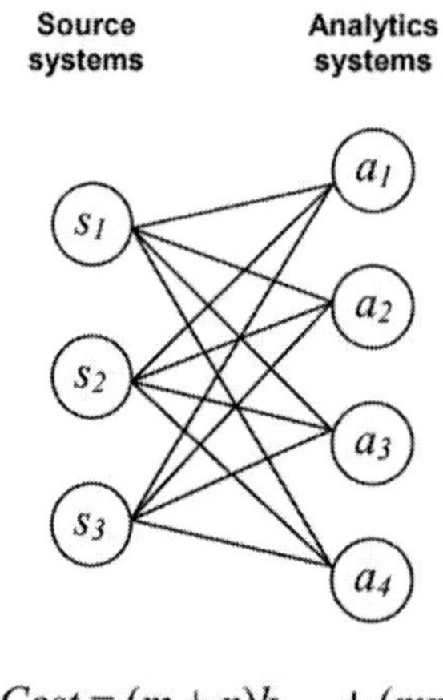

$$Cost = (m + n)k_{spec} + (mn)k_{map}$$

Figure 1. Stovepipe topology

The first architecture is the stovepipe topology as illustrated in Figure 1. Costs are considered to consists of specification costs (k_{spec}) and mapping costs (k_{map}). Specification costs are related to the specification of the schema of each system and, in this case, they are assumed to be constant for all systems. Mapping costs (k_{map}) are the costs related to the mapping of each different source system to all the different target systems and, in this case, they are also assumed to be constant for each pair of systems. Assuming there are m source systems and n target systems. Given that the total mapping cost $(mn)k_{map}$ is proportional to the size of the graph, the total implementation cost of such a topology would increase exponentially as depicted by the equation at the bottom of Figure 1 [14]. This also implies that a bounded input (e.g., adding a new source system) may lead to an unbounded output which is highly discouraged by NST [12].

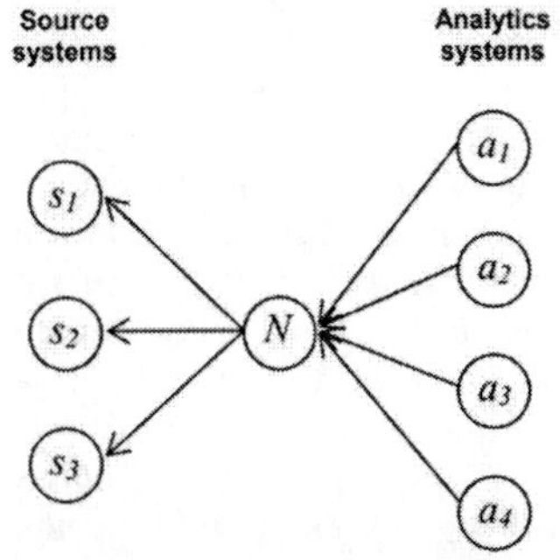

$$Cost = k_N + (m+n)k_{spec} + (m+n)k_{map}$$

Figure 2. Numeraire topology

The second architecture is the numeraire topology as illustrated in Figure 2. Costs are also considered to consist of specification costs (k_{spec}) and mapping costs (k_{map}). However, by introducing an intermediate metadata layer that decouples the target systems from the source systems, the resulting total mapping cost is no longer dependent on the size of the overall graph and only on the total number of source and target systems which might be equal to $(m+n)$. Additionally, the cost of specifying such an intermediate metadata layer is (k_N). Moreover, such an architecture uses a 'pull' strategy that departs from the inputs needed for analyses in the target systems to define the outputs that the different source systems must deliver. The total implementation cost of such a topology would increase just linearly over time as depicted by the equation at the bottom of Figure 2 [14]. Another advantage is that this architecture will remain more stable over time as a bounded input will lead to a bounded output as suggested by NST. This could only be achieved if the interfaces of the different systems in such an architecture are well insulated to comply with the *data version transparency* and *action version transparency* principles of NST. In other words, interfaces should encapsulate changes in the data and program structures within each system to avoid pervasive ripple effects on other systems [12]. Therefore, this architecture will be used to this data harmonization project [14].

III. Data Harmonization Methodology

In order to conduct any data harmonization endeavor, a sound methodology is needed to guide users. Therefore, a data harmonization methodology has been developed for this project consisting of three steps as follows. Step 1 will comprise the definition of high-level requirements in terms of business questions that need to be (graphically) answered for business users and decision makers. Finally, in Step 3, more detailed requirements will be specified for each of the three dimensions of data harmonization.

A. Defining high-level requirements (step 1)

Step 1 will comprise the definition of high-level requirements in terms of business questions that need to be (graphically) answered for business users and decision makers

B. Defining a data harmonization architecture (step 2)

Departing from the outputs of Step 1, a data harmonization architecture and its components will be designed in Step 2 following the *numeraire topology* in a *'pull fashion'*. In alignment to NST, the interfaces of the different systems within such a topology must be *data version transparent* and *action version transparent* to isolate changes in each system from other components within the overall data harmonization architecture [12].

C. Defining a low-level requirements (step 3)

Finally, in Step 3, more detailed requirements will be specified for each of the three dimensions of data harmonization as follows.

The technical harmonization requirements will cover the technical concerns of converting the data from the source systems to a format that can be stored and queried in the same storage implementation. Some of these requirements will be what serialization format will be used or what type of inferencing will be performed (*cached* or *just-in-time*). The semantic harmonization requirements will be needed to map the data fields in the different source system to their respective representations of the domain of discourse in the form of an ontology. As a matter of academic rigor and to make this methodology more generalizable, semantic harmonization principles found in the academic literature have been aligned to Normalized Systems Theory (NST) [12] [14].

Data quality harmonization is the last dimension whose requirements will be needed to bring the quality of the data in all the different source systems to a level suited to for answering the predefined business questions from Step 1. This will be done by using certain data quality metrics.

After the definition of these requirements, the data in each source will be harmonized independently from the other ones to isolate the concerns inherent to each systems and delivering loosely coupled outputs as suggested by the *Separation of Concerns* and *Separation of States* theorems from NST [12]. Accordingly, the data in each source will be converted into a RDF graph by using the CONSTRUCT command from SPARQL [10]. However, the identification and specification of dependencies between such RDF graphs are crucial since they represent the connection points between them. Therefore, an iterative approach will be followed to identify these connection points and to specify them in a way that facilitates the integration of such individual graphs into federated ones.

IV. Data Harmonization Planning

A business case, provided by D. Allemang, and A. Keen, will be used to illustrate the data harmonization methodology mentioned above. It is fictitious and has been formulated to show a realistic business scenario. Such a business scenario in this consists of unraveling the rather complex and nested ownership and control relationships between companies listed in different US stock markets and other companies. A listed company is defined as: '*a company whose shares can be traded on a country's main stock market*' [15]. AMEX, NASDAQ and NYSE are the three main stock markets in the United States that list the stocks of different companies, such as Facebook, Amazon and Apple. That being said, it would be of great value for brokers, banks, hedge funds and investors in general to have a sight of the companies that either own any, or are owned by any of these listed companies. Therefore, the planning of this data harmonization project will follow the methodology described above as follows.

A. Defining high-level requirements (step 1)

Based on the description above, the following high-level business questions have been formulated:

- What companies are listed by AMEX, NASDAQ and NYSE?
- What are the parent companies and subsidiaries of these listed companies?
- Where are all these companies located?

Additionally, the results obtained from the data harmonization process meant to answer these questions will be used to generate user-friendly visualizations for business people by means of Business Intelligence tools.

B. Defining a data harmonization architecture (step 2)

The source systems containing the data needed to answer these questions are listed as follows:

- Datasets that contain data about the companies listed on AMEX, NASDAQ and NYSE have been retrieved from NASDAQ's website [16].
- The Global Legal Entity Foundation (GLEIF) is an organization aimed at providing unique identifiers to legal entities. Additionally, they provide datasets about ownership and control relationships between these legal entities. Therefore, the dataset containing data on ownership relationships between listed companies and other companies have been imported from GLEIF's website [17].
- Additionally, a dataset containing further information (e.g., postal codes and names) of the legal entities registered by GLEIF has been imported as well [18].
- The last source system consists of datasets on postal codes and their coordinates retrieved from the GeoNames organizations [19].

As metadata layer of such an architecture, data.world is an open data platform and has been selected because of its user-friendly interface and API capabilities. More specifically, data.world will be the platform in which the different source systems will be integrated and from which outputs for the target systems will be exported through its APIs. Finally, Tableau is a Business Intelligence interface that allows users to import data and visualize them in a wide variety of forms for further analysis. Therefore, this is the target system chosen for this project.

C. Defining a low-level requirements (step 3)

The source systems containing the data needed to answer these questions are listed as follows:

- **Technical harmonization.** Because of the limited scope of this work, the technical harmonization requirements to each source will be considered to be rather simple. All datasets used in this project will be exported as .csv-files to data.world's platform in a straightforward way. However, this would not be the case if the data would need to be retrieved from a relational database through SQL queries or an API. Therefore, no requirements will be defined regarding such concerns. Moreover, the way triples will be inferred must be determined. Inferred triples can either be saved (i.e., *cached*) or inferred at the spot (i.e., *just-in-time*). However, this choice entails important change management implications because cached triples will need to be deleted if their source changes or no longer exists whereas that would not be necessary for just-in-time triples. Given that this project will have a static nature instead of a dynamic one in which sources constantly change, the data in each source system will be converted to and saved as cached triples by using CONSTRUCT queries in SPARQL and saving them in graphs. Additionally, these triples will be saved in an RDF serialization file format known as *turtle*. Such a *turtle* file can be stored and queried by any RDF store. Since URIs represent the dependencies and intersections between graphs, URIs should be standardized and properly managed across graphs. Otherwise, this would result in lots fragmented triples that are not integrable one to another.
- **Semantic harmonization.** The data fields from each data source will be mapped to their respective meanings according to FIBO. As a matter of academic rigor, semantic harmonization principles were aligned to NST and will serve as a foundation to formulate the requirements for this part of the project as follows. As first semantic harmonization requirement, technical and semantic harmonization should be done separately. Secondly, classes should be separated from inference rules. Thirdly, standardized vocabularies, such as the ones provided by FIBO should be reused. Finally, the different concepts in the datasets should be mapped to their respective meanings in FIBO via declarative CONSTRUCT queries in SPARQL [12] [14].
- **Data quality harmonization.** In order to define the requirements for data quality harmonization, data quality will be measured through different metrics provided for this work. Based on the needs of business users and by using these metrics, data will be adjusted if necessary. This will be done separately for each dataset.

V. Data Harmonization Execution

The planning formulated above has been executed as follows. Firstly, data harmonization has been performed on the individual datasets which, in turn, were converted to individual *named* graphs. Secondly, the goal of defining them as *named* graphs is to have the ability to import them for federated queries in which several graphs are integrated and retrieved at the same time as also done in the next execution step of this work [10]. Finally, the query results were exported to Tableau for further graphical analysis. Each of these steps are described in more detail below. The entire project can be found on https://data.world/carlostubbax1/masters-thesis.

A. Data harmonization step

The four datasets mentioned above were harmonized and converted to four different graphs. For example, the dataset about ownership and control relationships has been mapped to FIBO and converted to a graph (see Figure 3). It can be noticed that the subject of the property *fibo-fnd-oac-oac:ownsAndControl* is the URI of the LEI of the parent company while the object is the one of the subsidiary. Additionally, this property could be considered as transitive given that, if A owns B and B owns C, A owns C. Therefore, *owl:TransitiveProperty* has been used to represent that as an inference rule. For example, given that General Motors Company owns Opel Bank GmbH and Opel Bank GmbH owns Opel Bank GmbH (Niederlassung Griecheland), the query engine will infer that General Motors Company also owns Opel Bank GmbH (Niederlassung Griecheland).

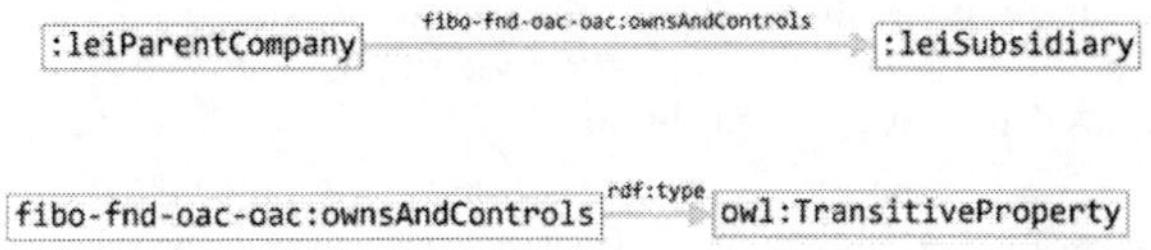

Figure 3. The *fibo-fnd-oac-oac:ownsAndControl* relationship

The namespace *https://lei.info/* has been used to generate standardized URIs of the LEIs of the companies in the datasets. Using that namespace allowed me to generate a URI for each legal entity identifier that can be recycled across several graphs or even across the semantic web. Additionally, this allows users to merge this graph to more graphs enabling its reusability.

For the purpose of data quality harmonization, the timeliness of the ownership relationships is considered to be important since relationships can change due to mergers, acquisitions, registrations problems, etc. Therefore, a timeliness metric was used to clean out ownership relationships that are not considered to be up-to-date. Such a metric is given by the equation below [20].

$$Q_{Time}(w, A) := exp(-decline(A) * age(w, A)$$

$Q_{Time}(w, A)$ denotes the probability that an data field may still be valid. $decline(A)$ depicts the marginal probability that a certain attribute value may become invalid within one period of time. $age(w, A)$ represents the duration between the last update of the data field and the current date which can be represented by variable t. In this case, the decline ratio was obtained by calculating the average percentage of ownership relationships registered by GLEIF that become inactive within just on month. The resulting ratio was 0.0193 or 1.93 percent. The value of t for each ownership relationship was determined by calculating the difference between the time each ownership relationship was updated and the current date. In turn, this was used to calculate the timeliness ratio of each consolidation relationships in the equation below [20].

$$Q_{Time}(t) := e^{-0.0193*t}, \forall t > 0$$

However, since SPARQL does not support this function, the Padé approximant was used to estimate such ratios as shown by the equation below [21].

$$e^{-0.0193*t} \approx \frac{(-0.0193 * t + 3)^2 + 3}{(-0.0193 * t - 3)^2 + 3}, \forall t > 0$$

Variable t represents the time period (measured in months) between the last update of each ownership relationship and 10th July 2019 which is the day the ratios were calculated. Based on this, only ratios above 0.7165 were considered to be up-to-date at a significance level of 5 percent. This means that only relationships with ratios above that threshold would be converted and saved as triples in the graph on ownership relationships. In other words, only ownership relationships with a probability higher than 71.65 percent of being up-to-date are considered for further analysis while the rest is excluded.

During the technical harmonization part, the work performed during the semantic and data quality harmonization parts has been saved in the form of triples in a turtle file called *GLEIF-Who-owns-Whom2.ttl*.

B. Data federation step

The four individual graphs made in the data harmonization step have been merged in multiple ways to build different larger graphs through federated queries. Using standardized URIs as explained earlier was crucial for this since URIs represent the intersections and dependencies between triples and graphs.

C. Results visualization step

The results of such federated queries have been exported to Tableau through data.world's APIs to answer the business questions formulated during the planning of this data harmonization project. Some of the results will be shown below. All queries can be found on https://data.world/carlostubbax1/masters-thesis.

1) How many companies are listed by AMEX, NASDAQ and NYSE?: After filtering out repeated values, 5,818 companies listed by any of these three exchanges were found.

TABLE I. Belgian subsidiaries of Johnson & Johnson and their addresses.

Name	*Location*
AMO Belgium BVBA	1831 Machelen
GMED Healthcare BVBA	1831 Machelen
J.C. General Services CVBA/SCRL	2340 Beerse
Janssen Infectious Diseases-Diagnostics BVBA	2340 Beerse
Janssen Pharmaceutica NV	2340 Beerse
Janssen-Cilag NV	2340 Beerse
Johnson & Johnson Belgium Finance Company CVBA	2340 Beerse
Johnson & Johnson Medical NV	1831 Machelen
Omrix Biopharmaceuticals NV	1831 Machelen

2) What Belgian companies are owned by Johnson & Johnson and were are their headquarters?: The graph pattern in the federated query necessary to answer this question has been constrained to only generate matches of companies owned by Johnson & Johnson and located in Belgium. The results of such a query are listed in Table I. There are 9 Belgian subsidiaries of Johnson & Johson and all of them are located in Machelen or Beerse.

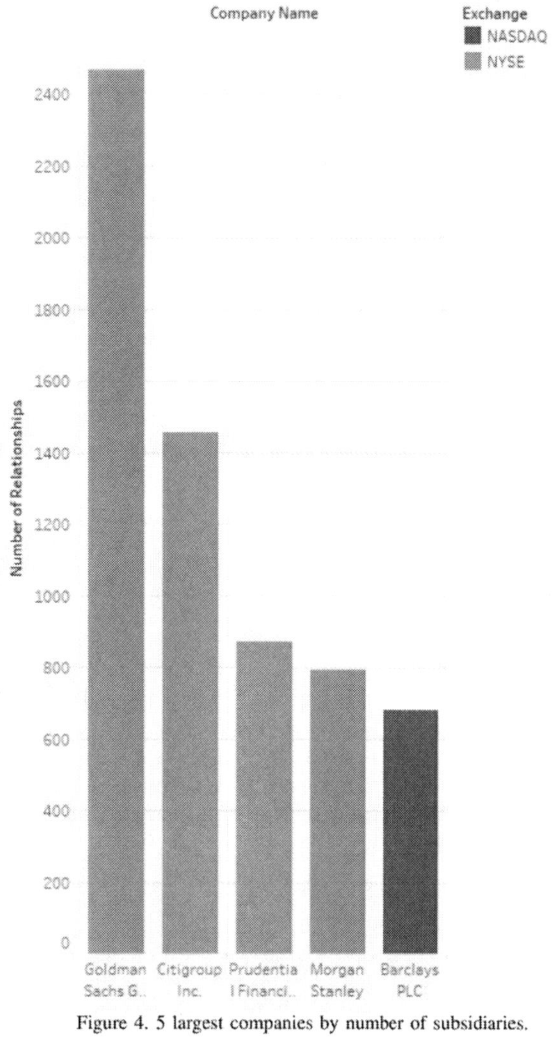

Figure 4. 5 largest companies by number of subsidiaries.

3) What are the five listed companies with the largest number of subsidiaries?: The results of a SPARQL-query meant to answer this question have been sent to Tableau to generate Figure 4. As graphically illustrated, Goldman Sachs is the company with the largest number of subsidaries followed by Citigroup and Prudentia on the second and third places respectively. It can also be seen that all companies in this top 5 come from the financial sector and 4 of them are listed on the New York Stock Exchange (NYSE).

VI. CONCLUSION

A. Discussion

The execution and results of this data harmonization work illustrate how data from heterogenous sources can be integrated through the use of ontologies and other Semantic Web technologies that allow computers to assign richer context to data by exploiting the power of computer inferencing. This has been shown by first converting several datasets into individual graphs before merging them into different federated graphs that served to answer various business questions about ownerships relations of companies listed in the main stock exchanges in the United States. Furthermore, these answers were exported to Tableau to generate visualizations that are more visually appealing to business users and decision makers.

The main contribution of this work is that it systematically illustrates how data harmonization can be conducted with ontologies and Semantic Web technologies by business users to integrate heterogenous datasets. Additionally, it also introduced Normalized Systems Theory to the body of knowledge on the Semantic Web and data harmonization. The main advantage of this approach is that data integration costs just grow linearly as the number of data sources and data destinations increase.

B. Recommendations

Since URIs represent the dependencies and intersections between graphs and triples, their proper design and management are crucial to ensure that graphs are integrable one to another. Therefore, standardization of URIs across graphs should be encouraged. Additionally, this may increase the reusability of graphs.

During the literature review of this work, little to none specification were found to operationalize the data quality requirements formulated in *BCBS239* [2]. One of these requirements is the timeliness principle for effective risk data aggregation and risk reporting. However, *BCBS239* provides no means nor specifications to measure the timeliness of data. Therefore, the timeliness metric used in this contribution could be used to solve that problem.

Since Semantic Web technologies are considered to be backed by a well-rooted theorical foundation provided by the World Wide Web Consortium (W3C) that may allow organizations to solve many of the interoperability problems they experience on a daily basis. Therefore, organizations should pay closer attention to these technologies.

C. Limitations

The first limitation of this work is that all datasets harmonized and integrated are .csv-files retrieved from the internet. In other words, this work is not representative of the heterogeneity in terms of data formats, sources and types that may normally found in most organizations. Therefore, this work does not capture the level of data source heterogeneity that most business and organizations deal with on a daily basis.

The second limitation of this work stems from the static nature of this data harmonization project that does not represent a more realistic dynamic business environment in which data may need to harmonized on a real-time basis. Therefore, this work does not offer an accurate representation of a dynamic data harmonization environment.

D. Further research

As a result of this research work, some hints for further research were identified. First, it would be interesting to use Normalized Systems Theory to study the modularity of ontologies. Second, it would be of value to study how the modelling languages of the Semantic Web could be used to model business processes as means to exploit the capabilities provided by machine inferencing to understand data flows within them.

REFERENCES

[1] V. R. Prevosto and L. Francis, "Data and Disaster: The Role of Data in the Financial Crisis," 2010, URL: https://www.casact.org/pubs/forum/10spforum/ [accessed: 2020-04-25].

[2] B. C. on Banking Supervision, "Principles for effective risk data aggregation and risk reporting," 2013, URL: https://www.bis.org/publ/bcbs239.pdf [accessed: 2020-04-25].

[3] W. H. Inmon, *Building the Data Warehouse*. John Wiley Sons, USA, 2005, ISBN: 978-0-471-56960-2.

[4] V. Chaudhary and T. Seth, "Big Data in Finance," 2015, URL: https://www.semanticscholar.org/paper/Big-Data-in-Finance-Seth-Chaudhary/75229e144e857f15c506e87898f8aa35ac1b9852 [accessed: 2020-04-05].

[5] P. Aven and D. Burley, Eds., *Building on multi-model databases: How to manage multiple schemas using a single platform*. O'Reilly, USA, May 2017, ISBN: 978-1-491-97788-0.

[6] T. Berners-Lee and J. Hendler, "The Semantic Web," 2001, URL: https://www.scientificamerican.com/article/the-semantic-web/ [accessed: 2020-04-25].

[7] D. Allemang and J. Hendler, *Semantic Web for the Working Ontologist*. Morgan Kaufmann, USA, 2011, ISBN: 978-0-12-385965-5.

[8] J. R. Burd, S. and J. Satzinger, *Systems Analysis Design in a Changing World*. Cengage Learning, USA, 2009, ISBN: 978-0-12-385965-5.

[9] R. I. Eifrem, E. and J. Webber, *Graph Databases*. OReilly, USA, 2015, ISBN: 978-1-491-93089-2.

[10] B. DuCharme, *Learning SPARQL*. OReilly, USA, 2013, ISBN: 978-1-449-37143-2.

[11] E. D. M. council, "FIBO OWL," 2010, URL: https://spec.edmcouncil.org/fibo/doc/ [accessed: 2020-04-05].

[12] M. H. De Bruyn, P. and J. Verelst, *Normalized Systems Theory. From Foundations for Evolvable Software Toward a General Theory for Evolvable Design*. NSI, Belgium, 2016, ISBN: 978-9-07716-0 09-1.

[13] K. D. V. S. M. Cunningham, J. A. and R. Verbeeck, "Nine Principles of Semantic Harmonization," in *Proceedings of the9^{th} AMIA Annual Symposium, 2017, Somecity, USA*. AMMIA, 2017, pp. 451–459.

[14] M. Flood, "Embracing change:
nancial informatics and risk analytics In: Quantitative Finance," 2009, URL: https://doi.org/10.1080/14697680802366037 [accessed: 2020-04-25].

[15] C. Dictionary, "listed company," 2020, URL: https://dictionary.cambridge.org/fr/dictionnaire/anglais/listed-company [accessed: 2020-04-25].

[16] NASDAQ, "Listed companies dataset," 2020, URL: https://www.nasdaq.com/screening/company-list.aspx [accessed: 2020-07-02].

[17] GLEIF, "level 2 who owns whom," 2020, URL: https://www.gleif.org/en/lei-data/access-and-use-lei-data/level-2-data-who-owns-whom [accessed: 2020-07-02].

[18] ——, "level 1 data who is who," 2020, URL: https://www.gleif.org/en/lei-data/access-and-use-lei-data/level-2-data-who-owns-whom [accessed: 2020-04-25].

[19] GeoNames, "Postal Codes," 2020, URL: ttp://download.geonames.org/export/zip/ [accessed: 2020-07-02].

[20] K. M. M. Heinrich, Bernd and M. Klier, "How to measure data quality? - A metric based approach." in *Proceedings of the 28th International Conference on Information Systems, 2007*. ICIS, 2007.

[21] Stackoverflow, "Approximation of e-x," 2011, URL: https://math.stackexchange.com/questions/71357/approximation-of-e-x [accessed: 2020-07-02].

Pattern-based Deployment Models Revisited: Automated Pattern-driven Deployment Configuration

Lukas Harzenetter, Uwe Breitenbücher, Michael Falkenthal, Jasmin Guth, and Frank Leymann

Institute of Architecture of Application Systems (IAAS), University of Stuttgart
Universitätsstrasse 38, 70569 Stuttgart, Germany
Email: {harzenetter, breitenbuecher, falkenthal, guth, leymann}@iaas.uni-stuttgart.de

***Abstract*—The manual deployment of cloud applications is error-prone and requires significant expertise. Therefore, many deployment automation technologies have been developed that enable deploying applications fully automatically by processing deployment models. However, while these technologies substantially simplify deployment, the manual creation of deployment models ironically poses similar challenges to manually deploying applications as technical expertise about the components to be deployed and their dependencies is required. Therefore, we introduced Pattern-based Deployment Models (PbDMs) in a previous work that allow using design patterns to model components in an abstract manner, which are then automatically replaced by concrete technologies. However, in many scenarios, the resulting deployment models still have to be subsequently adapted with regard to the configuration of the selected technologies, e. g., to configure a selected Platform as a Service (PaaS) offering, such as Amazon Beanstalk, for optimal scaling. Therefore, while our previous work only enables using design patterns to model components, in this paper we extend the proposed meta-model and algorithms by the possibility to specify behavioral aspects of components and relations also in the form of patterns. Moreover, we show how these annotated patterns can be automatically transformed into concrete configurations that reflect their semantics. We present a prototype and a case study to validate the extension's practical feasibility.**

***Keywords*-*Deployment Automation*; *Deployment Modeling*; *Patterns*; *Model-driven Architecture*; *TOSCA*.**

I. INTRODUCTION

Automating the deployment of applications is of vital importance as manual deployment is error-prone, time-consuming, and requires a significant amount of technical expertise [1]. Therefore, several *deployment automation technologies*, such as Chef, Terraform, or Kubernetes, have been developed to automate the deployment of applications. The majority of these technologies use *declarative deployment models* to describe the structure of an application to be deployed [2]. These models specify all components of the application to be deployed, their configurations, as well as their dependencies among each other [3]. For example, to describe the deployment of a Java 8 based application, a declarative deployment model may specify its components as follows: The application itself may be described as an instance of a Java 8 Web App that is hosted on an Amazon Elastic Beanstalk Environment to enable its automatic scaling. Additionally, it may be connected to a MySQL 5.7 database that is installed on an Ubuntu 18.04 Virtual Machine (VM) running on an Amazon EC2 instance.

However, while deployment technologies are an established means, the manual creation of deployment models ironically poses similar challenges to manually deploying applications: First, (i) modelers are required to have *significant technical expertise* in selecting appropriate components, such as web servers or operating systems. For example, considering the example, a modeler has to know which web servers supported by Beanstalk are able to run Java 8 Web Apps. This often results in (ii) *error-prone* modeling that requires testing the created models multiple times, which quickly becomes a (iii) *time-consuming* task. To tackle these issues, we introduced *Pattern-based Deployment Models (PbDM)* in a previous work [4], whereby we used patterns as first-class citizens in a declarative deployment model to describe components in an abstract manner. For example, instead of specifying a concrete web server for Beanstalk to run the Java 8 Web App, in a PbDM only the *Platform as a Service (PaaS)* pattern [5] needs to be modeled. Moreover, since PbDM cannot be executed as they only specify abstract semantics instead of executable technologies, we also presented algorithms to automatically refine all patterns in a PbDM to concrete technologies [4]. However, in many scenarios, the resulting deployment models have to be adapted with regard to the configuration of the refined components, e. g., to configure the scaling behavior of Beanstalk. Unfortunately, this again requires technical expertise and is error-prone. The reason for these problems is that only components are abstracted by patterns, not their configuration.

Therefore, we extend our proposed meta-model for PbDMs in this paper by the possibility to specify also *behavioral requirements* for components and relations in the form of abstract patterns. For example, instead of providing a concrete configuration of Beanstalk's scaling behavior, our new approach enables the annotation of the *Unpredictable Workload Pattern* [5] to the Java Web App, which implies that the underlying infrastructure needs to be elastic, but without the need to specify any technical configuration. Moreover, we also extend the refinement algorithms to support refining patterns annotated at components and relations. We validate the practical feasibility of the approach by a case study and a prototype.

Hereafter, Section II describes fundamentals, Sections III and IV introduce the new concepts while Sections V and VI explain our case study and prototype. Finally, Section VII describes related work and Section VIII concludes the paper.

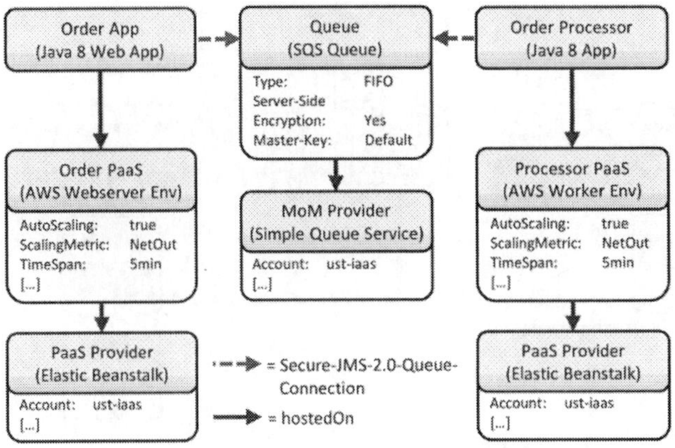

Figure 1. A declarative deployment model.

II. FUNDAMENTALS AND MOTIVATION

In this section, we introduce deployment automation concepts and technologies, as well as our motivating scenario.

A. Deployment Models and Automation

To automate the deployment of applications, many deployment automation technologies have been developed. Most of these technologies use *Deployment Models* to describe the desired application [3]. Deployment models can be categorized into two types: (i) *declarative deployment models* and (ii) *imperative deployment models* [3]. An imperative deployment model describes *how* a deployment is performed as an executable process including all technical activities and their execution order [3]. In contrast, a declarative deployment model describes *what* has to be achieved but provides no executable process. Thus, a deployment technology must interpret declarative models and derive the necessary steps [3]. In this paper, we focus on declarative models as they are (i) supported by various deployment technologies [2] and (ii) can be automatically transformed to imperative deployment models [1].

Declarative models state the desired outcome of a deployment in the form of the application's structure encompassing the components of the application, their configurations, and the dependencies between them [3]. An example consisting of components, relations, and their properties is depicted in Figure 1. It illustrates a frontend component called *Order App* and a backend component called *Order Processor*, both hosted on Elastic Beanstalk Environments. The Elastic Beanstalk Environments are configured to scale automatically, which is indicated by their "AutoScaling" properties. To communicate to another, the applications use a *Queue* that is hosted on the Simple Queue Service (SQS), whereas the Order App expects that each order is delivered and processed exactly once, which is hereby ensured by a queue of type "FIFO". Finally, the types of the components and relations are shown. The component types are depicted in braces, while the relation types are encoded by their stroke type and color. Thus, the Order App, e. g., is an instance of the *Java 8 Web App* while its relation to the Queue is of type *Secure-JMS-2.0-Queue-Connection*.

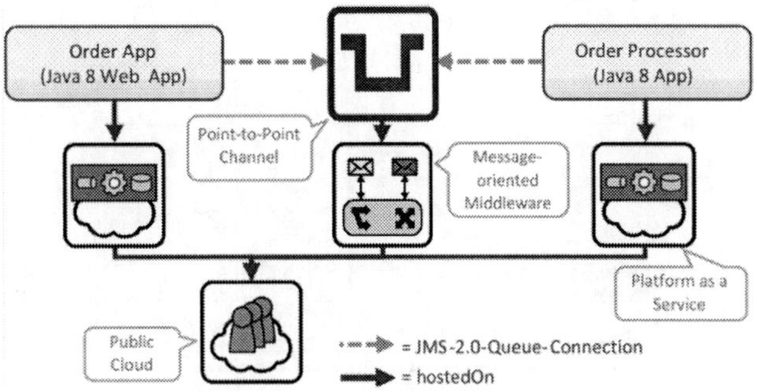

Figure 2. A Pattern-based Deployment Model (PbDM).

B. Pattern-based Deployment Models

However, even the creation of such simple models poses several challenges as it requires technical expertise in different technologies. For instance, it must be known whether Beanstalk supports Java 8 and which environment is appropriate, or whether an SQS Queue can be used at all since the apps require JMS connections. Thus, to reduce the modeling complexity, we previously introduced *Pattern-based Deployment Models (PbDM)* [4], which use Design Patterns [6] as first class model elements. Figure 2 shows an example PbDM representing the abstract semantics of the deployment shown in Figure 1. Herein, the *Cloud Computing Patterns* [5] and *Enterprise Integration Patterns* [7] are used to represent components in an abstract, technology-agnostic way: Instead of specifying concrete services, such as Beanstalk and SQS, the applications are hosted on *Platform as a Service (PaaS)* patterns [5] while a *Point-to-Point Channel* pattern [7] is used for communication that is hosted on a *Message-oriented Middleware (MoM)* pattern [5]. Thus, this model contains no details about technologies but only specifies the *abstract semantics* of the required components in the form of patterns, which is less error-prone and requires less technical expertise. We refer to patterns that represent the semantics of components as *Component Patterns*. Moreover, we also presented *refinement algorithms* [4] that replace Component Patterns with concrete technologies and providers.

However, in many cases, the refined deployment model requires additional manual configuration: For example, as the Order App's workload is unpredictable, the Beanstalk environment must be configured for automated scaling by specifying the "ScalingMetric" and the "TimeSpan" to define when scaling will be triggered. Additionally, the Order App requires the orders to be processed exactly once by the Order Processor. Thus, the modeler has to select the correct queue type, i. e., in the context of SQS "FIFO" instead of "Standard". Another difficulty often results from compliance requirements: If the orders issued by the Order App contain sensitive data, the communication between the applications must be secured using "Server-Side Encryption" and a "Master-Key". However, to configure all components and relations correctly via properties, immense technical expertise is required on each employed technology and again results in an error-prone and time-consuming model configuration step.

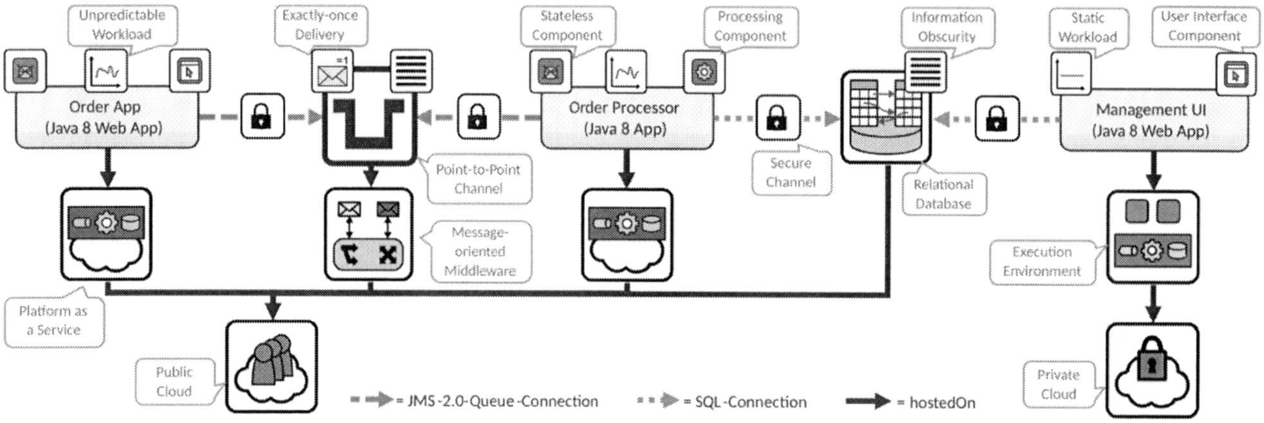

Figure 3. A Pattern-based Deployment and Configuration Model (PbDCM) following the metamodel defined in Figure 4.

III. Pattern-based Deployment and Configuration Models

To tackle the issue of subsequent manual model configuration, our first contribution is an extension of PbDMs to *Pattern-based Deployment and Configuration Models (PbDCMs)*, which support annotating *Behavior Patterns* [8] to components and relations to describe their desired behavior in an abstract way.

To provide the basis for demonstrating our new approach in a more complex case study, we first enlarge our motivating scenario as shown in Figure 3: We add the *Relational Database* Component Pattern [5] to store the results from the Processor as well as a management component called *Management UI* to maintain the database, which is hosted on *Execution Environment* [5] and *Private Cloud* [5] Component Patterns.

A. Overview of the Modeling Extension

To compensate the shortcomings, we extend PbDMs to *Pattern-based Deployment and Configuration Models*: Instead of using patterns only to abstract components by Component Patterns, we extend the metamodel to also allow annotating *Behavior Patterns* to components and relations: A Behavior Pattern abstractly describes behavioral requirements that must be respected by the deployment, e.g., that a component has to handle unpredictable workload. Figure 3 shows a PbDCM in which both apps have been annotated with Behavior Patterns, e.g., the Unpredictable Workload which implies the need for automatic scaling. To secure communication and to encrypt the storage, the relations between the applications are annotated with the *Secure Channel* pattern [9], while the Relational Database and the Point-to-Point Channel are annotated with the *Information Obscurity* pattern [9]. To ensure that the orders are processed only once, the Point-to-Point Channel is annotated with the *Exactly-once Delivery* pattern [5]. Moreover, patterns may specify additional semantics, e.g., the *Stateless Component*, the *User Interface Component* and the *Processing Component* patterns [5]. Thus, instead of specifying all technical configurations that realize these behaviors manually, our extension only requires to annotate desired behavior of components and relations in the form of Behavior Patterns.

B. Metamodel Extensions for PbDCMs

In this section, we describe the formal metamodel for PbDCMs, which is graphically illustrated in Figure 4. Hereby, the original PbDM metamodel [4] is extended by the grey elements, which provide the capabilities to define Behavior Pattern types and to annotate them to components and relations.

The new PbDCM metamodel and the original metamodel are based on the *Essential Deployment Metamodel (EDMM)* [2], which is a normalized metamodel that has been extracted from the 13 most used deployment technologies including, e. g., Terraform and the Topology Orchestration Specification for Cloud Applications (TOSCA) [10]. We use EDMM as basis metamodel to describe our approach in a technology-agnostic way instead of extending only one certain deployment technology. Since Section IV describes how PbDCMs can be automatically transformed into EDMM-compliant models containing only standard EDMM modeling constructs, the extension of EDMM only affects the design time while the refined models can be directly translated into any of the 13 supported deployment technologies that can be mapped to EDMM. To demonstrate the approach's practical feasibility, we show how the PbDCM metamodel can be realized using the TOSCA standard and how the models refined by our algorithms presented in Section IV can be consumed by a standard-compliant TOSCA runtime. Let $\mathcal{T}$ be the set of all PbDCMs, then $t \in \mathcal{T}$ is defined as a fifteen-tuple as follows:

$$t = (C_t, R_t, CP_t, CBP_t, RBP_t, CT_t, RT_t, CPT_t, CBPT_t, RBPT_t, PROP_t, type_t, supertype_t, properties_t, annotations_t)$$

1) Basis of the Metamodel: Following EDMM, a deployment model is a directed, weighted graph, in which nodes represent components, edges their relations. Components and relations are typed and specify properties to configure the deployment. EDMM defines more elements, such as Operations, which are, however, not affected by our approach. Thus, we omit them for the sake of simplicity. Our previous work of PbDMs extends this metamodel by *Component Patterns* that can be used as nodes [4]. Thus, the following elements of t are already defined by EDMM [2] and the metamodel of PbDMs [4]:

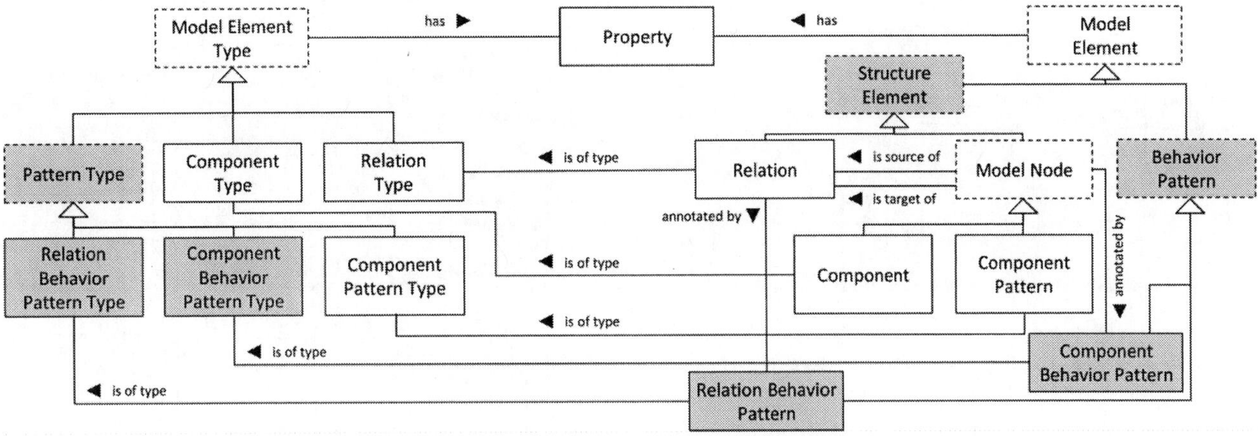

Figure 4. Metamodel of Pattern-based Deployment and Configuration Models (extensions to PbDMs are highlighted in grey).

- C_t is the set of *Components* in t. A *Component* $c_i \in C_t$ is a physical, functional, or logical unit of an application.
- CP_t is the set of *Component Patterns* in t. A $cp_i \in CP_t$ describes a *Component Pattern* that must be refined to a concrete *Component* before the application's deployment.
- The union of *Components* C_t and *Component Patterns* CP_t form the set of *Model Nodes* in t: $MN_t := C_t \cup CP_t$.
- $R_t \subseteq MN_t \times MN_t$ represents the set of *Relations* in t. A *Relation* $r_i = (mn_{source}, mn_{target}) \in R_t$ is a directed physical, functional, or logical dependency between exactly two *Model Nodes* $mn_{source}, mn_{target} \in MN_t$, where mn_{source} is the source and mn_{target} the target *Model Node* of the *Relation*.
- CT_t is the set of *Component Types* in t. A *Component Type* $ct_i \in CT_t$ specifies the semantics of a *Component* $c_j \in C_t$ that has this type assigned.
- CPT_t is the set of *Component Pattern Types* in t. A *Component Pattern Type* $cpt_i \in CPT_t$ specifies the semantics of a *Component Pattern* $cp_j \in CP_t$ that has this type assigned.
- RT_t is the set of *Relation Types* in t. A *Relation Type* $rt_i \in RT_t$ specifies the semantics of a *Relation* $r_j \in R_t$ that has this type assigned.
- $PROP_t \subseteq \Sigma^+ \times \Sigma^+$ is the set of *Properties* in t. A *Property* $pr_i = (Key, Value) \in PROP_t$ describes the configuration of a *Component*, *Relation*, *Pattern*, or their types. Its initial value is defined to be the *Empty Word* ε.

2) *Extension for Behavior Patterns:*

- CBP_t is the set of *Component Behavior Patterns* in t. A $cbp_i \in CBP_t$ represents a pattern annotated to a *Model Node* describing its desired behavior in an abstract way.
- RBP_t is the set of *Relation Behavior Patterns* in t. A $rbp_i \in RBP_t$ represents a pattern that is annotated to a *Relation* describing its behavior in an abstract way.
- $CBPT_t$ is the set of *Component Behavior Pattern Types* in t. A $cbpt_i \in CBPT_t$ specifies the semantics of a *Component Behavior Pattern* $cbp_j \in CBP_t$ that has this type assigend.
- $RBPT_t$ is the set of *Relation Behavior Pattern Types* in t. A $rbpt_i \in RBPT_t$ specifies the semantics of a *Relation Behavior Pattern* $rbp_j \in RBP_t$ that has this type assigned.
- The union set $SE_t := R_t \cup MN_t$ contains all *Structure Elements* in t, while the union set $BP_t := CBP_t \cup RBP_t$ contains all *Behavior Patterns* in t.
- The union of all *Structure Elements* SE_t and *Behavior Patterns* BP_t form the set of *Model Elements* ME_t in t: $ME_t := SE_t \cup BP_t$.
- The union set $MET_t := CT_t \cup RT_t \cup CPT_t \cup CBPT_t \cup RBPT_t$ contains all *Model Element Types* in t.
- $annotations_t$ is the map that assigns a *Structure Element* $se_i \in SE_t$ to its set of annotated *Behavior Patterns*.

$$annotations_t : SE_t \rightarrow \wp(BP_t) \quad (1)$$

The following maps are already defined by EDMM [2] and PbDMs [4]. Since we extended ME_t and MET_t, their mapping now include also *Behavior Patterns* and *Behavior Pattern Types*:

- $type_t$ is a map that assigns all *Model Elements* $me_i \in ME_t$ to their respective *Model Element Type* $met_j \in MET_t$ providing the semantics for the *Model Element*:

$$type_t : ME_t \rightarrow MET_t \quad (2)$$

- $supertype_t$ is the map that assigns each *Model Element Type* to its respective supertype. It associates a $met_i \in MET_t$ with a $met_j \in MET_t$ where $i \neq j$, i. e., that met_j is the supertype of met_i.

$$supertype_t : MET_t \rightarrow MET_t \quad (3)$$

- Additionally, $supertypes_t$ assigns a *Model Element Type* $met_i \in MET_t$ to all of its supertypes that can be transitively resolved. Thus, $supertypes_t$ is defined as:

$$supertypes_t : MET_t \rightarrow \wp(MET_t) \quad (4)$$

- $properties_t$ is the map that assigns each $met_i \in MET_t$ and $me_j \in ME_t$ its corresponding set of *Properties*.

$$properties_t : MET_t \cup ME_t \rightarrow \wp(PROP_t) \quad (5)$$

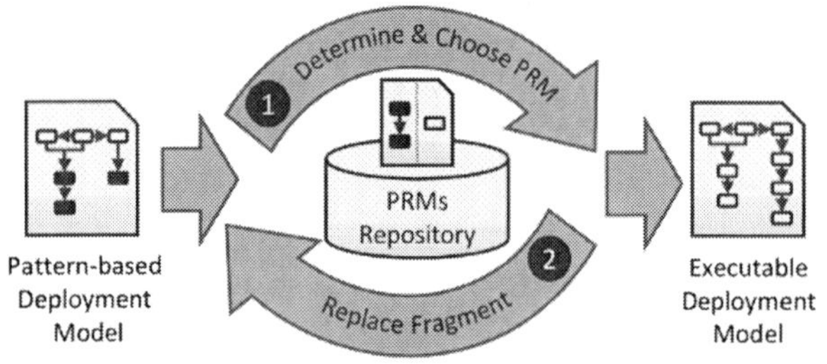

Figure 5. Refinement of PbDMs to executable models [4].

IV. Automatic Refinement to Executable Deployment Models

PbDCMs are not executable as the contained patterns only specify abstract semantics. Thus, to get an *Executable Deployment Model*, all *Component Patterns* need to be replaced by concrete *Components* and the additional semantics specified by the annotated *Behavior Patterns* must be considered by configuring the affected *Components* and *Relations* correctly. In our previous work [4], we presented *Pattern Refinement Models (PRMs)* and corresponding *refinement algorithms* to replace *Component Patterns* by concrete *Components*.

A. Pattern Refinement Models (PRMs)

To deploy a PbDM, we introduced algorithms to automatically replace *Component Patterns* by concrete technologies [4]. Hereby, *Pattern Refinement Models (PRMs)* define how *Component Patterns* can be refined to concrete components [4]. As illustrated in Figure 5, the refinement is an semi-automated, iterative process: All PRMs contained in a repository are analyzed whether they can refine certain *Component Patterns* contained in the PbDM to concrete *Components*. Appropriate PRMs are selected manually and automatically applied until the PbDM contains no more patterns resulting in an *Executable Deployment Model*, which requires only small manual additions.

A PRM consists of (i) a *Detector*, (ii) a *Refinement Structure*, and (iii) a set of *Relation Mappings*. The Detector is a PbDM fragment that specifies the structure of *Component Patterns* and their *Relations* the PRM can refine to concrete *Components*. Thus, if a fragment of a Detector matches a fragment in a PbDM, this PRM can refine exactly the matching subgraph. The Refinement Structure specifies how the Detector fragment can be refined to concrete *Components* and *Relations*. Hence, if a fragment in a PbDM matches a Detector fragment of a PRM, the PbDM fragment can be refined to the fragment specified in the PRM's Refinement Structure. For example, Figure 6 shows a PRM that refines the PaaS and the Public Cloud patterns to a concrete Webserver Environment hosted on AWS Beanstalk.

Moreover, to handle external relations of the mapped Detector fragment, we introduced *Relation Mappings* [4] defining which type of relations can be redirected from which *Model Node* in the Detector to which *Model Node* in the Refinement Structure. For example, the Relation Mapping in Figure 6 redirects all incoming *Relations* of type *hostedOn* that target the Public Cloud *Component Pattern* and that are not contained in the Detector to the Public Cloud *Component*.

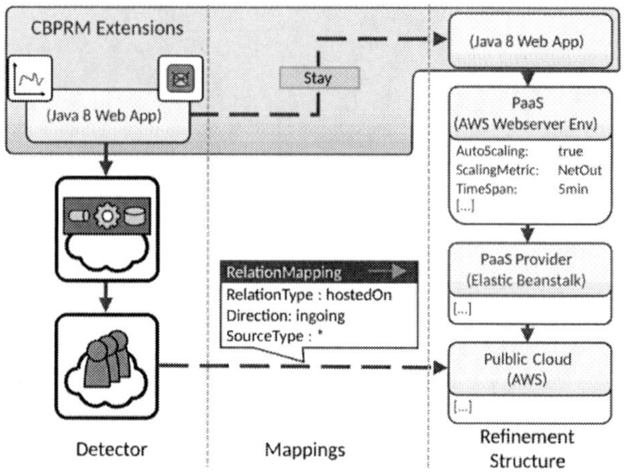

Figure 6. Exemplary CBPRM respecting Behavior Patterns.

B. Component and Behavior Pattern Refinement Models (CBPRMs)

In the original approach [4], PRMs were only used to refine *Component Patterns* by concrete *Components*. Therefore, Detector fragments of PRMs contained only *Component Patterns* and their *Relations*, but no business components as they were not affected by the refinement. Thus, only *Component Patterns* are considered if a PRM is applicable or not. However, our extended approach must consider *Behavior Patterns* that are attached to business *Components* or *Relations*, such as the Java 8 Web App shown in Figure 6. Hence, we extend PRMs to *Component and Behavior Pattern Refinement Models (CBPRMs)* to also support the refinement of *Behavior Patterns*.

The extension requires two changes: First, PRMs must be extended to use PbDCM fragments as Detector and Refinement Structure instead of PbDM fragments. Second, to consider *Behavior Patterns* during the refinement, also the affected business components must be modeled in the Detector to define which *Behavior Patterns* a CBPRM considers. This is, for example, shown in Figure 6: Herein, also the business *Component* Java 8 Web App is modeled in the CBPRM Detector including the two *Component Behavior Patterns* Unpredictable Workload and Stateless Component. This business *Component* is hosted on Platform as a Service and Public Cloud *Component Patterns*. Thus, this Detector specifies that the PaaS and Public Cloud *Component Patterns* can be refined by this CBPRM in a way that it respects the *Behavior Patterns* annotated at the Java 8 Web App, i.e. that its Refinement Structure is able to handle unpredictable workloads of stateless Java 8 Web Apps. Hence, this Detector is refined to an elastic PaaS-based solution on AWS including all required configuration properties, e. g., it specifies the “AutoScaling”, “ScalingMetric”, and “TimeSpan” *Properties* of Beanstalk to dynamically scale the application. Thus, when applying such a CBPRM, all annotated *Behavior Patterns* in the Detector must be considered by the Refinement Structure. Thereby, the Refinement Structure must not contain any of the Detector's or new patterns. Thus, each CBPRM removes the patterns it refines from the PbDCM model.

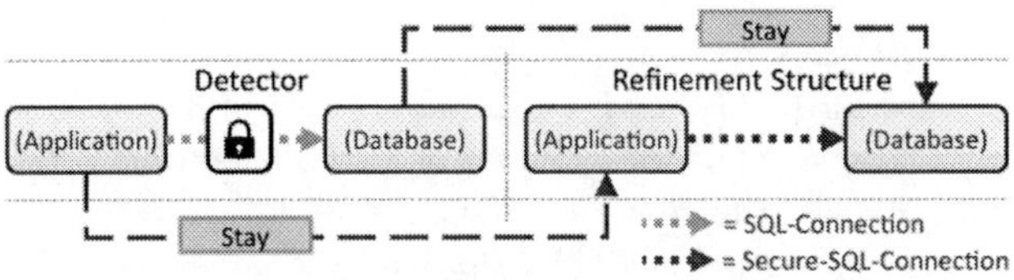

Figure 7. Exemplary CBPRM that refines Relations.

However, while business *Components* and their configuration *Properties* must not be changed during the refinement of *Component Patterns*, their annotated *Behavior Patterns* must be considered. Therefore, we introduce *Stay Mappings* as a second extension to PRMs, which state that a *Model Node* in a PbDCM mapping to a "staying" *Model Node* in the CBPRM's Detector must not be changed. For example, Figure 6 specifies that if the Detector can be mapped to a subgraph in the PbDCM, the *Model Node* of the PbDCM mapping to the Java 8 Web App of the Detector must stay as is, i.e., neither its type nor its configuration must change. Thus, business *Components* are essential to specify the pattern-component constellations a CBPRM can refine. For example, the CBPRM shown in Figure 6 states that it is able to refine Java 8 Web Apps hosted on PaaS and Public Cloud *Component Patterns* while considering the annotated Unpredictable Workload and Stateless Component *Component Behavior Patterns*. To specify where business *Components* will be located in the PbDCM after their annotated *Component Behavior Patterns* are refined, Stay Mappings are defined in CBPRMs. Hence, Stay Mappings are only required if *Behavior Patterns* are refined by a CBPRM.

Moreover, Stay Mappings enable the definition of CBPRMs that only refine a *Relation* between two *Model Nodes* that is annotated with a *Relation Behavior Pattern*. For example, as illustrated in Figure 7, it is possible to refine a *SQL-Connection* annotated with the *Secure Channel* pattern [9] between an application and a database to a *Secure-SQL-Connection* without changing neither the application nor the database. Thus, the application and the database stay in the given PbDCM while their *Relation* gets refined to a more concrete *Relation Type*.

C. Metamodel for CBPRMs

In the following, the metamodel for *Component and Behavior Pattern Refinement Models* is defined based on PRMs [4]. Let $CBPRM$ be the set of all Component and Behavior Pattern Refinement Models, then a $cbprm \in CBPRM$ is a four-tuple:

$$cbprm = (d_{cbprm}, rs_{cbprm}, RM_{cbprm}, S_{cbprm}) \quad (6)$$

The original metamodel of PRMs [4] is adopted for CBPRMs by exchanging PbDMs by PbDCMs as follows:

- $d_{cbprm} \in \mathcal{T}$ is a PbDCM fragment describing the *Detector* which can be refined by this CBPRM.
- $rs_{cbprm} \in \mathcal{T}$ is a PbDCM fragment that describes the *Refinement Structure* that refines the Detector fragment.
- RM_{cbprm} is the set of *Relation Mappings* describing the rules how external relations of *Model Nodes* in the Detector must be redirected to *Model Nodes* in the Refinement Structure. A $rm_i \in RM_{cbprm}$ is defined as:

$$rm_i = (mn_1, mn_2, rt, direction_{rt}, vt) \quad (7)$$

Herein, $mn_1 \in MN_{d_{cbprm}}$ and $mn_2 \in MN_{rs_{cbprm}}$ are *Model Nodes* of the Detector d_{cbprm} and the Refinement Structure rs_{cbprm}. $rt \in RT$ is the *Relation Type* of an external *Relation* that targets or sources the *Model Node* matching mn_1, while the *Relation*'s direction is defined as $direction_{rt} \in \{ingoing, outgoing\}$. $vt \in CT \cup CPT$ specifies the valid type of the *Relation*'s source *Model Node*, if it is ingoing, or target *Model Node* otherwise. To also refine *Behavior Patterns*, we introduce *Stay Mappings* in CBPRMs:

- S_{cbprm} is the set of Stay Mappings. A Stay Mapping $s_i = (mn_1, mn_2) \in S_{cbprm}$ is a pair of *Model Modes*, whereby $mn_1 \in MN_{d_{cbprm}}$ is matching a *Model Node* in a PbDCM that must stay as is at the place of the Refinement Structure's *Model Node* $mn_2 \in MN_{rs_{cbprm}}$.

D. Refinement Step 1: CBPRM Selection

Following our original approach [4], to refine *Component Patterns* in a PbDM, first all applicable PRMs are determined. A PRM is applicable iff (i) its Detector fragment can be found as a subgraph of *compatible Structure Elements* in the PbDM and (ii) all external *Relations* of all mapped *Model Nodes* in the PbDM can be redirected by the CBPRM's Relation Mappings [4]. To find two compatible *Structure Elements* their types and annotated *Behavior Patterns* must be considered. Thus, a *Structure Element* in a CBPRM's Detector is only compatible to a *Structure Element* in a PbDCM iff (i) their types are compatible and (ii) all *Behavior Patterns* the CBPRM defines in its Detector are also annotated at a matching *Structure Element* in the PbDCM. To determine the compatibility of two *Structure Elements* in our algorithms, we introduce a formal *Compatibility Rule* similarly to Breitenbücher [11]: A *Structure Element* $se_1 \in SE_{d_{cbprm}}$ of a Detector d_{cbprm} is matching a *Structure Element* $se_2 \in SE_t$ in a PbDCM t iff (i) the type of se_2 or one of its *supertypes* is equal to the type of se_1, (ii) all *annotations* defined at se_1 are also annotated at se_2, (iii) all *Properties* that are set in se_1 are equally set in se_2 or se_1 specifies wildcard values "*", which means that any non-empty value is allowed for a *Property*. Based on this, we define the *Compatibility Operator* "$\vec{\approx}$" as follows:

$$\begin{aligned} se_1 \vec{\approx} se_2 :\Leftrightarrow \Big(& type_{d_{cbprm}}(se_1) \in supertypes_t(se_2) \\ & \wedge \big(\forall b_x \in annotations_{d_{cbprm}}(se_1) \exists b_y \in annotations_t(se_2) \\ & \big(type_{d_{cbprm}}(b_x) = type_t(b_y)\big)\big) \\ & \wedge \big(\forall p_i \in properties_{d_{cbprm}}(se_1) \\ & \exists p_j \in properties_t(se_2) \ \big(\pi_1(p_i) = \pi_1(p_j) \wedge \\ & \big(\pi_2(p_i) = \pi_2(p_j) \vee (\pi_2(p_i) = \text{“*”} \wedge \pi_2(p_j) \neq \varepsilon)\big)\big)\big)\Big) \end{aligned}$$

The set of $SubgraphMappings_{d_{cbprm},t}$ contains all possible subgraph mappings that exist between a CBPRM's Detector d_{cbprm} and a PbDCM t. A Subgraph Mapping $sm_i \in SubgraphMappings_{d_{cbprm},t}$ is defined as the set of *Element Mappings* between *Structure Elements*: An *Element Mapping* $em_j = (se_1, se_2) \in sm_i$ is defined as a tuple of *Structure Elements*, where the *Structure Elements* $se_1 \in SE_{d_{cbprm}}$ and $se_2 \in SE_t$ are compatible, i. e., $se_1 \vec{\approx} se_2$ holds.

E. Refinement Step 2: CBPRM Application

The refinement of an applicable CBPRM $cbprm$ that has been selected to refine a matching subgraph in a PbDCM t is described in Figure 8. Thus, to apply the $cbprm$ to t, they are both passed alongside the Subgraph Mapping sm containing the Element Mappings between the $cbprm$'s Detector and t. Hereby, Lines 1, 2, 11–20, and 23 are used from the original algorithm [4] and are adapted to support *Behavior Patterns* and *Stay Mappings*: First, all *Structure Elements* defined in the Refinement Structure are added to t (Line 1), then all affected *Relations* must be redirected to their new source or target (Lines 3–20). Therefore, all *Relations* that are in- or outgoing of a *Model Node* in t that is part of the subgraph sm (Line 2) must be investigated to redirect (i) *Relations* between added and staying *MNs* (Lines 4–10), and (ii) external *Relations* according to the Relation Mappings defined in the $cbprm$ (Lines 12–19).

To redirect the *Relations* that are in- or outgoing of staying *Model Nodes*, the *Relations* added by the $cbprm$'s Refinement Structure must be considered as the type of the *Relation* can change. Therefore, all *Relations* that are in- or outgoing of a *Model Node* that has been added from the Refinement Structure and that is part of a Stay Mapping (Line 4) must be redirected to the existing *Model Node* in t. For example, by adding the Refinement Structure defined in the CBPRM illustrated in Figure 6 to the PbDCM shown in Figure 3, the Java 8 Web App, the PaaS environment, the PaaS Provider, and the Public Cloud *Components*, as well as all three *Relations* are added. However, as there is a *Component* in the PbDCM that maps to the Java 8 Web App, the added application only serves as a placeholder, where the actual application must be located. Hence, the *Relation* between the placeholder and the PaaS environment must be redirected to the actual Java 8 Web App *Component* in the PbDCM. Thus, all *Relations* in t that have been added from $cbprm$'s Refinement Structure and are either the source or the target of a *Model Node* that is part of a Stay Mapping must be redirected to the corresponding staying *Model Node* that already exists in t. Hence, if the staying *Model Node* was the source, the *Relation's* source must be changed, or its target otherwise (Lines 5 to 9).

Similarly, external *Relations* that are in- and outgoing from the mapped subgraph in t must be redirected to the new *Model Nodes* that have been added from the $cbprm$. For example, based on the Relation Mapping defined for ingoing *Relations* of type *hostedOn* at the Public Cloud in Figure 6, all of these *Relations* must be redirected to the new Public Cloud *Component* of type AWS. Therefore, all *Relations* in t that are the source or the target of the currently processed *Model Node*, and that are not part of the subgraph (Line 12) must be redirected to the added *Model Node* as dictated by the $cbprm$'s Relation Mappings. Thus, for each *Relation* r_j that is in- or outgoing of the current *Model Node* mn_2 in t the following conditions must hold: (i) the *Relation Type* defined in the Relation Mapping must be in the supertypes of r_j, (ii) the direction defined in the Relation Mapping must be equal to the direction of r_j, and (iii) the corresponding source or

---

1: $SE_t := SE_t \cup SE_{rs_{cbprm}}$
2: **for all** $\big((mn_1, mn_2) \in sm : mn_2 \in MN_t\big)$ **do**
3: // *Redirect added Relations of the RS to staying MNs*
4: **for all** $\big(r_y \in R_t : r_y \in R_{rs_{cbprm}} \wedge \exists mn_i \in MN_{rs_{cbprm}} \big((mn_1, mn_i) \in S_{cbprm} \wedge (mn_i = \pi_1(r_y) \vee mn_i = \pi_2(r_y))\big)\big)$ **do**
5: **if** $\big(mn_i = \pi_1(r_y)\big)$ **then**
6: $\pi_1(r_y) := mn_2$ // *update the source of* r_y
7: **else**
8: $\pi_2(r_y) := mn_2$ // *update the target of* r_y
9: **end if**
10: **end for**
11: // *Apply Relation Mappings: redirect external Relations*
12: **for all** $\big(r_j \in R_t : (mn_2 = \pi_1(r_j) \vee mn_2 = \pi_2(r_j)) \wedge \nexists r_z (r_z, r_j) \in sm\big)$ **do**
13: $relationMapping := rm_x \in RM_{cbprm} : \big(\pi_1(rm_x) = mn_1 \wedge \pi_3(rm_x) \in supertypes_t(r_j) \wedge \pi_4(rm_x) = \text{DIRECTION}(r_j) \wedge \pi_5(rm_x) \in supertypes_t(\texttt{sourceTarget}(r_j, mn_2))\big)$
14: **if** $\big(\text{DIRECTION}(r_j) = outgoing\big)$ **then**
15: $\pi_1(r_j) := \pi_2(relationMapping)$ // *update the source*
16: **else if** $\big(\text{DIRECTION}(r_j) = ingoing\big)$ **then**
17: $\pi_2(r_j) := \pi_2(relationMapping)$ // *update the target*
18: **end if**
19: **end for**
20: **end for**
21: // *Collect all Model Elements to remove from t*
22: $ME_{del} := \{se_i \in SE_t : \exists se_1 \in SE_{d_{cbprm}}\big((se_1, se_i) \in sm \, (\nexists mn_3 \in MN_{rs_{cbprm}} (se_1, mn_3) \in S_{cbprm})\big)\} \cup \{bp_j \in BP_t : \big(\exists (se_1, se_2) \in sm\big(\exists bp_x \in annotations_{d_{cbprm}}(se_1) \big(type_t(bp_j) = type_{d_{cbprm}}(bp_x)\big)\big)\big)\} \cup \{mn_k \in MN_{rs_{cbprm}} : \exists mn_1 \in MN_{d_{cbprm}}((mn_1, mn_k) \in S_{cbprm})\}$
23: $ME_t := ME_t \setminus ME_{del}$

Figure 8. The extended apply refinement algorithm. It gets the following inputs: $(cbprm \in CBPRM, t \in T, sm \in SubgraphMappings_{d_{cbrm}, t})$.

target *Model Node*, depending on the direction, must be of the same type as defined in the Relation Mapping (Line 13). Then, the *Relation* r_j is redirected to its new source or target *Model Node* which has been added from the $cbprm$ (Lines 14 to 19). For example, if the CBPRM shown in Figure 6 is applied to the Order App in Figure 3, all *Relations* of type *hostedOn* that are ingoing at the Public Cloud *Component Pattern* are redirected to the Public Cloud *Component* of type AWS. Hence, the Message-oriented Middleware, the Platform as a Service the Order Processor is hosted on, and the Relational Database are hosted on AWS after the CBPRM has been applied.

Finally, all *Model Elements* that are part of the subgraph must be deleted as they have been refined to concrete technologies (Lines 22 to 23). This also includes all *Behavior Patterns* annotated at any mapped *Structure Elements*. However, all staying *Model Nodes* mapped by the $cbprm$'s Detector must not be deleted, while all placeholder *Model Nodes* added from $cbprm$'s Refinement Structure must be removed from t.

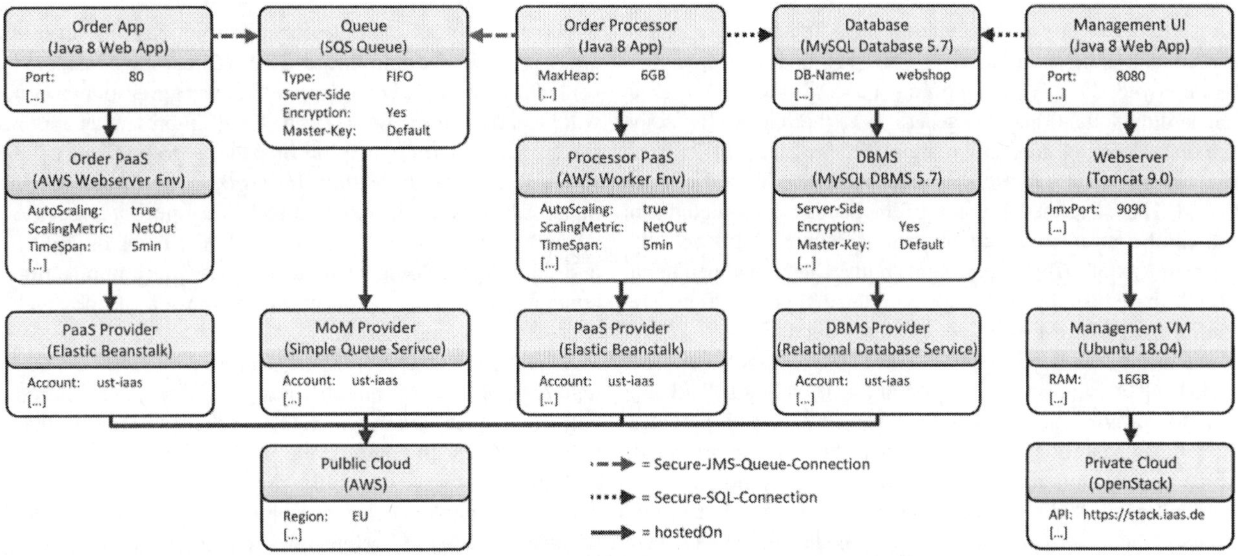

Figure 9. Executable EDMM deployment model, which results from refining the PbDCM shown in Figure 3.

V. Case Study

In the following, we describe a possible refinement of the PbDCM introduced in Figure 3 to an executable deployment model which is shown in Figure 9: All *Component Patterns* hosted on the Public Cloud pattern have been refined to concrete services offered by Amazon (AWS). Thus, the PaaS patterns hosting the *Order App* and the *Order Processor* have been refined to *Elastic Beanstalk Environments* that are preconfigured for automatic scaling to realize the Unpredictable Workload and Stateless Component patterns. Moreover, the types of the *Order App* and the *Order Processor* ensured that appropriate CBPRMs were chosen to refine the PaaS pattern to appropriate Beanstalk environments, i. e., to an *AWS Webserver Env* and to an *AWS Worker Env* respectively.

To realize the Exactly-Once Delivery pattern, the Point-to-Point Channel has been refined to a pre-configured "FIFO" *SQS Queue*, which is hosted on the *Simple Queue Service* offered by AWS. Further, the *Relational Database* pattern was refined to (i) a *MySQL Database 5.7*, (ii) a *MySQL Database Management System (DBMS) 5.7*, and (iii) the *Relational Database Service* offered by AWS. This is required, since a DBMS is obligatory to run a database, while the Relational Database Service provides and maintains the DBMS. To compensate the annotated Information Obscurity pattern, the SQS Queue and the DBMS are configured to use "Server-Side Encryption". Similarly to the Relational Database pattern, the Execution Environment pattern hosting the Management UI has been refined to multiple *Components*: An *Ubuntu 18.04* and a *Tomcat* webserver are needed since the Management UI is a Java 8 Web App and requires an underlying webserver.

Moreover, we created a video [12][13] showing the described case study in detail, i. e., how the PbDCM shown in Figure 3 can be refined to the executable deployment model illustrated in Figure 9 in an automated manner using our prototype.

VI. Prototypical Validation

To prove the practical feasibility of the extended modeling concept, we implemented a prototype based on the *Topology Orchestration Specification for Cloud Applications (TOSCA)* [10] and the open-source ecosystem OpenTOSCA [14][15] TOSCA is a standardized modeling language for automating the deployment and management of cloud applications in a portable way. We chose TOSCA as our basis as it is ontologically extensible [16] and can be mapped to EDMM as follows:

In TOSCA, a declarative deployment model can be expressed by a so-called *Topology Template*. Thereby, *Components* and *Relations* in a PbDCM are represented in TOSCA as *Node Templates* and *Relationship Templates*, which are instances of *Node Types* and *Relationship Types*, respectively. Thus, similar to our extended metamodel where, e. g., *Component Types* define the semantics for *Components*, Node Types and Relationship Types are defining the semantics for the Node and Relationship Templates. We realize *Component Patterns* and *Component Pattern Types* also as Node Templates and Node Types. To differentiate "Pattern Node Types" from "normal" Node Types in TOSCA, a *Tag* in the Node Type is used. Thus, all instances of Node Types having this pattern-tag identifies the corresponding Node Templates as *Component Patterns*.

To annotate Node Templates in a Topology Template by *Behavior Patterns*, *Policies* can be used in TOSCA. The semantics of a Policy is hereby defined by a *Policy Type*. Hence, *Relation Behavior Patterns* and *Component Behavior Patterns* can be mapped to Policies, while *Relation Behavior Pattern Types* and *Component Behavior Pattern Types* are represented by Policy Types in TOSCA. However, according to the TOSCA Specification [10], Relationship Templates cannot be annotated using Policies. Thus, we extended the TOSCA metamodel to support annotating Policies at Relationship Templates during modeling time. This, however, does not influence the standard compatibility of our implementation since Topology Templates that contain patterns are abstract PbDCMs, and, hence, cannot be deployed directly. By refining a PbDCM in TOSCA, a standard compliant model is generated as the refined Topology Template does not contain any more patterns, i. e., all Policies attached to Node and Relationship Templates have been removed. Thus, a refined Topology Template is standard conform and can be automatically deployed. Moreover, since we only use elements of a Topology Template that can be mapped to an EDMM-based deployment model, a refined Topology Template conforms to EDMM as no policies are contained.

Our prototype is part of the OpenTOSCA ecosystem [15]. OpenTOSCA is an implementation of the TOSCA standard and consists of three components: (i) Winery [17], which provides modeling capabilities, (ii) the OpenTOSCA Container [18], which enables automated orchestration and provisioning, and (iii) the OpenTOSCA UI, offering management functionality to the user. Since our concept focuses on modeling, we extended Winery to support the modeling of *Behavior Patterns*, and the creation and refinement of PbDCMs and CBPRMs.

VII. Related Work

Diverse approaches in the context of MDA and deployment models mention patterns, nevertheless we present selected related work sharing the definition of patterns by Alexander et al. [6] as proven solutions solving recurring problems.

PbDCMs and their refinement is based on the concept of *Model-driven Architecture (MDA)* [19]: A PbDCM represents a *Platform Independent Model (PIM)*, which is, in the context of MDA, transformed into a *Platform Specific Model (PSM)*, represented by the refinement to an executable deployment model. There are diverse approaches to transform a PIM into a PSM present. For instance, the approach of Mellor et al. [20] requires a definition and implementation of a mapping between the abstract metamodel and the metamodel of the target platform. Within our approach, the CBPRMs can be automatically applied, and, thus, combine the mapping and implementation.

Multiple approaches address the transformation of deployment models. The approach of Breitenbücher [11] enables the management of composite cloud applications by an automated relization of management patterns in topologies. Furthermore, Saatkamp et al. [21][22] use logic programming to formalize the problem and context domain of patterns enabling an automated detection and resolving of problems within deployment models. Moreover, the approaches of Eilam et al. [23][24] and Arnold et al. [25][26] focus on an automated transformation of deployment models using predefined transformation steps. Nevertheless, within all of the mentioned approaches patterns are not used to model and define the deployment model.

Hallstrom and Soundarajan [27] refine patterns into subpatterns representing realization variants of abstract patterns which leads to a hierarchy of patterns. Falkenthal et al. [28] introduce a similar approach, which refines patterns into concrete technologies. They further present concrete solutions of patterns capturing reusable implementation realizations, such as code snippets [29][30], as well as aggregation operators which allow the combination of multiple concrete solutions into an overall solution [31]. The introduced CBPRMs can be considered as concrete solutions, a combination through aggregation operators will be part of future work. Eden et al. [32] present an approach for an automated application of patterns to add source code to a given program. Within this work, patterns are specified on an abstract level and realized in a specific program in advance. Even though, those works do not focus on modeling and defining deployment models by a pattern application, a combination of our approach with the presented ones will be considered in future work.

Schürr [33] presents *Triple Graph Grammars (TGGs)* to define graph transformations in a general manner. Therefore, correspondence graphs in TGGs specify correspondences between nodes. In contrast, the presented Relation Mappings in CBPRMs focus on redirecting external relations to the exchanged graph fragment. Bolusset and Oquendo [34] introduce a software architecture refinement approach using *transformation patterns* based on rewriting logic. Similarly, Lehrig [35] introduces the *Architectural Template (AT)* method to apply patterns in terms of reusable modeling templates to software architectures. In contrast, transformation patterns and ATs define rewriting rules of architectures and do not use patterns as components to be refined to concrete technologies.

Di Martino et al. [36] describe the composition of cloud services to cloud applications using patterns. Further, they introduce a semantic model of patterns describing business processes, cloud applications, and mappings to required cloud resources for their implementation [37]. Contrary, those mappings cannot be used to describe or refine deployment models.

VIII. Conclusion & Future Work

Using the Pattern-based Deployment and Configuration Model (PbDCM) approach, the deployment becomes more variable as *Component Patterns* can be automatically refined to different technologies and vendors for each deployment. For example, while one modeler chooses AWS as a public cloud provider, a second one may choose the Google Cloud. Moreover, PbDCMs reduce the required knowledge how technologies must be configured to meet non-functional requirements as *Behavior Patterns* can be annotated at *Structure Elements* to abstractly specify their requirements. Thus, if an application experiences Unpredictable Workload [5], the pattern can be annotated to the corresponding *Components*, which are then automatically refined to an appropriate configuration. For example, configurations required by the General Data Protection Regulation (GDPR) can be realized by an appropriate selection of behavioral patterns, such as the Secure Channel pattern [9].

However, to detect applicable CBPRMs that are able to refine patterns in a PbDCM, our approach builds upon isomorphic subgraph matching. Thus, if any *Structure Element* in a PbDCM is changed by applying a CBPRM, another CBPRM, which may have been applicable before, may not be applicable anymore as the detector subgraph cannot be found. Hence, the order in which CBPRMs are applied is important and may result in different solutions. We plan to tackle this issue in future work by generating possible permutations of CBPRMs. Moreover, to close the gap between abstract architectures and deployment models we plan to combine the approach of Guth and Leymann [38] with the presented one. Thereby, first architectures are described using abstract patterns [38] which are then refined to more concrete patterns [28], and replaced by concrete technologies using the presented approach. Finally, we plan to use the *Cloud Data Patterns for Confidentiality* [39] to enhance the security of data stored in cloud environments.

ACKNOWLEDGMENT

This work was partially funded by the German Research Foundation (DFG) project SustainLife (379522012).

REFERENCES

[1] U. Breitenbücher *et al.*, "Combining Declarative and Imperative Cloud Application Provisioning based on TOSCA," in *International Conference on Cloud Engineering (IC2E 2014)*. IEEE, Mar. 2014, pp. 87–96.

[2] M. Wurster *et al.*, "The Essential Deployment Metamodel: A Systematic Review of Deployment Automation Technologies," *Software-Intensive Cyber-Physical Systems (SICS)*, Aug. 2019.

[3] C. Endres *et al.*, "Declarative vs. Imperative: Two Modeling Patterns for the Automated Deployment of Applications," in *Proceedings of the 9th International Conference on Pervasive Patterns and Applications (PATTERNS)*. Xpert Publishing Services, Feb. 2017, pp. 22–27.

[4] L. Harzenetter *et al.*, "Pattern-based Deployment Models and Their Automatic Execution," in *11th IEEE/ACM International Conference on Utility and Cloud Computing (UCC 2018)*. IEEE Computer Society, Dec. 2018.

[5] C. Fehling, F. Leymann, R. Retter, W. Schupeck, and P. Arbitter, *Cloud Computing Patterns: Fundamentals to Design, Build, and Manage Cloud Applications*. Springer, Jan. 2014.

[6] C. Alexander, S. Ishikawa, and M. Silverstein, *A Pattern Language: Towns, Buildings, Construction*. Oxford University Press, Aug. 1977.

[7] G. Hohpe and B. Woolf, *Enterprise Integration Patterns: Designing, Building, and Deploying Messaging Solutions*. Addison-Wesley, 2004.

[8] E. Gamma, R. Helm, R. Johnson, and J. Vlissides, *Design Patterns: Elements of Reusable Object-oriented Software*. Addison-Wesley, 1994.

[9] M. Schumacher, E. Fernandez-Buglioni, D. Hybertson, F. Buschmann, and P. Sommerlad, *Security Patterns: Integrating Security and Systems Engineering*. John Wiley & Sons, Inc., Jan. 2006.

[10] OASIS, *TOSCA Simple Profile in YAML Version 1.3*, Organization for the Advancement of Structured Information Standards (OASIS), 2019.

[11] U. Breitenbücher, "Eine musterbasierte Methode zur Automatisierung des Anwendungsmanagements," Dissertation, University of Stuttgart, Faculty of Computer Science, Electrical Engineering, and Information Technology, 2016.

[12] L. Harzenetter, "Demonstration Video," 2019, URL: https://youtu.be/zmU35Detr60 [accessed: 2020-02-18].

[13] ——, "Demonstration TOSCA Repository," 2019, URL: https://github.com/lharzenetter/tosca-definitions [accessed: 2020-02-18].

[14] University of Stuttgart, "OpenTOSCA," 2019, URL: https://github.com/OpenTOSCA [accessed: 2020-02-18].

[15] U. Breitenbücher *et al.*, "The OpenTOSCA Ecosystem - Concepts & Tools," in *European Space project on Smart Systems, Big Data, Future Internet - Towards Serving the Grand Societal Challenges - Volume 1: EPS Rome 2016,*. SciTePress, 2016, pp. 112–130.

[16] A. Bergmayr *et al.*, "A Systematic Review of Cloud Modeling Languages," *ACM Computing Surveys (CSUR)*, vol. 51, no. 1, Feb. 2018.

[17] O. Kopp, T. Binz, U. Breitenbücher, and F. Leymann, "Winery – A Modeling Tool for TOSCA-based Cloud Applications," in *Proceedings of the 11th International Conference on Service-Oriented Computing (ICSOC 2013)*. Springer, Dec. 2013, pp. 700–704.

[18] T. Binz *et al.*, "OpenTOSCA – A Runtime for TOSCA-based Cloud Applications," in *Proceedings of the 11th International Conference on Service-Oriented Computing (ICSOC 2013)*. Springer, Dec. 2013, pp. 692–695.

[19] R. Soley *et al.*, "Model driven architecture," *OMG white paper*, vol. 308, no. 308, p. 5, 2000.

[20] S. J. Mellor, K. Scott, A. Uhl, and D. Weise, "Model-driven architecture," in *Advances in Object-Oriented Information Systems*. Springer, 2002, pp. 290–297.

[21] K. Saatkamp, U. Breitenbücher, O. Kopp, and F. Leymann, "Application Scenarios for Automated problem Detection in TOSCA Topologies by Formalized Patterns," in *Papers From the 12th Advanced Summer School on Service Oriented Computing*. IBM Research Division, Oct. 2018, pp. 43–53.

[22] ——, "An Approach to Automatically Detect Problems in Restructured Deployment Models based on Formalizing Architecture and Design Patterns," *SICS Software-Intensive Cyber-Physical Systems*, pp. 1–13, 2019.

[23] T. Eilam *et al.*, "Managing the configuration complexity of distributed applications in Internet data centers," *Communications Magazine*, vol. 44, no. 3, pp. 166–177, Mar. 2006.

[24] T. Eilam, M. Elder, A. V. Konstantinou, and E. Snible, "Pattern-based Composite Application Deployment," in *Proceedings of the 12th IFIP/IEEE International Symposium on Integrated Network Management (IM 2011)*. IEEE, May 2011, pp. 217–224.

[25] W. Arnold, T. Eilam, M. Kalantar, A. Konstantinou, and A. Totok, "Pattern Based SOA Deployment," in *Proceedings of the Fifth International Conference on Service-Oriented Computing (ICSOC 2007)*. Springer, Sep. 2007, pp. 1–12.

[26] ——, "Automatic Realization of SOA Deployment Patterns in Distributed Environments," in *Proceedings of the 6th International Conference on Service-Oriented Computing (ICSOC 2008)*. Springer, Dec. 2008, pp. 162–179.

[27] J. O. Hallstrom and N. Soundarajan, "Reusing Patterns through Design Refinement," in *Formal Foundations of Reuse and Domain Engineering*. Springer, 2009, pp. 225–235.

[28] M. Falkenthal *et al.*, "Leveraging Pattern Application via Pattern Refinement," in *Proceedings of the International Conference on Pursuit of Pattern Languages for Societal Change (PURPLSOC 2015)*. epubli, Jun. 2015, pp. 38–61.

[29] M. Falkenthal, J. Barzen, U. Breitenbücher, C. Fehling, and F. Leymann, "From Pattern Languages to Solution Implementations," in *Proceedings of the Sixth International Conferences on Pervasive Patterns and Applications (PATTERNS 2014)*. Xpert Publishing Services, May 2014, pp. 12–21.

[30] M. Falkenthal and F. Leymann, "Easing pattern application by means of solution languages," in *Proceedings of the 9th International Conferences on Pervasive Patterns and Applications (PATTERNS)*. Xpert Publishing Services (XPS), 2017, pp. 58–64.

[31] M. Falkenthal, J. Barzen, U. Breitenbücher, and F. Leymann, "On the Algebraic Properties of Concrete Solution Aggregation," *SICS Software-Intensive Cyber-Physical Systems*, Aug. 2019.

[32] A. Eden, A. Yehudai, and J. Gil, "Precise Specification and Automatic Application of Design Patterns," in *Proceedings of the 12th IEEE International Conference Automated Software Engineering (ASE 1997)*. IEEE, Nov. 1997, pp. 143–152.

[33] A. Schürr, "Specification of graph translators with triple graph grammars," in *Graph-Theoretic Concepts in Computer Science*. Springer Berlin Heidelberg, 1995, pp. 151–163.

[34] T. Bolusset and F. Oquendo, "Formal Refinement of Software Architectures Based on Rewriting Logic," in *Proceedings of the International Workshop on Refinement of Critical Systems*, 2002, pp. 200–202.

[35] S. M. Lehrig, "Efficiently Conducting Quality-of-Service Analyses by Templating Architectural Knowledge," Dissertation, University of Stuttgart, Faculty of Computer Science, Electrical Engineering, and Information Technology, 2018.

[36] B. Di Martino, G. Cretella, and A. Esposito, "Cloud services composition through cloud patterns," in *Adaptive Resource Management and Scheduling for Cloud Computing*. Springer, 2015, pp. 128–140.

[37] B. Di Martino, A. Esposito, S. Nacchia, and S. A. Maisto, "A semantic model for business process patterns to support cloud deployment," *Computer Science - Research and Development*, vol. 32, no. 3, pp. 257–267, 2017.

[38] J. Guth and F. Leymann, "Pattern-based rewrite and refinement of architectures using graph theory," *Software-Intensive Cyber-Physical Systems (SICS)*, pp. 1–12, Aug. 2019.

[39] S. Strauch, U. Breitenbücher, O. Kopp, F. Leymann, and T. Unger, "Cloud Data Patterns for Confidentiality," in *Proceedings of the 2nd International Conference on Cloud Computing and Services Science (CLOSER 2012)*. SciTePress, Apr. 2012, pp. 387–394.

Efficiently Detecting Disguised Web Spambots (with Mismatches) in a Temporally Annotated Sequence

Hayam Alamro

Department of Informatics
King's College London, UK
Department of Information Systems
Princess Nourah bint Abdulrahman University
Riyadh, KSA
email: hayam.alamro@kcl.ac.uk

Costas S. Iliopoulos

Department of Informatics
King's College London, UK
email: costas.iliopoulos@kcl.ac.uk

***Abstract*—Web spambots are becoming more advanced, utilizing techniques that can defeat existing spam detection algorithms. These techniques include performing a series of malicious actions with variable time delays, repeating the same series of malicious actions multiple times, and interleaving legitimate (decoy) and malicious actions. Existing methods that are based on string pattern matching are not able to detect spambots that use these techniques. In response, we define a new problem to detect spambots utilizing the aforementioned techniques and propose an efficient algorithm to solve it. Given a dictionary of temporally annotated sequences $\overline{S}$ modeling spambot actions, each associated with a time window, a long, temporally annotated sequence T modeling a user action log, and parameters f and k, our problem seeks to detect each degenerate sequence $\tilde{S}$ with c indeterminate action(s) in $\overline{S}$ that occurs in T at least f times within its associated time window, and with at most k mismatches. Our algorithm solves the problem exactly, it requires linear time and space, and it employs advanced data structures, bit masking and the Kangaroo method, to deal with the problem efficiently.**

Keywords–Web spambot; Indeterminate ; Disguised; Actions log.

I. Introduction

A spambot is a computer program designed to do repetitive actions on websites, servers or social media communities. These actions might be harmful, such as carrying out certain attacks on websites/ servers or may be used to deceive users such as involving irrelevant links to increase a website ranking in search engine results. Spambots can take different forms that are designed according to a spammer desire such as using web crawlers for planting unsolicited material or to collect email addresses from different sources like websites, discussion groups or newsgroups with the intent of building mailing lists for sending unsolicited or phishing emails. Usually, Spammers create fake accounts to target specific websites or domain specific users and start sending predefined designed actions which are known as predefined scripts. Therefore, websites administrators are looking for automated tools to curtail the actions of web spambots. Although there are attempts to prevent spamming using anti-spambots tools, the spammers try to adopt new forms of spambots by manipulating spambots' actions behaviour to appear as it were coming from a legitimate user to bypass the existing spam-filter tools. One of the main popular techniques used in web spambots is *content-based* which inject repetitive keywords in meta tags to promote a website in search engines, as well as *link-based* techniques that add links to a web page to increase its ranking score in search engines. There are several works for preventing the use of content-based or link-based techniques by web spambots [1]–[6]. However, they focus on identifying the content or links added by spambots, rather than detecting the spambot based on their actions. There are also techniques that analyze *spambot behavior* [5] [7]. These techniques utilize supervised machine learning to identify the source of spambot, rather than detecting the spambot. More relevant to our work are string pattern matching-based techniques that detect spambots based on their actions (i.e., based on how they interact with the website these spambots attack) [8] [9]. These techniques model the user log as a large string (sequence of elements corresponding to actions of users or spambots) and common/previous web spambot actions as a dictionary of strings. Then, they perform pattern matching of the strings from the dictionary to the large string. If a match is found, then they state that a web spambot has been detected. For example, the work by Hayati et.al [8] proposes a rule-based, on-the-fly web spambot detection technique, which identifies web spambots by performing string matching efficiently using tries. The work of [9] improves upon [8] by considering spambots that utilize decoy actions (i.e., injecting legitimate actions, typically performed by users, within their spam actions, to make spam detection difficult) and using approximate pattern matching based on the *FPT* algorithm to detect such spambots. However, both [8] and [9] are limited in that they consider consecutive spambot actions. This makes them inapplicable in real settings where a spambot needs to be detected from a log representing actions of both users and spambots, as well as settings where a spambot injects legitimate actions in some random fashion within a time window. The reason that the works of [8] and [9] are inapplicable in these settings is that they do not take into account temporal information of neither the sequence (i.e., the user log) nor the pattern (i.e., the spambot actions). Recently, Artificial Intelligence (AI) has been employed in security purposes to recognize cyber crimes and to reduce the time and money needed for manual tasks and threats monitoring at businesses. In our paper, we use one of the main approaches for AI-based threats detection which is based on monitoring behavior of a stream of data in a log file and try to detect the places of spambots. To the best of our knowledge, our contribution is novel as no other work takes into account the temporal information of a sequence of actions in a user log, nor the estimated time window of a pattern of actions in a dictionary. These challenges made finding an effective solution to our problem a new challenge as there is no other work addressing the issue of time (the spambot can pause and speed up) or errors (deceptive or unimportant actions). It is worth mentioning that our methods are not comparable to others as they address different issues. The other challenge that we faced was when conducting our laboratory experiments for our algorithm as there was no publicly available data set modeling the real temporal annotated sequence of a user log. The only available is the public data sets (WEBSPAM-UK2006/7) which are a collection of assessments and set of host names and based on the spamicity measure to decide whether a web page is a spam, non-spam or undecided.

In this work, we focus on time annotated sequences, where each action is associated with a time stamp. Our goal is to detect one or more spambots, by finding frequent occurrences of indeterminate spambot actions within a time window that can also occur with mismatches. Our work makes the following specific contributions:

1. We introduce an efficient algorithm that can detect one or more sequences of indeterminate (non solid) actions in text T in linear time. We ignore the temporal factor in describing this algorithm to facilitate the process of clarification and focus on detecting disguised web spambots efficiently. It is worth mentioning that our algorithm can compute all occurrences of a sequence $\tilde{S}$ in text T in $O(m + logn + occ)$, where m is the length of the degenerate sequence $\tilde{S}$, n is the length of the text T and occ is the number of the occurrences of the sequence $\tilde{S}$ in text T.

2. We propose an efficient algorithm for solving (f, c, k, W)-Disguised Spambots Detection with indeterminate actions and mismatches. Our algorithm takes into account temporal information, because it considers time-annotated sequences and because it requires a match to occur within a time window. The latter requirement models the fact that spambots generally perform a series of disguised actions in a relatively short period of time. Our algorithm is a generalization of the previous problem and based on constructing a *generalized enhanced suffix array*, *bit masking* with help of *Kangaroo method* which help in locating indeterminate spambots with mismatches fast. Our proposed algorithm (f, c, k, W)-Disguised Spambots Detection with indeterminate actions can find all occurrences of each $\tilde{S}_i$ in $\overline{S}$, such that $\tilde{S}_i$ occurs in T at least f times within the window W_i of $\tilde{S}_i$ and with at most k mismatches according to Hamming distance.

The rest of the paper as follows. In Section II, detailed literature review, In section III we introduce notations and background concepts. In Section IV, we formally define the problems we address. In Section V, we formally detail our solutions and present our algorithms. In Section VI, we present experimental results. In Section VII, we conclude.

II. Literature Review

Web spam usually refers to the techniques that the spammers used to manipulate search engine ranking results to promote their sites either for advertising purposes, financial benefits or for misleading the user to a malicious content trap or to install malware on victim's machine. For these purposes, spammers can use different techniques such as *content-based* which is the most popular type of web spam, where the spammer tries to increase term frequencies on the target page to increase the score of the page. Another popular technique is through using *link-based*, where the spammer tries to add lots of links on the target page to manipulate the search engine results [10] [11]. Ghiam et al. in [11] classified spamming techniques to link-based, hiding, and content-based, and they discussed the methods used for web spam detection for each classified technique. Roul et al. in [10] proposed a method to detect web spam by using either content-based, link-based techniques or a combination of both. Gyongyi et al. in [12] proposed techniques to semi-automatically differ the good from spam page with the assistance of human expert whose his role is examining small seed set of pages to tell the algorithm which are 'good pages' and 'bad pages' roughly based on their connectivity to the seed ones. Also, Gyongyi et al. in [13] introduced the concept of spam mass and proposed a method for identifying pages that benefit from link spamming. Egele et al. [14] developed a classifier to distinguish spam sites from legitimate ones by inferring the main web page features as essential results, and based on those results, the classifier can remove spam links from search engine results. Furthermore, Ahmed et al. [15] presented a statistical approach to detect spam profiles on online social networks (OSNs). The work in [15] presented a generic statistical approach to identify spam profiles on online social networks. For that, they identified 14 generic statistical features that are common to both Facebook and Twitter and used three classification algorithms (naive Bayes, Jrip and J48) to evaluate features on both individual and combined data sets crawled from Facebook and Twitter networks. Prieto et al. [16] proposed a new spam detection system called Spam Analyzer And Detector (SAAD) after analyzing a set of existing web spam detection heuristics and limitations to come up with new heuristics. Prieto et al. in [16] tested their techniques using Webb Spam Corpus(2011) and WEBSPAM-UK2006/7, and they claimed that the performance of their proposed techniques is better than others system presented in their literature. On the other side, other contributions try to detect web spambot using supervised machining learning. In this regard, Dai et al. [17] used supervised learning techniques to combine historical features from archival copies of the web and use them to train classifiers with features extracted from current page content to improve spam classification. Araujo et al. [18] presented a classifier to detect web spam based on qualified link (QL) analysis and language model (ML) features. The classifier in [18] is evaluated using the public WEBSPAM-UK 2006 and 2007 data sets. The baseline of their experiments was using the precomputed content and link features in a combined way to detect web spam pages, then they combined the baseline with QL and ML based features which contributed to improving the detecting performance. Algur et al. [19] proposed a system which gives spamicity score of a web page based on mixed features of content and link-based. The proposed system in [19] adopts an unsupervised approach, unlike traditional supervised classifiers, and a threshold is determined by empirical analysis to act as an indicator for a web page to be spam or non-spam. Luckner et al. [20] created a web spam detector using features based on lexical items. For that, they created three web spam detectors and proposed new lexical-based features that are trained and tested using WEBSPAM-

UK data sets of 2006 and 2007 separately, then they trained the classifiers using WEBSPAM-UK 2006 data set but they use WEBSPAM-UK 2007 for testing. In the end, the authors based on the results of the first and second detectors as a reference for the third detector where they showed that the data from WEBSPAM-UK 2006 can be used to create classifiers that work stably both on the WEBSPAM-UK 2006 and 2007 data sets. Moreover, Goh et al. [21] exploited web weight properties to enhance the web spam detection performance on a web spam data set WEBSPAM-UK 2007. The overall performance in [21] outperformed the benchmark algorithms up to 30.5% improvement at the host level and $6-11\%$ improvement at the page level. At the level of online social networks (OSNs), the use of social media can be exploited negatively as the impact of OSNs has increased recently and has a major impact on public opinion. For example, one of the common ways to achieve media blackout is to employ large groups of automated accounts (bots) to influence the results of the political elections campaigns or spamming other users' accounts. Cresci et al. [22] proposed an online user behavior model represents a sequence of string characters corresponding to the user's online actions on Twitter. The authors in [22] adapt biological DNA techniques to online user behavioral actions which are represented using digital DNA to distinguish between genuine and spambot accounts. They make use of the assumption of the digital DNA fingerprinting techniques to detect social spambots by mining similar sequences, and for each account, they extract a DNA string that encodes its behavioral information from created data set of spambots and genuine accounts. After that, Cresci et al. [23] investigate the major characteristics among group of users in OSNs. The study in [23] is an analysis of the results obtained in DNA-inspired online behavioral modeling in [22] to measure the level of similarities between the real behavioral sequences of Twitter user accounts and synthetic accounts. The results in [23] show that the heterogeneity among legitimate behaviors is high and not random. Later, Cresci et al. in [24] envisage a change in the spambot detection approach from reaction to proaction to grasp the characteristics of the evolved spambots in OSNs using the logical DNA behavioral modeling technique, and they make use of digital DNA representation as a sequence of characters. The proactive scheme begins with modeling known spambot accounts with digital DNA, applying genetic algorithms to extract new generation of synthetic accounts, comparing the current state-of-art detection techniques to the new spambots, then design novel detection techniques.

III. Background and Main Terminologies

Let $T = a_0a_2\dots a_{n-1}$ be a string of length $|T| = n$ over an alphabet Σ of size $|\Sigma| = \sigma$. The empty string ε is the string of length 0. For $1 \le i \le j \le n$, $T[i]$ denotes the ith symbol of T, and $T[i,j]$ the contiguous sequence of symbols (called *factor* or *substring*) $T[i]T[i+1]\dots T[j]$. A *substring* $T[i,j]$ is a suffix of T if $j = n$ and it is a prefix of T if $i = 1$. A string p is a *repeat* of T iff p has at least two occurrences in T. In addition p is said to be *right-maximal* in T iff there exist two positions $i < j$ such that $T[i, i+|p|-1] = T[j, j+|p|-1] = p$ and either $j+|p| = n+1$ or $T[i, i+|p|] \neq T[j, j+|p|]$. A *degenerate or indeterminate string* , is defined as a sequence $\tilde{X} = \tilde{x}_0\tilde{x}_1\dots\tilde{x}_{n-1}$, where $\tilde{x}_i \subseteq \Sigma$ for all $0 \le i \le n-1$ and the alphabet Σ is a non-empty finite set of symbols of size $|\Sigma|$. A *degenerate symbol* $\tilde{x}$ over an alphabet Σ is a non-empty subset of Σ, i.e. $\tilde{x} \subseteq \Sigma$ and $\tilde{x} \neq \emptyset$. $|\tilde{x}|$ denotes the size of $\tilde{x}$ and we have $1 \le \tilde{x} \le |\Sigma|$. A degenerate string is built over the potential $2^{|\Sigma|}-1$ non-empty subsets of letters belonging to Σ. If $|\tilde{x}| = 1$, that is $|\tilde{x}|$ repeats a single symbol of Σ, we say that $\tilde{x}_i$ is a *solid symbol* and i is a *solid position*. Otherwise, $\tilde{x}_i$ and i are said to be a *non-solid symbol* and *non-solid position* respectively. For example, $\tilde{X} = ab[ac]a[bcd]bac$ is a degenerate string of length 8 over the alphabet $\Sigma = \{a,b,c,d\}$. A string containing only solid symbols will be called a solid string. A *conservative degenerate string* is a degenerate string where its number of non-solid symbols is upper-bounded by a fixed position constant c [25], [26]. The previous example is a conservative degenerate string with $c = 2$.

A *suffix array* of T is the lexicographical sorted array of the suffixes of a string T i.e., the suffix array of T is an array $SA[1\dots n]$ in which $SA[i]$ is the ith suffix of T in ascending order [27]–[29]. The major advantages of *suffix arrays* over *suffix trees* is the space as the space needed using suffix trees becomes larger with larger alphabets such as Japanese characters, and it is useful in computing the frequency and location of a substring in a long sequence (corpus) [28]. $LCP(T_1, T_2)$ is the length of the longest common prefix between strings T_1 and T_2 and it is usually used with SA such that $LCP[i] = lcp(T_{SA[i]}, T_{SA[i-1]})$ For all $i \in [1..n]$ [27] [30].

IV. Problems Definitions

The two main problems that the paper will address can be defined as follows.

Problem A: Disguised (Indeterminate) Actions

Some spambots might attempt to disguise their actions by varying certain actions. For example, a spambot takes the actions $ABCDEF$, then $ACCDEF$, then $ABDDEF$ etc. This can be described as $A[BC][CD]DEF$. They try to deceive by changing the second and third action. The action $[BC]$ and $[CD]$ are variations of the same sequence. We will call the symbols A, C, D, E, F solid, the symbols $[BC]$ $[CD]$ indeterminate or non-solid and the string $A[BC][CD]DEF$ degenerate string which is denoted by $\tilde{S}$. In fact, they can disguise any of the actions. In this case, we are not concern which actions will be disguised but we assume that the numbers of attempts to disguise is limited. Let us assume that the number of disguised actions is bounded by a constant c. For the moment, we will ignore the temporal factor of the disguises at this problem to facilitate the clarification of the discovery of the spambot actions, and we will consider the temporal factor in describing problem B as it is a generalization of problem A. Actually, we combine both temporal and fake actions discovery by apply both algorithms simultaneously. For now, let us consider the series of actions taking place on the server.

Definition IV.1. Given a sequence $T = a_1 \dots a_n$, find all occurrences of $\tilde{S} = s_1s_2\dots s_m$ in T, where s_i might be solid or indeterminate.

Problem B: Disguised Actions (with k Mismatches)

It is a generalization of *Problem A* with k errors such that the sequence of spambot actions $\tilde{S}$ is *degenerate* actions with errors, and the number of errors is bounded by a constant k. Our aim is to detect new suspicious spambots which are resulting from changing other disguised actions by spammers such that using few mismatches in its spambot actions $\tilde{S}$ to appear like actions issued by a genuine user.

Definition IV.2. Given a sequence $T = a_1 \dots a_n$ and an action sequence $\tilde{S} = s_1 s_2 \dots s_m$, find all occurrences of $\tilde{S}$ in T where s_i might be solid or indeterminate with *hamming distance* between $\tilde{S}$ and T is no more than k mismatches.

V. ALGORITHMS

In the following, we discuss our algorithms for the two aforementioned problems which they include (preprocessing) as preliminary stage.

A. Preprocessing

Our algorithms require as input sequences temporally annotated actions. These temporally annotated sequences are produced from user logs consisting of a collection of *http* requests. Specifically, each request in a user log is mapped to a predefined index key in the sequence and the date-time stamp for the request in the user log is mapped to a time point in the sequence.

B. Problem A: Disguised (indeterminate) actions

In order to design an efficient algorithm for this problem, we need to use the following steps that will make the algorithm fast.

Step 1: For each *non-solid* s_j occurring in degenerate pattern $\tilde{P} = s_1 \dots s_m$, we substitute each s_j with '#' symbol, where '#' is not in Σ. Let $\hat{P}$ be the resulting pattern from substitution process and will be considered as a *solid* pattern, see (Figure 1 **Step1**) and (Table I).

TABLE I. CONVERTING $\tilde{P}$ TO $\hat{P}$

$\tilde{P}$	A	B	[GX]	C	[AD]	F
$\hat{P}$	A	B	$\#_1$	C	$\#_2$	F

Step 2: Compute the *suffix array* for the sequence of actions T. Since the *suffix array* is sorted array of all suffixes of a given string, we can apply *binary search* algorithm with the suffix array to find a pattern of spambot actions in a text of actions in $O(mlogn)$ time complexity, where m is the the length of the pattern P and n is the length of the text T. Our algorithm uses Manber and Myers algorithm which is described in [31], which uses a suffix array for on-line string searches and can answer a query of type "Is P a substring in T?" in time $O(m + logn)$. The algorithm in [31], uses a sorted *suffix array*, *binary search* against the suffix array of T and auxiliary data structures *Llcp, Rlcp* which they are precomputed arrays and hold information about the *longest common prefixes (lcps)* for two subranges *(L...M)* and *(M...R)* of binary search. Subsequently, the algorithm speeds up the comparison and permits no more than one comparison for each character in P to be compared with the text T. The method is generalised to $O(m+logn+occ)$ to find all occurrences of P by continuing on the adjacent suffixes to the first occurrence of P in *suffix array*, see (Figure 1 **Step2**).

Step 3: At this stage, we consider each *non-solid* position s_j in $\hat{P}$ which is represented by '#' as an allowed mismatch with the corresponding action a_i in T as '#' is not in Σ. To query whether that a_i belongs to the set of actions in '#', the algorithm uses a *bit masking* operation. For example, suppose we want to see whether the action 'X' in text T belongs to one of the set actions $[GX]$ in $\hat{P}$ which is represented by '$\#_1$', see Table I, we assume that each action in degenerate symbol represents bit '1' among other possible actions, and '0' otherwise. Furthermore, The current compared action a_i in T is always represented by bit '1'. Thereafter, the algorithm uses *And* bit wise operation between the two sets $[GX]$ and $[X]$ such that $[11] \bigwedge [01] = [01]$ which means that $[X] \in [GX]$. To do that, the algorithm uses the *suffix array* and *binary search* to find the pattern match, and for each '#' in the sequence is encountered, the algorithm consider it as an allowed mismatch and get into the *verification* process to check whether the action a_i in T is one of the actions in '#'. However, each *non-solid* position s_j in $\hat{P}$ is numbered sequentially starting from 1 up to the number of indeterminate symbols c. Consequently, we refer to that position for each pattern of spambots actions with the number of the pattern $\hat{P}_r$ and the number of $\#_l$, where $1 \le r \le \Sigma\hat{P}$ and $1 \le l \le \Sigma\# \in \hat{P}_r$, see (Figure 1 **Step3**).

```
Input: Action sequence T, spambots dictionary S̄ where each spambot P̃ ∈ S̄
Output: all matching P̃ found in T
procedure LOCATE ALL LOCATIONS OF P̂ WITH INDETERMINATE ACTIONS IN T
▷ Step1: (Substitution)
    for each P̃_r ∈ S̄ do
        P̂_r ← P̃_r
        m ← |P̂_r|
        l ← 1
        for (j = 0 to m − 1) do
            if (P̂_r[j] is non solid) then
                P_r[j] ← #_l
                l ← l + 1
            end if
        end for
    end for
▷ Step2: (actions matching)
    Build the suffix array SA for the text of actions T
    for each P̂_r ∈ S̄ do
        Apply the binary search with LCPs arrays of Manber and Myer in [31]
        For each current action a_i in SA compared to non solid symbol represented
    by '#_l' in P̂_r ▷ go to: step 3
    end for
▷ Step3: (verification process)
    mask = 1 ⋀ hashMatchTable[P̂_r #_l][ascii[a_i]]
    if mask = 1 then
        continue
    else                                                    ▷ not match
        exit matching
    end if
end procedure
```

Figure 1: Problem A: Locate spambots with indeterminate actions

Verification process: At this stage, the algorithm does a bit level masking operation using the logical operator 'And' between the current compared action a_i in T and the corresponding *non-solid* position in $\hat{P}$ which is represented by '$\#_l$'. As we mentioned before, the algorithm assumes each current compared action a_i in T is represented by a bit '1', and each '$\#_l$' of each pattern reveals its original set of actions by setting bit '1' at each action belongs to its set and '0' otherwise using a match table called *hashMatchTable*, see Table II. To access the corresponding column in *hashMatchTable* directly, the columns are indexed by the *(ascii code)* of each character belongs to the actions alphabets in Σ and ordered from 65 to 90 which are the ascii code of capital letters (or 97 to 122 for small letters). Thus, the algorithm can apply the following formula ($1 \bigwedge hashMatchTable[\hat{P}_r\#_l][ascii[a_i]]$) to find whether that current comparing action a_i in T has a match with one of the actions in '$\#_l$' where '1' is the corresponding bit of a_i, see (Figure 1 **Step3**) and (Table II).

TABLE II. HASHMATCHTABLE OF THE PATTERN $\hat{P_1} = AB[GX]C[AD]F$ WHERE ITS COVERSION IS $\hat{P_1} = AB\#_1C\#_2F$

asscii(a_i)	65	66	67	68	..	71	...	88	89	90
a_i	A	B	C	D	..	G	...	X	Y	Z
$\hat{P_1}\#_1$	0	0	0	0		1	...	1	0	0
$\hat{P_1}\#_2$	1	0	0	1		0	...	0	0	0
...	...	...	...	...		...	...	...	...	...
$\hat{P_r}\#_l$	...	...	...	...		...	...	...	...	...

Theorem 1. Algorithm (Figure 1) computes the occurrence of the pattern $\hat{P}$ in text T in $O(mlogn)$ time using *suffix array* with *binary search.* □

Theorem 2. Algorithm (Figure 1) can compute all occurrences of the pattern $\hat{P}$ in text T in $O(m + logn + occ)$ time using an *enhanced suffix array* with auxiliary data structure *LCP*, *binary search* and *bit masking*. □

C. Problem B: Disguised Actions (with k Mismatches)

The problem we solve is referred to as (f, c, k, W)-Disguised Spambots Detection which is a generalization of problem A and defined as follows:

Problem. (f, c, k, W)-Disguised Spambots Detection with indeterminate actions. Given a temporally annotated action sequence T (a_j, t_j), a dictionary $\overline{S}$ containing sequences $\hat{S}_i$ each has a c non-solid symbol (represented by #), associated with a time window W_i, a minimum frequency threshold f, and a maximum Hamming distance threshold k, find all occurrences of each $\hat{S}_i \in \overline{S}$ in T, such that each $\hat{S}_i$ occurs: (I) at least f times within its associated time window W_i, and (II) with at most k mismatches according to Hamming distance.

The problem we introduce in our work considers spambots that perform indeterminate sequence of malicious actions multiple times. Thus, we require an indeterminate sequence which has c non-solid symbol(s) to appear at least f times and within a time window W_i, to attribute it to a spambot. In addition, we consider spambots that perform decoy actions, typically performed by real users. To take this into account, we consider mismatches. We assume that the dictionary and parameters are specified based on domain knowledge (e.g., from external sources or past experience).

1) Our algorithm for solving (f, c, k, W)-Disguised Spambots Detection: The algorithm is based on constructing a *generalized enhanced suffix array* data structure, *bit masking* with help of *Kangaroo method* [32], to find the *longest common subsequence* LCS between a sequence of actions in T and an action sequence $\hat{S}_i$ with at most k mismatches in linear time.

Definition V.1. The *Enhanced suffix array (ESA)* is a data structure consisting of a suffix array and additional tables which can be constructed in linear time and considered as an alternative way to construct a *suffix tree* which can solve pattern matching problems in optimal time and space [33], [34].

Definition V.2. The *Generalized enhanced suffix array (GESA)* is simply an enhanced suffix array for a set of strings, each one ending with a special character and usually is built to find the *longest common sequence* LCS of two strings or more. *GESA* is indexed as a pair of identifiers (i_1, i_2), one identifying the string number, and the other is the lexicographical order of the string suffix in the original concatenation strings [35].

To do so, we start with algorithm (Figure 2). First, our algorithm extracts the actions of the temporally annotated action sequence T into a sequence T_a such that it contains only the actions $a_0 \dots a_n$ from T (step 2). Then, we generalize the enhanced suffix array to a collection of texts T_a and set of action sequences $\overline{S_{\hat{S}_i}}$ separated by a special delimiter at the end of each sequence (step 5) as follows:

Input: Temporally annotated action sequence T, spambot dictionary $\overline{S}$, k, f
Output: All occurrences for each spambot $\hat{S}_i$ in dictionary $\overline{S}$

1: **procedure** DISGUISED SPAMBOTS DETECTION WITH K MISMATCHES
2: $T_a \leftarrow$ *all extracted action sequences with same their order from* T
3: $n \leftarrow |T_a|$
4: // Create $GESA$, where each index consists of a pair (i_1, i_2)
5: $GESA(T_a, \overline{S_{\hat{S}_i}}) \leftarrow T_a!_0\hat{S}_1!_1\hat{S}_2!_2 \dots \hat{S}_r!_r$
6: Create $GESA^{R'}$ from $GESA$
7: Initialize $hashMatchTable[no.of\#][26]$
8: **for each** spambot sequence $\hat{S}_i \in \overline{S}$ **do** ▷ Start matching
9: $occ \leftarrow 0, occur[] \leftarrow empty, sus\_spam \leftarrow empty$
10: // Calculate LCS between $\hat{S}_i$ and T_a
11: $m \leftarrow GESA^R[i], (m_1, m_2) \leftarrow GESA[m].(i_1, i_2)$
12: // Find the closest T_a sequence suffix j which is identified by $i_1 = 0$ and closest to m either before or after m
13: $j \leftarrow m - 1$ ▷ ($j \leftarrow m + 1$) in case closest j is after m
14: `Find_Occ`:
15: **while** $j \geq 0$ and $i_1 \neq 0$ **do** ▷ $(j < n)$ & $(i_1 \neq 0)$ in case closest j is after m
16: $j \leftarrow j - 1$ ▷ $j \leftarrow j + 1$ in case closest j is after m
17: **end while**
18: **if** $j \geq 0$ and $i_1 = 0$ **then** ▷ $((j < n)$ & $(i_1 = 0))$ in case closest j is after m
19: $(j_1, j_2) \leftarrow GESA[j].(i_1, i_2)$
20: Find_LCS(T_a, $\hat{S}_i$, j_2, m_2, n, k, occ, $occur[]$, $\overline{S}$, sus_spam, $hashMatchTable$)
21: $j \leftarrow j - 1$ ▷ $j \leftarrow j + 1$ in case closest j is after m
22: **if** $j \geq 0$ **then** ▷ $j < n$ in case closest j is after m
23: // Find other occurrences of suspicious spambot from $\hat{S}_i$
24: **go to** `Find_Occ`
25: **else**
26: Output $sus\_spam, occur[]$
27: **end if**
28: **end if**
29: **end for**
30: **end procedure**

Figure 2: Problem B: Disguised spambots detection with k mismatches

$$GESA(T_a, \overline{S_{\hat{S}_i}}) = T_a!_0\hat{S}_1!_1\hat{S}_2!_2 \dots \hat{S}_r!_r$$

Such that, $\hat{S}_1 \dots \hat{S}_r$ are set of spambots sequences that belong to dictionary $\overline{S_{\hat{S}_i}}$, and $!_0, \dots, !_r$ are special symbols not in Σ and smaller than any alphabetical letter in T_a and smaller than '#' with respect to an alphabetical order. We will refer to a collection of tables (GESA, GESA^R, LCS, T, $\overline{S_{\hat{S}_i}}$) to find disguised spambots within a time window t such that given a temporally annotated action sequence $T = (a_0, t_0), (a_1, t_1) \dots (a_n, t_n)$, an action sequence $\hat{S} = s_1 \dots s_m$

and an integer t, we will compute $j_1, j_2, \ldots, j_m$ such that $a_{j_i} = s_i$, $1 \leq i \leq m$ and $\sum_{i=1}^{m} t_{j_i} < t$ or $t_{j_m} - t_{j_1} < t$ with Hamming distance between T_a and $\hat{S}$ no more than k mismatches. For example, suppose we have the following sequence actions:
$T_a = ABBABGCDFCBACAFAABGDFF$ and an indeterminate spambot sequence: $\hat{S} = B\#_1C\#_2F$, where $\#_1 = [GX]$ and $\#_2 = [AD]$ in the original sequence $\tilde{S}$. Hence, the $GESA(T_a, \hat{S}) = T_a!_0\hat{S}!_1$, where all sequences are concatenated in one string separated with a unique delimiter ! and the reference indexing of the GESA will consist of 29 index as shown in Figure 3. Our algorithm includes initialization for *hashMatchTable* to do *bit masking* (see Figure 2, step 7). For each spambot sequence $\hat{S}_i$ in the spambots dictionary $\overline{S_{\hat{S}_i}}$, the algorithm calculates the *longest common sequence* LCS between $\hat{S}_i$ and T_a starting at position 0 in sequence $\hat{S}_i$ and position j in sequence T_a such that the common substring starting at these positions is maximal (see Figure 2, steps 8-24). Since the suffixes of these two sequences are represented in the lexicographical order at $GESA(T_a, \overline{S_{\hat{S}_i}})$, we need to look up the closest suffix j (which belongs to the other sequence in T_a) to the sequence $\hat{S}_i$. This can be achieved by using $GESA^R$ table which retains all the lexicographical ranks of the suffixes of the $GESA$ (see Figure 2, step 6). After locating the suffix index of the pattern $\hat{S}_i$, (see Figure 5, rank 10 in $GESA^R(i)$ column as an example), then, the closest suffix j will be the closest neighbour to that suffix and belongs to the sequence T_a (which is identified by an integer number i_1 and equal to 0). More precisely, the length of the longest common sequence at position $GESA(i)$ and matching substring of $GESA(j)$ is given as follows:

0	1	2	3	4	5	6	7	8	9	10	11	12	13	14	15	16	17	18	19	20	21	22	23	24	25	26	27	28
A	B	B	A	B	G	C	D	F	C	B	A	C	A	F	A	A	B	G	D	F	F	[illegible]	B	#1	C	#2	F	[illegible]

Figure 3: Concatenation strings of $T_a!_0\hat{S}!_1$

$$LCS(\hat{S}_i, T_a) = max(LCP(GESA(i_1, i_2), GESA(j_1, j_2)) = l_0$$

Where l_0 is the maximum length of the *longest common prefix* matching characters between $GESA(i_1, i_2)$ and $GESA(j_1, j_2)$ until the first mismatch occur (or one of the sequences terminates). Next, the second step in our algorithm involves finding the length of the longest common subsequence starting at the previous mismatch position l_0 which can be achieved using *Kangaroo method* (see Figure 4) as follows:

$$max(LCP(GESA(i_1, i_2 + l_0 + 1), GESA(j_1, j_2 + l_0 + 1)) = l_1$$

Where l_1 is the maximum length of the *longest common prefix* matching characters between $GESA(i_1, i_2+l_0+1)$ and $GESA(j_1, j_2+l_0+1)$ until the second mismatch occur (or one of the sequences terminates). Once our algorithm encounters '#' at the pattern, it will get into the verification process (see Figure 4, steps 27-32) that we described in problem A (using *bit masking* and *hashMatchTable*). Our algorithm will continue in using *Kangaroo method* to find other k mismatches until the number of mismatches is greater than k or one of the sequences terminates. Subsequently, to find other occurrences of the spambot $\hat{S}_i$ in T_a, Figure 2 continues finding the second closest suffix j that belongs to the sequence T_a simply from $GESA$, see Figure 5.

1: **function** FIND_LCS(T_a, $\hat{S}_i$, j_2, m_2, n,k, occ, ref : $occur[]$, $\overline{S}$, ref : $sus\_spam, hashMatchTable[][26]$) ▷ ref: to return parameter's value to algorithm Figure 3
2: $l \leftarrow 0$; $k\_mis \leftarrow 0$
3: **while** $k\_mis < k$ and $l < n$ and $l < |\hat{S}_i|$ **do**
4: **while** $T_a[j_2 + l] = \hat{S}_i[0 + l]$ **do**
5: $sus\_spam \leftarrow sus\_spam + T_a[j_2 + l]$
6: $l \leftarrow l + 1$
7: **end while**
8: **if** $\hat{S}_i[0 + l] =' \#'$ **then**
9: **go to** Verification process
10: **if** match **then**
11: $sus\_spam \leftarrow sus\_spam + T_a[j_2 + l]$
12: $l \leftarrow l + 1$
13: **else**
14: $k\_mis \leftarrow k\_mis + 1$
15: **end if**
16: **end if**
17: **end while**
18: **if** $|sus\_spam| = |\hat{S}_i|$ **then**
19: $a\_time \leftarrow 0$
20: **for** $pos = j_2$ to $|\hat{S}_i|$ **do**
21: $a\_time \leftarrow a\_time + T[t_{pos}]$
22: **end for**
23: **if** $a\_time \leq W_i$ **then**
24: $occ \leftarrow occ + 1$; $occur[occ] \leftarrow j_2$
25: **end if**
26: **end if**
27: ▷ **Verification process:**
28: **if** $hashMatchTable[\hat{S}_i[0 + l]][ascii[T_a[j_2 + l]]] = 1$ **then**
29: $match \leftarrow true$
30: **else**
31: $match \leftarrow false$
32: **end if**
33: **end function**

Figure 4: Problem B: LCS with *Kangaroo* method

i	$GESA[i]$	Suffix	$GESA^R[i]$
0	(1,28)	$!_1$	5
1	(0,22)	$!_0b\#_1c\#_2f!_0$	13
2	(1,24)	$\#_1c\#_2f!_1$	11
3	(1,26)	$\#_2f!_1$	6
4	(0,15)	$aabgdff!_0b\#_1c\#_2f!_1$	14
5	(0,0)	$abbabgcdfcbacafaabgdff!_0b\#_1c\#_2f!_1$	27
6	(0,3)	$abgcdfcbacafaabgdff!_0b\#_1c\#_2f!_1$	19
7	(0,16)	$abgdff!_0b\#_1c\#_2f!_1$	20
8	(0,11)	$acafaabgdff!_0b\#_1c\#_2f!_1$	25
9	(0,13)	$afaabgdff!_0b\#_1c\#_2f!_1$	18
10	(1,23)	$b\#_1c\#_2f!_1$	12
11	(0,2)	$babgcdfcbacafaabgdff!_0b\#_1c\#_2f!_1$	8
12	**(0,10)**	$b\underline{a}cafaabgdff!_0b\#_1c\#_2f!_1$	17
13	(0,1)	$bbabgcdfcbacafaabgdff!_0b\#_1c\#_2f!_1$	9
14	**(0,4)**	$bgcdfcbacafaabgdff!_0b\#_1c\#_2f!_1$	24
15	(0,17)	$bg\underline{d}ff!_0b\#_1c\#_2f!_1$	4
16	(1,25)	$c\#_2f!_1$	7
17	(0,12)	$caf\ aabgdff!_0b\#_1c\#_2f!_1$	15
18	(0,9)	$cbacafaabgdff!_0b\#_1c\#_2f!_1$	28
19	(0,6)	$cdfcbacafaabgdff!_0b\#_1c\#_2f!_1$	21
20	(0,7)	$dfcbacafaabgdff!_0b\#_1c\#_2f!_1$	26
21	(0,19)	$dff!_0b\#_1c\#_2f!_1$	23
22	(1,27)	$f!_1$	1
23	(0,21)	$f\ !_0b\#_1c\#_2f!_1$	10
24	(0,14)	$faabgdff!_0b\#_1c\#_2f!_1$	2
25	(0,8)	$fcbacafaabgdff!_0b\#_1c\#_2f!_1$	16
26	(0,20)	$\underline{f}\ f!_0b\#_1c\#_2f!_1$	3
27	(0,5)	$gcdfcbacafaabgdff!_0b\#_1c\#_2f!_1$	22
28	(0,18)	$gdff!_0b\#_1c\#_2f!_1$	0

Figure 5: $GESA$ for the sequences T_a,$\hat{S}$ and illustration of occurrences of $\hat{S}$ in T_a at $i = 12, 14$ and 15 and $k = 2$, where $\#_1 = [GX]$ and $\#_2 = [AD]$

As we can see from Figure 5, there are three occurrences for spambot $\hat{S}$ in T_a with up to $k = 2$ mismatches. The first occurrence is illustrated using blue color at $i = 12$ with one mismatch ($k = 1$). The second occurrence is illustrated using violet color at $i = 14$ with zero mismatch ($k = 0$) and the last occurrence is illustrated using green color at $i = 15$ with two mismatches ($k = 2$). All curved arrows represent the *Kangaroo* jumps, and the underlines represent mismatches places. Finally, at each occurrence of $\hat{S}_i$ in the sequence T_a, algorithm (Figure 4) checks its time window using the dictionary $\overline{S}$ and T such that it sums up each time t_i associated with its action a_i in T starting at the position j_2 in $GESA(j_1, j_2)$ until the length of the spambot $|\hat{S}_i|$ and compares it to its time window W_i. If the resultant time is less than or equal to W_i, algorithm (Figure 4) considers that the pattern sequence corresponds to a spambot and terminates (see Figure 4, steps 18-26), so that the control returns to algorithm (Figure 2). Once the frequency number hits a predefined threshold f, the sequence and its occurrences will be output by algorithm Figure 2.

VI. Experimental Evaluation

We implemented our algorithm in C++ and ran it on an Intel i7 at 3.6 GHz. Our algorithm uses linear time and space. It constructs the suffix array by *almost pure Induced-Sorting* [36], to build our GESA for the concatenated sequences (T_a and data dictionary $\overline{S}$), and then it applies the *bit masking* and *Kangaroo* method to detect all uncertain actions. We use synthetic data to test our method, because we are not aware of publicly available datasets of real spambot behavior and modeling the real temporal annotated sequence of a user log.

TABLE III. Results for the number of detected desguised spambots and runtime. Dictionary size $|\overline{S}| = 100, 200$ and 500 (include 20, 50 and 100 disguised sequences respectively) with $f = 2$, and Hamming distance threshold $k = 0$, 1 and 2.

$\lvert\overline{S}\rvert : \lvert\#\rvert$	$\lvert T\rvert$	$\lvert T_{inj}\rvert$	Disguised actions			Time (min)		
			$k=0$	$k=1$	$k=2$	$k=0$	$k=1$	$k=2$
100 : 20	10,000	13,004	85	142	376	0.036	0.038	0.043
	25,000	28,100	97	152	302	0.223	0.225	0.237
	50,000	52,924	93	154	542	0.890	0.894	0.974
	100,000	103,028	90	161	758	3.705	3.751	3.795
200 : 50	10,000	16,060	206	313	976	0.137	0.148	0.160
	25,000	30,876	306	422	1726	0.555	0.582	0.586
	50,000	55,856	202	258	946	1.976	1.957	2.094
	100,000	105,878	203	337	1512	7.422	7.781	7.966
500 : 100	10,000	25,088	630	856	2141	2.294	2.255	2.367
	25,000	39,736	602	811	2488	2.440	2.575	2.582
	50,000	64,666	582	791	2854	6.621	6.779	6.929
	100,000	114,812	640	902	4110	21.515	21.744	22.207

However, the use of synthetic data does not affect our findings, because our method is guaranteed to detect all specified patterns in any temporally annotated sequence. Also note that we do not compare with existing works because no existing method can solve this problem. We used a random string generator to generate: (I) temporally annotated sequences with 26 distinct characters and sizes in $\{10000, 25000, 50000, 100000\}$, and (II) dictionaries with size in $\{100, 200, 500\}$. In every generated temporally annotated sequence T, we injected each sequence in $\overline{S}$ to random locations $f \in \{2, 5, 10\}$ times, to obtain the web-spambots user log T_{inj}. We also changed some sequences in $\overline{S}$, to simulate disguised and mismatch actions. Specifically, we replaced 20% of actions of selected sequences in $\overline{S}$ by '$\#$' symbol which represents an indeterminate symbol that corresponds to one or more action in T_{inj}, to simulate disguised actions. Also, we changed one random element in 25% of randomly selected sequences, to simulate a mismatch, and two random elements in another 25% of randomly selected sequences, to simulate two mismatches. The window length (W_i) for each sequence in $\overline{S}$ was selected randomly in $[5, 125]$. Table III shows the impact of the dictionary size $|\overline{S}|$ on the disguised spambot actions (with mismatches) and runtime. From this table we observe the following:

- For the same ($|\overline{S}| : |\#|$) and $|T|$ and varying k, the number of detected actions increases, as our algorithm by construction detects all actions with at most k mismatches (so the actions for a larger k include those for all smaller k's). Interestingly, the sequences which have disguised actions (represented by '#' symbol) are detected as the normal sequences due to the use of *bit masking* operation and *hashMatchTable*. Also, it is noticeable that the runtime is hardly affected by k, due to the use of the *Kangaroo* method, which effectively speeds up the finding of occurrences of spambots. For example, the time for the disguised spambots detection at $k = 1$ and $k = 2$, when ($|\overline{S}| : |\#| = 500 : 100$) and ($|T| = 25,000$) is relatively the same, despite the big difference in the number detected spambots.
- For the same ($|\overline{S}| : |\#|$) and k and varying $|T|$, the number of detected actions does not directly depend on $|T|$; it depends on the size of the injected actions to T, which generally increases with ($|\overline{S}| : |\#|$). The runtime increases with $|T|$, since our algorithm always detects all actions in T.
- For the same $|T|$ and k and varying ($|\overline{S}| : |\#|$), the number of detected actions increase with ($|\overline{S}| : |\#|$) as our algorithm always detects all actions in the dictionary, and the runtime also increases with the dictionary size.

Table IV shows the impact of the frequency f on the disguised spambot actions and runtime. For this table, we observe the following:

TABLE IV. Results for the number of detected disguised spambots and runtime. Dictionary size ($|\overline{S}| : |\#| = 100 : 20$) with $f = 2, 5$ and 10, and Hamming distance threshold $k = 0$, 1 and 2.

f	$\lvert T\rvert$	$\lvert T_{inj}\rvert$	Disguised actions			Time (min)		
			$k=0$	$k=1$	$k=2$	$k=0$	$k=1$	$k=2$
2	10,000	13,004	85	142	376	0.036	0.038	0.043
	25,000	28,100	97	152	302	0.223	0.225	0.237
	50,000	52,924	93	154	542	0.890	0.894	0.974
	100,000	103,028	90	161	758	3.705	3.751	3.795
5	10,000	17,510	209	345	715	0.085	0.088	0.092
	25,000	32,750	243	376	497	0.345	0.353	0.357
	50,000	57,310	234	379	894	1.073	1.091	1.144
	100,000	107,570	224	382	1075	4.184	4.147	4.247
10	10,000	25,020	417	681	1264	0.179	0.191	0.203
	25,000	40,500	488	751	1149	0.514	0.532	0.539
	50,000	64,620	466	751	1475	0.528	1.494	1.456
	100,000	115,140	451	755	1609	4.713	4.948	5.045

- For the same f and $|T|$ and varying k, the detected actions for any k include all actions with at most k mismatches. Also, the runtime is hardly affected by k and disguised actions, due to the use of the *Kangaroo* method and *bit masking* operation.
- For the same f and k and varying $|T|$, the number of detected actions does not increase with $|T|$, as it depends on the size of injected actions which generally depends on ($|\overline{S}| : |\#|$), as explained above. The runtime increases because our algorithm always detects all actions in T.

- For the same $|T|$ and k and varying f, the number of detected actions increases as our algorithm always detects all injected actions. Interestingly though the algorithm scales well with f, especially when $|T|$ is large. This is due to the use of the Generalized enhanced suffix array (GESA) which finds all subsequent occurrences of a detected action occurrence directly from the adjacent suffixes to the first occurrence suffix.

VII. Conclusion

We have introduced two efficient algorithms that can detect spambots of malicious actions with variable time delays. One can detect one or more indeterminate sequences in a web user log using *Manber and Myers* algorithm and *bit masking* operation. The second proposed a generalized solution for solving (f, c, k, W)-Disguised Spambots Detection with indeterminate actions and mismatches. Our algorithm takes into account temporal information, because it considers time-annotated sequences and because it requires a match to occur within a time window. The problem seeks to find all occurrences of each conservative degenerate sequence corresponding to a spambot that occurs at least f times within a time window and with up to k mismatches. For this problem, we designed a linear time and space inexact matching algorithm, which employs the *generalized enhanced suffix array* data structure, *bit masking* and *Kangaroo* method to solve the problem efficiently.

References

[1] J. Yan and A. S. El Ahmad, "A low-cost attack on a microsoft captcha," in CCS. ACM, 2008, pp. 543–554.

[2] A. Zinman and J. S. Donath, "Is britney spears spam?" in CEAS, 2007.

[3] S. Webb, J. Caverlee, and C. Pu, "Social honeypots: Making friends with a spammer near you." in CEAS, 2008, pp. 1–10.

[4] P. Heymann, G. Koutrika, and H. Garcia-Molina, "Fighting spam on social web sites: A survey of approaches and future challenges," IEEE Internet Computing, vol. 11, no. 6, 2007, pp. 36–45.

[5] P. Hayati, K. Chai, V. Potdar, and A. Talevski, "Behaviour-based web spambot detection by utilising action time and action frequency," in International Conference on Computational Science and Its Applications, 2010, pp. 351–360.

[6] F. Benevenuto, T. Rodrigues, V. Almeida, J. Almeida, C. Zhang, and K. Ross, "Identifying video spammers in online social networks," in International workshop on Adversarial information retrieval on the web. ACM, 2008, pp. 45–52.

[7] A. H. Wang, "Detecting spam bots in online social networking sites: a machine learning approach," in CODASPY, 2010, pp. 335–342.

[8] P. Hayati, V. Potdar, A. Talevski, and W. Smyth, "Rule-based on-the-fly web spambot detection using action strings," in CEAS, 2010.

[9] V. Ghanaei, C. S. Iliopoulos, and S. P. Pissis, "Detection of web spambot in the presence of decoy actions," in IEEE International Conference on Big Data and Cloud Computing, 2014, pp. 277–279.

[10] R. K. Roul, S. R. Asthana, M. Shah, and D. Parikh, "Detecting spam web pages using content and link-based techniques," Sadhana, vol. 41, no. 2, 2016, pp. 193–202.

[11] S. Ghiam and A. N. Pour, "A survey on web spam detection methods: taxonomy," arXiv preprint arXiv:1210.3131, 2012.

[12] Z. Gyongyi, H. Garcia-Molina, and J. Pedersen, "Combating web spam with trustrank," in Proceedings of the 30th international conference on very large data bases (VLDB), 2004.

[13] Z. Gyongyi, P. Berkhin, H. Garcia-Molina, and J. Pedersen, "Link spam detection based on mass estimation," in Proceedings of the 32nd international conference on Very large data bases. VLDB Endowment, 2006, pp. 439–450.

[14] M. Egele, C. Kolbitsch, and C. Platzer, "Removing web spam links from search engine results," Journal in Computer Virology, vol. 7, no. 1, 2011, pp. 51–62.

[15] F. Ahmed and M. Abulaish, "A generic statistical approach for spam detection in online social networks," Computer Communications, vol. 36, no. 10-11, 2013, pp. 1120–1129.

[16] V. M. Prieto, M. Álvarez, and F. Cacheda, "Saad, a content based web spam analyzer and detector," Journal of Systems and Software, vol. 86, no. 11, 2013, pp. 2906–2918.

[17] N. Dai, B. D. Davison, and X. Qi, "Looking into the past to better classify web spam," in Proceedings of the 5th international workshop on adversarial information retrieval on the web, 2009, pp. 1–8.

[18] L. Araujo and J. Martinez-Romo, "Web spam detection: new classification features based on qualified link analysis and language models," IEEE Transactions on Information Forensics and Security, vol. 5, no. 3, 2010, pp. 581–590.

[19] S. P. Algur and N. T. Pendari, "Hybrid spamicity score approach to web spam detection," in International Conference on Pattern Recognition, Informatics and Medical Engineering (PRIME-2012). IEEE, 2012, pp. 36–40.

[20] M. Luckner, M. Gad, and P. Sobkowiak, "Stable web spam detection using features based on lexical items," Computers & Security, vol. 46, 2014, pp. 79–93.

[21] K. L. Goh, R. K. Patchmuthu, and A. K. Singh, "Link-based web spam detection using weight properties," Journal of Intelligent Information Systems, vol. 43, no. 1, 2014, pp. 129–145.

[22] S. Cresci, R. Di Pietro, M. Petrocchi, A. Spognardi, and M. Tesconi, "Dna-inspired online behavioral modeling and its application to spambot detection," IEEE Intelligent Systems, vol. 31, no. 5, 2016, pp. 58–64.

[23] ——, "Exploiting digital dna for the analysis of similarities in twitter behaviours," in 2017 IEEE International Conference on Data Science and Advanced Analytics (DSAA). IEEE, 2017, pp. 686–695.

[24] S. Cresci, M. Petrocchi, A. Spognardi, and S. Tognazzi, "From reaction to proaction: Unexplored ways to the detection of evolving spambots," in Companion Proceedings of the The Web Conference 2018, 2018, pp. 1469–1470.

[25] C. Iliopoulos, R. Kundu, and S. Pissis, "Efficient pattern matching in elastic-degenerate strings," arXiv preprint arXiv:1610.08111, 2016.

[26] M. Crochemore, C. S. Iliopoulos, R. Kundu, M. Mohamed, and F. Vayani, "Linear algorithm for conservative degenerate pattern matching," Engineering Applications of Artificial Intelligence, vol. 51, 2016, pp. 109–114.

[27] S. J. Puglisi, W. F. Smyth, and A. H. Turpin, "A taxonomy of suffix array construction algorithms," acm Computing Surveys (CSUR), vol. 39, no. 2, 2007, pp. 4–es.

[28] M. Yamamoto and K. W. Church, "Using suffix arrays to compute term frequency and document frequency for all substrings in a corpus," Comput. Linguist., vol. 27, no. 1, Mar. 2001, pp. 1–30.

[29] J. Kärkkäinen, P. Sanders, and S. Burkhardt, "Linear work suffix array construction," JACM, vol. 53, no. 6, 2006, pp. 918–936.

[30] T. Kasai, G. Lee, H. Arimura, S. Arikawa, and K. Park, "Linear-time longest-common-prefix computation in suffix arrays and its applications," in Annual Symposium on Combinatorial Pattern Matching. Springer, 2001, pp. 181–192.

[31] U. Manber and G. Myers, "Suffix arrays: a new method for on-line string searches," siam Journal on Computing, vol. 22, no. 5, 1993, pp. 935–948.

[32] M. Nicolae and S. Rajasekaran, "On pattern matching with k mismatches and few don't cares," IPL, vol. 118, 2017, pp. 78–82.

[33] M. I. Abouelhoda, S. Kurtz, and E. Ohlebusch, "Replacing suffix trees with enhanced suffix arrays," J. Discrete Algorithms, vol. 2, 2004, pp. 53–86.

[34] M. Abouelhoda, S. Kurtz, and E. Ohlebusch, Enhanced Suffix Arrays and Applications, 12 2005, pp. 7–1.

[35] F. A. Louza, G. P. Telles, S. Hoffmann, and C. D. Ciferri, "Generalized enhanced suffix array construction in external memory," AMB, vol. 12, no. 1, 2017, p. 26.

[36] G. Nong, S. Zhang, and W. H. Chan, "Linear suffix array construction by almost pure induced-sorting," in DCC, 2009, pp. 193–202.

Analysis of Spatiotemporal Patterns of Changes in Brightness of Nighttime Lights (NTL) in the Former USSR Territory

Michail Zhizhin
Earth Observation Groupe, Payne Institute
Colorado School of Mines
Golden CO, USA
e-mail: mzhizhin@mines.edu

Alexey Poyda
Kurchatov Complex of NBICS Nature-like Technologies
NRC "Kurchatov Institute"
Moscow, Russia
e-mail: Poyda_AA@nrcki.ru

Alexander Troussov
Institute of Applied Economic Research,
RANEPA
Moscow, Russia
e-mail: Troussov-av@rane.ru

Sergey Maruev
Institute Of Economics, Mathematics and IT
RANEPA
Moscow, Russia
e-mail: Maruev@ranepa.ru

***Abstract*—The distribution of brightness of nighttime lights (NTL) at the Earth's surface in the visible band of the electromagnetic spectrum is a new forward-looking data source for socio-economic studies. Visual and statistical analysis of this distribution in time and space requires new mathematical and geo-informational methods of cooperative processing of many raster images and vector data (geographical maps) together with socio-economic analytics. The current research develops new means of the spatiotemporal analysis, reveals basic problems of applied monitoring, and outlines forward-looking approaches to their solution.**

Keywords-Earth Remote Sensing; Night-time lights; data mining; big data; spatio-temporal analysis; socio-economic applications.

I. Spatiotemporal Statistical Analysis of Patterns of NTL Dynamics

Basic data for the applied analysis of changes in NTL in the visible spectrum are received in the form of a continuous sequence of images from two constellations of American low-Earth-orbit heliosynchronous meteorological satellites Defense Meteorological Satellite Program (DMSP) and Joint Polar Satellite System (JPSS) with a 1 km spatial resolution [1], [2]. Monthly maps of the mean brightness of cloudless and moonless NTL created on the basis of VIIRS/DNB data were used for the analysis of statistics of changes in urban NTL.

Figure 1 demonstrates an example of a brightness distribution map of Moscow in the DNB channel. Yellow color corresponds to pixels with higher brightness, blue – to pixels with lower brightness.

In order to create the map, the data were compressed with the use of a logarithmic function for the purpose of multiplexing the range of accepted data. The obtained image was laid over a map in the Google Earth application. The map contains several distinct large objects: the Kremlin and city center are much brighter even after a logarithmic compression; blue color corresponds to large forest park; major highways are clearly visible. Nevertheless, it is clearly seen that the borders of districts with high and low brightness are blurred. It is associated with the spatial resolution of images and the fact that detection coordinates (the center of a pixel in which the light source is reflected) differ from the coordinates of the source itself, so in the course of several flyovers one and the same light source corresponds to a "cloud" of detections with different coordinates.

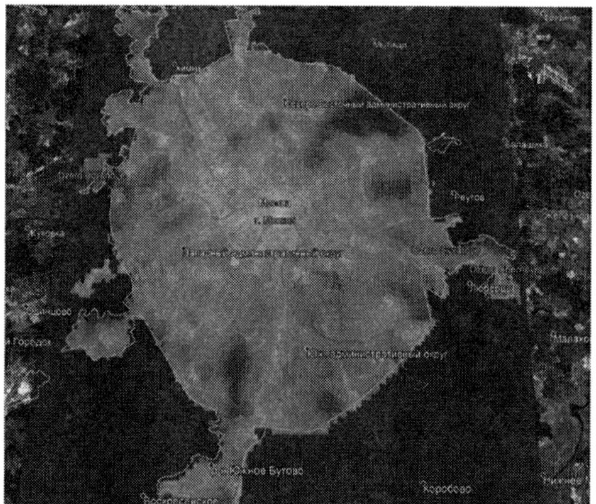

Figure 1. Brightness distribution maps of Moscow in the VIIRS / DNB spectrum channel.

Figure 2 demonstrates an example of a time sequence of the mean brightness value of pixels obtained in Moscow that was formed starting from January 2017 till July 2019.

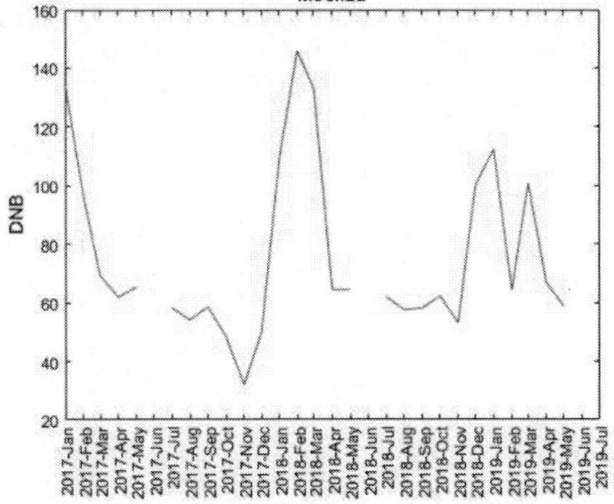

Figure 2. Time sequence with monthly intervals formed by averaging brightness indications of all pixels in the DNB channel that correspond to Moscow.

The graph is characterized by the absence of indications in several summer months and an abnormal increase in brightness during winter months. Manual exclusion of abnormal indications can ensure more precise results but has two significant drawbacks:

1) Subjectivity of the analysis. Different specialists can keep different months and consequently obtain different trends. It is hard to answer which trend is the right one and which is not;

2) Labor intensity. If it is necessary to analyze several hundreds of cities, manual exclusion of indications will require large labor inputs.

As of now, we have fulfilled the automatic exclusion of abnormal indications with the help of the RANSAC algorithm [3].

The algorithm includes two basic steps: generation of a hypothesis and its testing. In the generation step, a random subset is chosen from the whole sample of data. It is supposed that the chosen subset does not contain any abnormalities. Optimal model parameters are selected for the chosen subset. The class of the model is defined beforehand. For example, if it is a linear model of the form $ax + by + c = 0$, it is necessary to evaluate the coefficients a, b and c.

In the testing step, all points of the input sample are tested for abnormality. The process of testing depends on the examiner. For example, in the case of a linear model, it can be fulfilled on the basis of the distance between the point and the line of the examined model: if it is larger than a given parameter, then the point is considered abnormal.

Once all points are tested for belonging to the model, the overall number of abnormal points is estimated. If at this iteration the number of abnormalities is the smallest one among all previous iterations, the result is saved as an intermediate one. If the number of iterations has not reached the limit (indicated by the examiner), a new iteration begins; otherwise, the intermediate result returns.

Thus, while using RANSAC, it is necessary to define a set of parameters including:

- Model on the basis of which the data will be evaluated;
- Metric for the separation of points in the corresponding models and abnormalities;
- Number of iterations sufficient for the construction of a consistent model.

In this case, we selected a linear model and used the distance between the point and the line as an abnormality filtration metric. As of now, we used the following equation:

$$TH = 9 \times \frac{STD}{STD\_M}, \tag{1}$$

where TH stands for the admission threshold, STD defines the root mean square deviation of the time sequence of the mean brightness indications of the examined city, and STD_M is the root mean square deviation of the time sequence of the mean brightness indications of Moscow.

The results of the RANSAC algorithm application for Moscow are demonstrated in Figure 3.

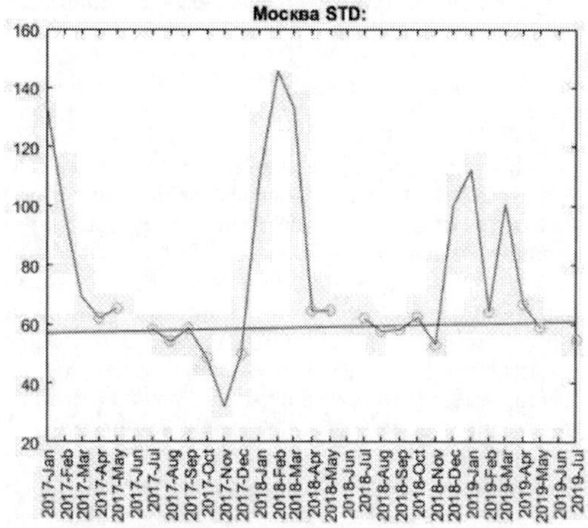

Figure 3. Results of the RANSAC algorithm application for Moscow (excluding Novomoskovsky Administrative Okrug, Troitsky Administrative Okrug, and Zelenogradsky Administrative Okrug).

Indications belonging to the model are marked by green points and the red line shows the linear trend.

Figure 3 demonstrates that the algorithm excluded those points that corresponded to the increase in urban brightness in winter. However, apart from brightness increase, the observations from November 2017 were also excluded due to a downturn in the signal level. The reason for such a significant downfall requires further examination but whatever it is, the question arises as to whether such months should be excluded from the calculations.

In this case, a large time interval is examined and the linear trend is consequently defined, so it is implied that the analysis is long-term and the changes are gradual. In this regard, it seems logical to exclude both upward and downward abnormalities in the signal level.

II. Applications of the Pattern Recognition Method in Terms of Time Sequences of NTL Brightness

A detailed analysis of changes in NTL over time can be carried out with the help of time sequences that are obtained by summing up and averaging the light sources' brightness in a limited region over a short period of time.

Four index types aimed at analyzing regional time sequences of the total brightness are presented in this section:

1) MNL – mean nighttime lights;

2) SDNL – standard deviation of nighttime lights [5] for the analysis of spatiotemporal characteristics of changes in artificial lighting in the examined region;

3) TNL – total nighttime lights;

4) ACTNL – area corrected total nighttime lights.

MNL indicates the mean level of artificial lighting in the examined area. For integral quantization values of the brightness of the DMSP / OLS sensor, the formula (2) takes the following form:

$$MNL_{OLS} = \frac{\sum_{i=0}^{63} C_i DN_i}{\sum_{i=0}^{63} C_i}, \tag{2}$$

where DN_i defines the i-th level of grey color ($i = 0$–2^6) in a DMSP/OLS image, C_i stands for the number of pixels that correspond to the given level of grey color within the examined region.

Figure 4 demonstrates a time sequence of indexes of the annual mean radiance MNL_{OLS} in the vicinity of the city of Grozny for the period from 1992 to 2013. DN_i images from different satellites F10 — F18 were compared with the use of cross-calibration according to the method [6]. The graph demonstrates downfalls in the brightness of the nighttime radiance during the First and the Second Chechen Wars and a stable positive trend in the postwar reconstruction period.

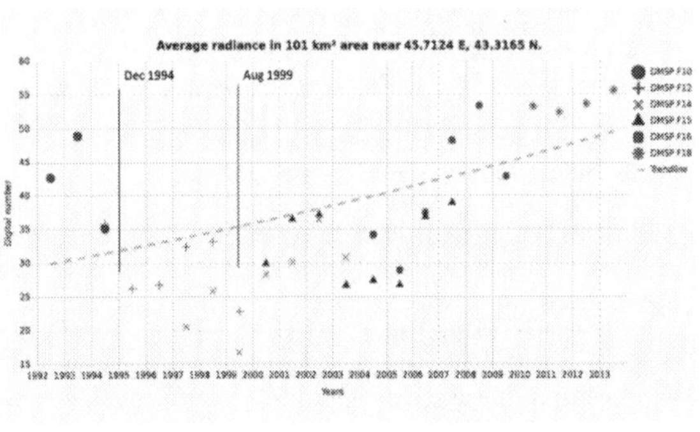

Figure 4. Time sequence of indexes of annual mean radiance MNL_{OLS} in the vicinity of the city of Grozny, the Chechen Republic for the entire period of digital registration of nighttime images from the DMSP satellites from 1992 to 2013.

For the absolute values of brightness in the DNB channel of the VIIRS sensor on the JPSS satellites, the MNL index is defined according to formula (3):

$$MNL_{DNB} = \frac{\sum_{i \in R} DNB_i}{\|R\|}, \tag{3}$$

where $\|R\|$ corresponds to the number or power of the set of pixels within the region R.

SDNL allows estimating the level of spatial heterogeneity of artificial lighting in the examination area. Formula 4 takes the following form:

$$SDNL_{DNB} = \sqrt{\frac{1}{\|R\|-1} \sum_{i \in R} (DNB_i - MNL_{DNB})^2}, \tag{4}$$

Where MNL_{DNB} defines the mean pixel brightness in the examination region.

TNL refers to the amount of artificial lighting in the examination region. An integral quantization value of brightness of the DMSP/OLS sensor is defined by formula 5:

$$TNL_{OLS} = \sum_{i=0}^{63} C_i DN_i, \tag{5}$$

where DN_i defines the i-th level of grey color in a DMSP/OLS image, C_i stands for the number of pixels that correspond to the given level of grey color within the examined region.

For the absolute values of brightness in the DNB channel of the VIIRS sensor on the JPSS satellites, the TNL index is defined according to formula (6):

$$TNL_{DNB} = \sum_{i \in R} DNB_i, \tag{6}$$

where DNB_i stands for the brightness of the image in the i-th pixel within the examined region R.

ACTNL is used to compare the total NTL brightness in regions located at different latitudes. The necessity of a pixel area correction is underpinned by the fact that stable lights maps are constructed on a coordinate grid with a regular latitude and longitude interval that, as a rule, equals to 15″ . The selection of the interval is driven by the spatial resolution of the DNB channel of the VIIRS sensor that is equal to 750×750 m and accounts for approximately 20″ at the equator. In order to make an adequate comparison of the total brightness of equally large regions that are situated at different latitudes, it is necessary to make a trigonometric correction (formula 7) while using a raster NTL map:

$$ACTNL_{DNB} = \sum_{i \in R} \cos(\varphi_i) DNB_i, \tag{7}$$

where φ_i defines the latitude at which the pixel with the index i is located within the region R on the map that is constructed in the latitude-longitude projection.

Let us illustrate the possibilities of using the $ACTNL_{DNB}$ index for the analysis of regional socio-economic dynamics on the example of changes in the total radiance of stable

NTL in three Ukrainian cities: Kiev, Donetsk, and Luhansk for the period from 2012 to 2018. Taking into account potential stray light and increase in cloud amount at these latitudes in summer months, the analysis covered only mean brightness values of NTL from August-September to March-April of each year when the number of cloudless and moonless space images of each city is sufficient. The results of the analysis are summarized in Table 1.

Student's t-statistic was used for comparing the significance of the change in the mean values of the $ACTNL_{DNB}$ index before and after the beginning of the military conflict in Donbass. In this case, the null hypothesis supposes that the mean values of monthly $ACTNL_{DNB}$ indexes during the observation periods before and after the beginning of the military conflict have not changed. In other words, the total brightness of all NTL within the city remains unchanged. As shown in Table 1, the null hypothesis is confirmed only in Kiev: despite a minor negative trend, the mean brightness before and after May 2014 can be considered constant. The situation is different in the cases of Donetsk and Luhansk. Here, there is 99,999% confidence in the presence of a gradual decrease in brightness right after the beginning of the military conflict in the ratio of 0.6 and 0.47 to the prewar rates correspondingly.

TABLE I. MEAN VALUES OF THE $ACTNL_{DNB}$ INDEX AND LEAPS IN THE MEAN VALUES BEFORE/AFTER MAY 2014

City	Mean $ACTNL_{DNB}$ before May 2014, nW	Mean $ACTNL_{DNB}$ after May 2014, nW	Ratio of $ACTNL_{DNB}$ before and after	Significant difference	Level of statistical significance, %
Kiev	10442	9432	0,90	No	29,0000
Donetsk	4629	2779	0,60	Yes	99,9999
Luhansk	959	448	0,47	Yes	99,9999

It is known that the total brightness of NTL correlates with the city population. That is why a gradual change in the $ACTNL_{DNB}$ index can be interpreted as a correlation between the prewar and postwar populations of the city. The feasibility of this interpretation can be implicitly verified by comparing the prewar indexes and the population presuming that the latter indications are credible. Such a comparison is provided in Table 2. It demonstrates that the correlations between the population and the total brightness of NTL in the case of the selected cities are divergent: Luhansk was comparatively dimmer than Kiev, while Donetsk, on the contrary, was comparatively brighter.

TABLE II. CORRELATION BETWEEN THE MEAN VALUES OF THE $ACTNL_{DNB}$ INDEX AND POPULATION BEFORE MAY 2014.

Comparison	Population as of 2013, thou.	Correlation between population	Correlation between $ACTNL_{DNB}$
Donetsk / Kiev	950 / 2 800	0,34	0,44
Luhansk / Kiev	426 / 2 800	0,15	0,09

The non-parametric Mann-Kendall test (M-K test)

The M-K test was developed for defining spatiotemporal characteristics of fluctuations in artificial lighting. The M-K test is a method of non-parametric analysis of trends, the main advantage of which is that it is independent of the actual distribution of samples and avoids problems associated with single abnormalities [7].

The M-K statistics are calculated in the following way (formulas 8-12):

$$U = \frac{\tau}{\sqrt{Var(\tau)}}, \quad (8)$$

where

$$\tau = \frac{S}{n(n-1)-1}, \quad (9)$$

$$S = \sum_{i=1}^{n} \sum_{j=i+1}^{n} sign(x_j - x_i), \quad (10)$$

$$sign(x_j - x_i) = \begin{cases} 1, \text{if } x_j > x_i \\ 0, \text{if } x_j = x_i \\ -1, \text{if } x_j < x_i \end{cases}, \quad (11)$$

$$Var(\tau) = \frac{2(2n+5)}{9n(n-1)}, \quad (12)$$

where the time sequence x_i (i = 1, 2,..., n); i < j; i = 1, 2,..., n; j = i + 1, 2,..., n is tested for monotone changes. If the value of U is positive, this means that the artificial lighting expands and the larger this value is, the more significant this expansion is.

The possibility of the use of the M-K test for analyzing regional socio-economic dynamics is demonstrated on the example of changes in the total brightness of stable NTL in the territory of Ukraine and border regions in Russia and Belorussia for the period from 2012 to 2018. Input data account for images of NTL averaged over the course of one month of observations. Taking into account potential stray light on the DNB sensor, increase in the amount of clouds at these latitudes in summer months, and increased fluctuation in brightness of NTL in winter because of snow, the analysis covered only mean brightness values of NTL in September of each year. In order to distinguish settlements and transportation routes in the wake of "clutter" from forest fires and campfires, the stable NTL image as of 2016 was used.

The results of a pixel-by-pixel calculation of the M-K test for the entire examination region are demonstrated in Figure 14. The obtained values are wide-spread: -150...130. In order to improve the map visualization, a range of colors from red (maximal negative trend -10) through white (medium, no trend observed) to black (maximal positive trend +10) is used.

For the period from 2012 to 2018, there is a consistent negative trend in the brightness of urban radiance in the entire territory of military conflicts in the Donetsk People's Republic, the Luhansk People's Republic, and Transnistria.

The obtained results correspond to the results of other research groups that relied on different data in their studies.

For example, German researchers Julia Bluszcz and Marica Valente in their work «The War in Europe: Economic Costs of the Ukrainian Conflict» used the "potential opportunities" approach for estimating the influence of the military conflict in Ukraine on the national GDP. In their work, the researchers evaluate the influence of the military conflict on the national GDP by defining the difference in prewar and postwar GDP rates that are extrapolated to postwar years.

Suppose that $i=1,\dots,J+1$ denotes the control group countries and $t=1,\dots,T$ defines such time periods that $1 \leq T_0 < T$ corresponds to the prewar period. Let $Y_{i,t}^N$ represent per capita GDP in Ukraine. Suppose that Ukraine is the only country participating in the military conflict and other countries J are not affected by the war. It is also supposed that none of the countries expects the outbreak of the war till the period of time T and that after the conflict there will be no negative side effects on the control regions J. Let us consider $(J \times 1)$ – an optimal weight vector $W^* = (w_2, \dots, w_{J+1})'$ *with* $w_i \geq 0$ *for* $i = 2 \dots J+1$ and $w_2 + \dots + w_{J+1} = 1$, so that $Y_{1,t}^N = \sum_2^{J+1} w_j Y_{j,t}$. The purpose of this analysis is to estimate the influence of the military conflict on the Ukrainian GDP that is defined as follows:

$$a_{1,t} = \frac{1}{T-T_0} \sum_{t>T_0} \left[Y_{1,t} - \sum_{j=2}^{J+1} w_j Y_{jt} \right]. \tag{13}$$

The estimation of optimal weights W^* is fulfilled with the use of a nested optimization procedure. First and foremost, internal optimization minimizes Euclidean distance between X_1 and X_0W, $(r+k) \times 1$ and $(r+k) \times (J)$ matrices correspondingly containing k covariants and r linear combinations of prewar results that are used as predictors (formula 14):

$$W^* = \arg\min_{W} \| X_1 - X_0 W \| v = \sqrt{(X_1 - X_0 W)' V (X_1 - X_0 W)}. \tag{14}$$

where V denotes a symmetric diagonal matrix with nonzero matrix elements with the size of $(r+k) \times (r+k)$ in which diagonal elements $v = (v_1, \dots, v_{r+k})$ are predictors' weights assigned to the selected variables. V^* can be estimated in such a manner that the root mean square error in results is minimized for the outbreak of the war according to formula 15:

$$V^* \arg\min_V \left(Y_1 - Y_0 W^*(V) \right)' \left(Y_1 - Y_0 W^*(V) \right), \tag{15}$$

where Y_1 and Y_0 are the linear combinations of prewar rates of Ukraine and the control group countries that can be, for example, averaged for some prewar periods of time. Once the estimation of weights of the control group countries W^* and predictors V is made, the result of synthetic Ukraine is calculated as a weighted linear combination of results of the control group countries (formula 16):

$$\sum_{j=2}^{J+1} w_j Y_{j,t} = Y_{1,t}^N. \tag{16}$$

The authors estimate that, due to this war Ukraine's per capita GDP decreased by 15.1% (1438.90$) on average over the period 2013 – 2017. The estimation also shows that, due to the Donbass war, Donetsk's and Luhansk's average GRP for 2013-2016 decreased by 43% (4630$) and 52% (3326$), respectively.

The results obtained by German researchers perfectly correspond to the results obtained by the authors of this research on the basis of comparison of mean values of the $ACTNL_{DNB}$ index that is calculated according to remote sensing data before and after May 2014.

III. Conclusion

The current research presents new methods of visualization of changes in NTL brightness at the Earth's surface underpinned by economic, sociologic, and political factors. A quantitative analysis of time sequences of the integral NTL brightness over a limited area in Russia is aggravated by interseasonal changes in albedo because of snow (see [4]). The current research provides a new method of distinguishing interseasonal abnormalities on the basis of the RANSAC algorithm. After the separation of abnormalities in NTL brightness associated with climate characteristics, it is possible to apply pattern recognition for time sequences in the form of stepwise changes and trends associated with different socio-economic and political phenomena. This research presents the results of such analysis for Eastern Ukrainian cities affected by the military conflict since spring 2014.

References

[1] C. D. Elvidge, K. E. Baugh, M. Zhizhin, F. C. Hsu, and T. Ghosh, "VIIRS night-time lights," International Journal of Remote Sensing, vol. 38, No. 21, pp. 5860-5879, 2017, DOI: 10.1080/01431161.2017.1342050.

[2] C. D. Elvidge, K. E. Baugh, M. Zhizhin, and F. C. Hsu, "Why VIIRS data are superior to DMSP for mapping nighttime lights," Proceedings of the Asia-Pacific Advanced Network, Vol. 35, No. 62, pp. 62-69, 2013.

[3] S. Choi, T. Kim, and W. Yu, "Performance Evaluation of RANSAC Family," Proceedings of the British Machine Vision Conference (BMVC), London, UK. September 7–10, pp. 1-12, 2009.

[4] N. Levin, "The impact of seasonal changes on observed nighttime brightness from 2014 to 2015 monthly VIIRS DNB composites," Remote Sensing of Environment, vol. 193, pp. 150-164, 2017.

[5] W. Jiang, G. He, T. Long, C. Wang, Y. Ni, and R. Ma, "Assessing light pollution in China based on nighttime light imagery," Remote Sensing of Environment, vol. 9, p. 135, 2017.

[6] F. C. Hsu, K. E. Baugh, T. Ghosh, M. Zhizhin, and C. D. Elvidge, "DMSP-OLS radiance calibrated nighttime lights time series with intercalibration," Remote Sensing of Environment, vol. 7, No. 2, pp. 1855-1876, 2015.

[7] L. C. Smith, "Trends in Russian arctic river-ice formation and breakup, 1917 to 1994," Physical Geography, vol. 21, pp. 46-56, 2000.

Reliability Displays in Building Information Modeling A Pattern Approach

Alexander G. Mirnig and Manfred Tscheligi
Center for Human-Computer Interaction
University of Salzburg
Salzburg, Austria
firstname.lastname@sbg.ac.at

Peter Fröhlich, Johann Schrammel and Michael Gafert
Center for Technology Experience
AIT Austrian Institute of Technology GmbH
Vienna, Austria
firstname.lastname@ait.ac.at

Damiano Falcioni
BOC Asset Management GmbH
Vienna, Austria
damiano.falcioni@boc-eu.com

***Abstract*—Process management systems allow the user to, among other things, predict possible outcomes of larger processes and make decisions based on a pool of data available to the system. What can greatly influence the success of such processes is the *reliability* of the data that feeds the system's output. This, however, is usually not part of such systems and is left to the experience and expertise of the individual user. Design patterns are a method that can capture and communicate such implicit expert knowledge. In this paper, we present initial solutions for integrating reliability indicators in process management. Based on expert stakeholder requirements from the use case Building Information Modeling (BIM), we created three initial solutions for the realization of reliability displays in this context, which we abstracted into three draft patterns. These solutions pertain to expertise-based rights management, visualisation of entry timeliness, and communicating reliability via penalty indicators.**

Keywords–Patterns; reliability displays; process management, building information modeling.

I. Introduction

When working with large quantities of data, then any decision that is made based on that data must operate under the basic assumption that the data is accurate to a sufficient degree. In practice, this *reliability* of data is subject to fluctuation, depending on the type of data, where it came from or by whom it was fed into the system, and a number of similar factors. It would be very helpful, then, to have an indicator for the reliability of the data the system bases its output on in addition to whichever output the system generates via its primary functionality (sum calculations, predictions, a.s.o.). Such values, that could allow to determine the reliability of any individual piece of data, are usually not integrated and it is left to the user, to determine how reliably the data he/she is working with is in the end.

Reliability displays are displays or User Interface (UI) elements intended to address this gap and introduce indicators to convey reliability information. Such displays add an additional dimension to data displays: in addition to showing the data itself to the user, they also convey how reliable the output can or should be expected to be by the user. This information can be very valuable for predictions (e.g., weather forecasts) or contexts with high degrees of variability (e.g., automated driving [1]), although such displays or indicators are not yet widely integrated or researched and, as a result, not yet used within process management or BIM.

In this paper, we present an attempt to design reliability indicators for process management in the BIM context. Following a pattern approach [2], we decided to generate intitial design patterns based on stakeholder requirements. From initial expert interviews, we extracted reliability requirements for the BIM context. For three of these, we then generated high- to mid-level solutions, which we present as pattern drafts. These are intended to serve as the basis for continued efforts to design UI reliability indicators.

II. Related Work

In the following, we provide an overview of relevant literature and state-of-the art for BIM and process management, reliability displays, and design patterns.

A. Process Management and BIM

There is a growing belief that digital transformation in the architecture and construction industry can only happen if four key parameters are properly addressed: digital data, digital access, automation and connectivity [3]. The common denominator of all these factors is the utilization of BIM as both the backbone for the launch of new processes and new service features to the architecture, engineering and construction industry, as well as the link between the various stakeholders involved in the renovation and construction value chain [4].

Using BIM methodologies and tools has been proposed to yield large benefits for the construction/renovation sector, most importantly by: (i) reducing critical mistakes and omissions and (ii) improving collaboration between stakeholders, subsequently enabling lower costs through less rework, greater speed by removal of additional documentation efforts, and higher quality due to closer control. Other direct benefits of BIM for renovation projects, include reduction of uncertainties regarding the post-renovation performance, early visualization of renovation impact to get consensus from building owners, improved collaboration between stakeholders leading to fewer conflicts, mistakes and re-works on site.

As for building owners and financiers, BIM are conceived as a way to make the estimation process more accurate and facilitate more visibility and interaction in the overall design/build process for the owners of a building, enabling them to take a more active role in determining the final outcome of capital-intensive projects. This appears even more relevant in building renovation processes, an area with the largest untapped potential for energy saving and reduction in greenhouse gas emissions [5], where BIM tools can help in the identification of the renovation options that can deliver the best value for money. This requires the availability of specific BIMR (BIM-based renovation) tools that can accurately estimate the impact of renovation options and lead the involved stakeholders through an efficient implementation path (see [6] for a detailed description of state-of-the-art renovation workflow models for BIM-based renovation process management).

Despite its clear benefits for all stakeholders involved, BIM is still facing reluctance to uptake in the mainstream market [7], mainly due to a number of key factors such as the requirement for the entire construction value chain to use consistent BIM tools in order for any party to reap benefits, the investment in time required as a learning curve on behalf of architecture and construction professionals, the size and the processing load induced by BIM models.

B. Trust Calibration and Reliability Displays

Trust can be understood as a relation between at least two agents, in which one or more agents (trustors) depend on the achievement of another agent's (trustee) goals in a situation that is characterized by uncertainty and vulnerability (compare Ekman et al. [8], Mirnig et al. [9], and de Visser et al. [10]. Undertrust in a system occurs when the perceived capabilities are lower than the actual capabilities, and inversely, overtrust implies that the perceived capability is higher than the actual capability. Users can underestimate the consequences if a system fails, and/or users can underestimate the likelihood that a system will make serious mistakes at all. The trust in a system is calibrated when neither over- nor undertrust occur.

Trust calibration can play an important role in intelligent and predictive systems, to establish and guarantee their long-term acceptance. Schrammel et al. [11] have shown that in different fields of research and practice different techniques for trust calibration have been proposed, most importantly reliability displays, uncertainty indicators, awareness and intent displays and the communication of available alternatives. Reliability displays, which are the focus of our paper, directly communicate the reliability as estimated by the system to the user [12]. This normally includes only one value, which is frequently expressed as a percentage, i.e.: "I am 60% sure that the data is correct". The display of this information needs to be adapted to the application domain, and different interface elements are used depending on the domain.

C. Patterns

Design patterns are structured solution documentations to reoccurring problems [13]. Design patterns were originally conceptualised by Christopher Alexander [14][15] to capture individual solutions to reoccurring problems in the architecture domain. His idea later influenced other domains as well, most prominently software engineering [16], where patterns are still widely used to document solutions to both common and obscure problems encountered by software engineers.

Patterns feature a number of characteristics that separate them from "classical" means of documentation, such as guidelines: Since they are problem-based, they can cover both high- and low-level solutions, depending on how the individual problem is framed [17]. A side effect of this is that pattern collections are never complete in a standard sense – whenever a new problem within a specific context occurs, so does the need for an appropriate pattern. Since patterns also focus on providing ready-to-use along with a description of the problem context, they can be useful to make expert knowledge accessible to novices [18] and serve as a powerful knowledge transfer tool in this regard.

These features render patterns particularly suitable for capturing and communicating solution knowledge in new or rapidly evolving domains [2]. BIM is one such domain, which is currently evolving based on advances in digitalisation, data management, and measurement technologies. Isikdag and Underwood presented two design patterns for synchronous collaboration in BIM [19], showing that the pattern approach can be successfully used in this domain.

Since both BIM and reliability displays are relatively novel without the solid literature basis that other more traditionally rooted fields have, patterns seem particularly suitable to capture solution knowledge in these domains. In this paper, we therefore apply a pattern approach to create initial draft patterns for conveying reliability information in BIM applications, based on expert stakeholder requirements. After an overview of the related work in Section 2, we present the requirements gathering approach in Section 3, the resulting patterns in Section 4, and conclude in Section 5.

III. Gathering Requirements for Trustworthy Process Management

Following an iterative pattern approach [2], we first gathered expert stakeholder requirements, which we then prioritized and used as a basis for the design solutions and resulting patterns. To this end, we formulated the following two guiding research questions:

RQ1 Which factors are most indicative of the data reliability in BIM process management?

RQ2 How can these factors be integrated into UI designs to communicate data reliability to the user?

We address RQ1 in Sections III-B and III-C, RQ2 in Section IV.

A. Method

The method consisted of a stepwise process from the state of the art analysis and interviews to requirement derivation and pattern writing.

State of the art analysis: Based on analysis of previous work on trust calibration, we came up with common design approaches for the communication of reliability, uncertainty, awareness and intent, as well as of choice alternatives [11]. Examples from research and practice were collected, whereby the most detailed guidance was available in the area of automated driving, as here reliability displays have already been investigated in experimental research.

Interviews: In order to capture the requirements for BIMR and related trust calibration aspects in depth, we conducted semi-structured individual interviews, which followed a consistent agenda but could then expand on specific further topics brought up by the respondents. After filling in a consent form and providing background information about their job profile and specific expertise, participants were asked some introductory questions on BIMR, its relevant processes, involved software environments and major issues in the field. Then, participants were briefly introduced into the above described investigation topics of trust calibration and process management in BIMR, through showing and commenting a few illustrative slides on the concepts and related example applications and use cases.

Respondents were then asked to comment on the use case as to whether or not it corresponded to their own work situation and to which extent they saw differences. They were then also asked about the types of data they use in their BIMR projects and to draw the timeline of a typical renovation process. The participants were then debriefed and asked about their preparedness to provide feedback to the next stages of pattern generation. Three experts were asked to participate in the interviews: an architect proficient in BIMR for building (I1), a project manager for highway construction projects (I2), and an IT solution provider specialized in BIMR (I3).

Derivation of requirements: The responses were analysed as to their potential for the derivation of requirements for pattern writing. The gathered requirements were then consolidated across the three different interviews and allocated to 9 requirements (or requirement groups).

B. Interview Results

In general, the BIMR use case itself was seen by all three participants as a promising alternative to currently prevailing, less data-intensive renovation approaches. All three respondents confirmed that the integration of BIM is not yet common in standard construction industry processes, as data for most actors in the construction industry appears to be restricted to PDFs with 2D or 2.5D plans (I2). However, in the participants' view the number of customers demanding for more informed modeling, documentation and monitoring is growing. Based on the respondents' experience with BIM renovation so far, a number of benefits were identified, such as the improved communication opportunities between different involved stakeholders through the joint exploration of the same model from different viewpoints (I1-3), the interconnection between the construction and the accounting data with different preferences for their level of integration, (I1-3), clear guidance in construction processes, due to high-precision data (I2), long-term reliable data availability for asset management purposes (I2), and a better overview and verifiability in complex buildings (I2).

While each of the respondents described a 'typical BIMR process' with a different focus, several commonalities could be identified. The first BIMR process step consists in the detailed creation of a model of the initial conditions of the site. This is then used for the planning, cost estimation and offer creation for the different renovation phases of the renovation project. During each actual renovation phase, BIMs are then used to track the process on site, and often the data on used materials is also used for billing. In some cases (I2), the BIM is then provided also for the further asset management.

C. List of requirements

R1: The presentation of reliability displays should follow the degree of abstraction. Therefore, it is necessary to highlight upfront the level of detail of the model.

R2: The system should always highlight the properties and restrictions of the underlying model. To this end, potential uncertainties of the model in representing the reality should be highlighted. Furthermore, the nature of the analysed object with regard to the related expected uncertainty/accuracy should be shown. For instance, a more geometrically complex object could provide more precise insights than a simpler object, in comparison with standard planning tools.

R3: It should be possible to filter system output (both with regard to data protection and to usability).

R4: It should be possible to define who provided an input and the related chosen approach.

R5: There should be a clear indication on who provided an input, estimation or prognosis. In addition, the system should show how this input was provided, with regard to the applied method, the used system, the user role and expertise. For example, for an infrastructure construction manager, providing information on whether data has been collected by a drone each week, as opposed to less systematic data capture by ground personnel. Also, for architects or project managers it is worthwhile to check on whether the person entering the data comes from the same company, or from a company with processes that they are familiar with.

R6: The system should provide cues and detailed information on whether the considered building model or respective estimations have undergone previous reliability checks. For example, if the system shows whether or not certain specific software-based tests (e.g., with Solibri [20]) have been applied on some or all of the available aspects of the model (e.g., jointings of different building parts) and if it is clarified whether manual corrections have been applied to further plausibilize them, this will help the user get an initial understanding which parts of the model can be trusted to what degree. To make this indicator meaningful, it is necessary to also show whether the software output has been surveyed by an expert to disambiguate them and to filter for relevancy in the given context.

R7: In the case that Artificial Intelligence (AI) is involved in the processing of the data, it would be necessary to provide an indication on which underlying data and models a respective estimation or prognosis has been made. In this respect, best practice from the currently evolving field 'Explainable AI' should be considered [21].

R8: The time period of data input as well as its relation to the respective billing period should be displayed. This should encompass ranges of default threshold values beyond which the provided data is deemed unreliable. The underlying assumption is that a closer match of data input with the actual billing period indicates its level of detail and correctness, as with longer delays of data input human error is more likely. Naturally, data to be considered in the context of this requirement is attached to a concrete time specification, such as the date of the made payment and the timestamp of the corresponding project deliverable.

R9: The system should provide cues on which of the renovation project deliverables is subject to a contractual penalty related to quality or time delays. In case of existence of such a penalty, a higher reliability is ascribed to it by project managers.

IV. From Requirements to UI Solutions

All requirements were discussed in an internal workshop with three UI experts. In the workshop, the requirements were prioritized regarding estimated effectiveness and feasibility of integrating with existing UIs. For the three highest priority requirements (R5, R8, and R9), solutions were then generated and brought into a minimal pattern draft format, including name, short description, problem, solution, and examples. These patterns are described in the following:

A. Draft Pattern 1: Expertise-Based User Roles

This pattern describes a solution to assign levels of expertise to user roles and communicate reliability of input data based on the combination of role and expertise level that entered it.

1) Problem: In the building construction context, there is often a large number of stakeholders who all contribute to one single project. This means that the data that feeds the process management system comes from a variety of sources and not all of them can be assumed to be equally reliable. In particular, the reliability of the data will depend on whether

1) the individual who entered or supplied the data held the appropriate role to do so, and
2) their level of expertise was sufficient to reduce the possibility of oversights/errors to a standard minimum.

In addition, the reliability is also influenced by whether the data was imported directly from another system or whether it was entered by a human individual. All of this information is typically not provided by the system when working with or viewing individual data or data sets. Thus, the judgement regarding data reliability depends entirely on the user's own experience and familiarity with the context, including any individuals that might have provided data with in the system. This is suboptimal in general and becomes more severe the larger the project in question is.

2) Solution: The rights management needs to provide an account system that allows to assign different user roles and levels of expertise within each role. The accounts are then coded (e.g., via colors and/or acronyms) to allow quick information regarding:

1) Type (human or other system)
2) Role
3) Level of expertise

Item 1 can be handled indirectly by assigning no user account, role, or expertise information to anything that was automatically generated or imported from a different system. This means that in the eventual output, the user can quickly see where the data came from via the presence or absence of any user account indicators.

Item 2 is addressed by simply defining the appropriate number of roles within the context. These need to be set specific to the individual context and type of the project. Examples for such roles within the construction context are project manager, site manager, foreman, (shift) supervisor, etc.

Item 3 is addressed by further defining levels of expertise for each role. This pattern proposes a simple 3-level-system based on two metrics. This allows a comparably easy definition of levels by defining one threshold for each metric, then assigning the level of expertise based on whether both, one, or none of the thresholds are exceeded.

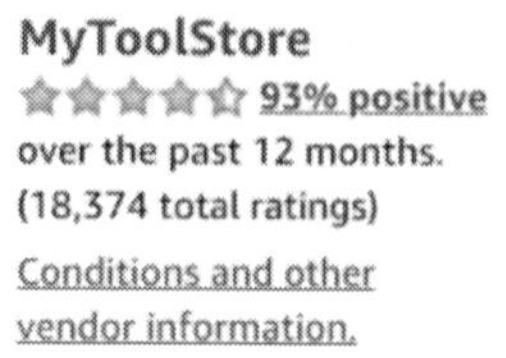

Figure 1. Example for seller reputation information from *Amazon*.

For example, within a project, there can and probably will be a role "project manager". For this role, the metrics could be defined as years of experience in the field (*M1*) and average size of previously managed projects ((*M2*). For both metrics, an expertise threshold is defined (e.g., 6 years for *M1*, EUR 300.000 for *M2*. If the threshold is exceeded, high expertise is assumed. Assuming a three-level-system with *L1* being the lowest and *L3* being the highest level of expertise, the user will be assigned *L1* if no threshold is exceeded, *L2* if the threshold in *M1* or *M2* is exceeded (but not the other, and *L3* if both thresholds are exceeded

Figure 3 provides an illustrative overview of such an account hierarchy and a suggestion for highlighting roles and levels via color coding in the eventual output. Note that Roles can also be entirely denoted via acronyms (e.g., 'PM' for 'project manager', 'SV' for 'supervisor', etc.) with one single color in different levels of brightness/saturation to donate the levels. This can be used to avoid color overload when working with a large volume of users and user roles.

3) Examples: This solution is strongly related to the following UI solutions, which address a similar problem space:

Seller-trustworthiness indicators on e-commerce sites. E-commerce sites that support re-selling on their platform (e.g., *Amazon*, cf. Figure 1) have the need to show indicators for the level of trustworthiness of the different individual sellers. Typical solutions here are to provide ratings by past customers, rank the sellers based on these ratings, and to provide historic and meta information (sales history, number of complaints, etc.)

Reputation indicators on expert-forums. In a similar manner, expert help forums, such as e.g., on *stack overflow* (cf. Figure 2) have the need to indicate the level of expertise of an individual user in order to provide context for the interpretation of the answer to a question. *Stack overflow* for example uses an elaborated reputation system based on scores, tags, and badges.

Skill endorsements on business networks (e.g., *LinkedIn*) or knowledge management systems. Also related is the possibility to endorse other users in a network for a specific skill, thereby providing valuable background information and social proof.

B. Draft Pattern 2: Reliability through Recency

This pattern describes a solution to communicate reliability through highlighting the temporal discrepancy between when data was first collected versus when it was entered into the system.

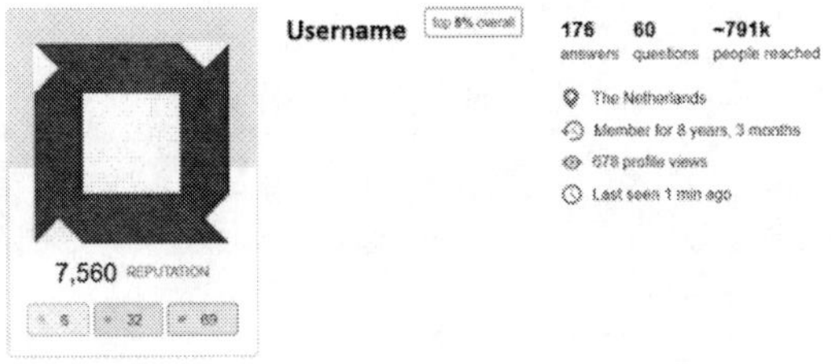

Figure 2. Example for expert reputation information from *stack overflow*.

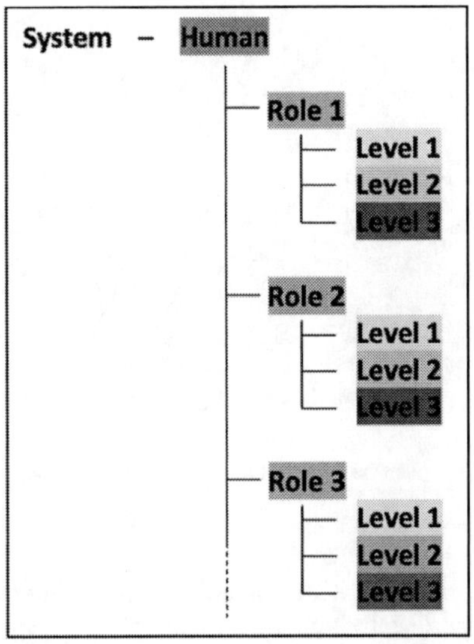

Figure 3. Overview of account hierarchy. User roles are further divided into three levels of expertise. Color coding allows distinction at a glance.

1) Problem: The more distant events are, the more difficult they are to retrace for any individual who was involved with them. As a result, written accounts, receipts, etc. become more important information carriers the more time has passed. Conversely, if the information available via documentation is incomplete, inaccurate, or otherwise insufficient, it becomes more difficult to correct such deficiencies, as additional documentation – if it had been available in the first place – might have been lost, archived, or otherwise hard to access. In addition, individuals who were involved in whichever activity that supplied the relevant data might no longer remember specifics that could have helped to detect or correct inaccuracies or supply missing information. Thus, it becomes necessary to distinguish data that was entered in time from data that was entered delayed, which is usually not supported by default.

2) Solution: The solution consists capturing and visualizing the temporal distance between data collection/availability and entry into the System. Upon entry, each data item is flagged with the date on which it was entered. In addition, each item requires an additional field in which the date of initial data collection or availability is entered. What is to be entered here depends on the documentation and data item but examples here are: billing date for invoices, market date for price estimates (e.g., price per barrel of raw oil at [day]), or the signature date for protocols.

Based on the hypothesis, that the closer these dates match, the more reliable the data is, reliability thresholds can be defined. This solution proposes a simple three-level system, which then corresponds to standard color coding via the traffic light metaphor (red-yellow-green). Level **red** denotes data that was entered late, level **green** denotes data that was entered in time. Level **yellow** can be used to flag entries that were not entered immediately but also without significant delay – e.g, everything that is entered within one week is flagged green, within two weeks yellow, and everything beyond two weeks in red.

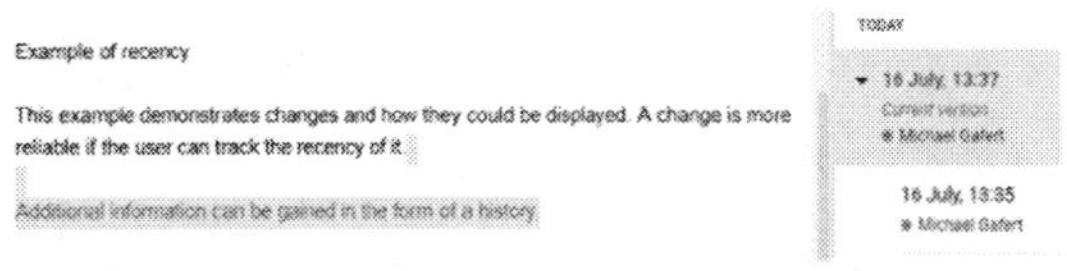

Figure 4. *Google Docs*'s version history. Each user has a unique color and changes are categorised by timestamps.

This way, delayed entries can be spotted at a glance and the reliability (or lack thereof) of individual items can be spotted at a glance. The delay-level of each entry can be easily visualized by simply showing the date fields and highlighting them in the appropriate color. In order to avoid visual overload, green level entries can be left unhighlighted with only level yellow and red ones being highlighted, as these are the more critical ones. In addition to the color coding, a numerical indicator of elapsed time (e.g., "xx days past") can be added.

As a direct consequence of requiring two dates for each item, this solution is only applicable to data items that can be associated with *documented* dates that are not identical with the entry dates by default.

3) Examples: Many text editing tools offer some kind of version history or version control to provide a sense of recency. *Google Docs*, for example, offers a simple version control depicted in Figure 4. Each continuously written text is tagged with a timestamp and the user who edited it.

A more advanced version control is offered by *GIT* [22]. Only specific users can change files and each change must be described in form of a commit message. Once a change is committed it will be added to the history. *GitHub*, a website implementing *GIT*, offers the ability to view these commits and their corresponding changes. Each change is marked (addition: green, deletion: red) in the corresponding file (see Figure 5).

WebStorm, an IDE (Integrated Development Environment) for developing *JavaScript* applications [23], also has the ability to display *GIT* commit messages. Instead of focusing on commits and their changes, it focuses on the files itself. Figure 6 shows that each line of code has an annotation with linked name and date. These values are extracted from the history and displayed alongside the file. Each user and timestamp have a different associated color and can therefor be differentiated.

C. Pattern Draft 3: Reliability through Penalties

This pattern describes a solution to convey reliability by associating data entries with information regarding whether the entry is tied to a monetary penalty or not.

1) Problem: Especially in larger projects, the level of care taken when reporting and resulting level of detail in reported

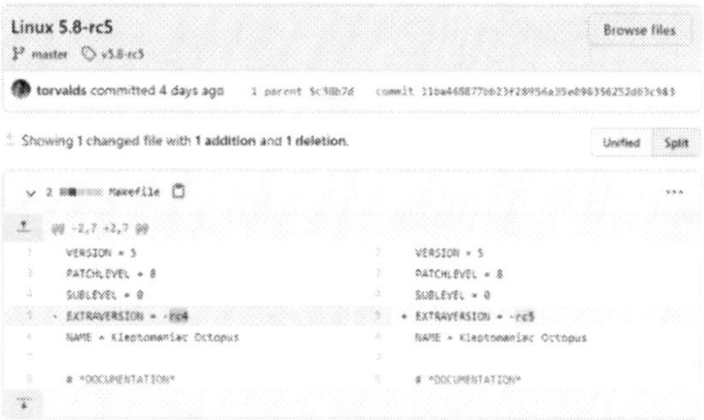

Figure 5. *GitHub's* commit overview with one addition marked green and a corresponding commit message. Excerpt from the Linux Kernel GitHub Page.

Figure 6. *WebStorm's* annotations display which user changed what line of code and marks it with a timestamp.

data can vary greatly between different stakeholder organizations as well as individuals within these organizations. This can be a result of different levels of interest and involvement between stakeholders in the project but also different degrees of repercussions in case results are not delivered at all or not in a timely (or otherwise satisfactory) manner. Depending on the level of interest/involvement and how close an individual's or organization's goal match the goals of the overall project, the more reliable can their input assumed to be. Such information, however, usually relies on personal knowledge and experience and is usually not captured within process or other management systems.

2) Solution: Contractually stipulated monetary penalties can be clearly traced and captured within a system. Whenever a data item or data set is associated with such a penalty, a visual indicator is added to show this (e.g., fulfilment of delivery is associated with a penalty in case of delays; data item date of delivery then shows a penalty indicator). Such an indicator can be a simple icon or text-based indicator and can operate in a binary fashion: if the indicator is present, then a penalty is attached to the data; otherwise, there is not. Since the presence of penalties can be a reliability indicator not only for individual data items or sets but also indicative of reliability within the entire project, including such indicators in hierarchical tree views is recommended. A top-level indicator shows whether there are any penalties in the project at all. Clicking on the top-level indicator expands all trees to the elements that are associated with penalties and highlights them. This provides both a high-level and lower-level reliability indicators as well as quick and efficient access to the latter.

3) Examples: Such hierarchical tree views are common in applications which have some kind of folder management. The text editor *Atom* [24] can forward tagged files in sub-directories up to the root node of the folder structure. The top-level in Figure 7 shows a root node called "top". It is marked orange because of a tag in a sub-directory. In this example the file is

Figure 7. Screenshot of the *Atom* text editor with *GIT* integration. The top item of the tree view (left) is colored orange as items inside the tree have uncommitted changes. All changed items are also visible as a list on the right.

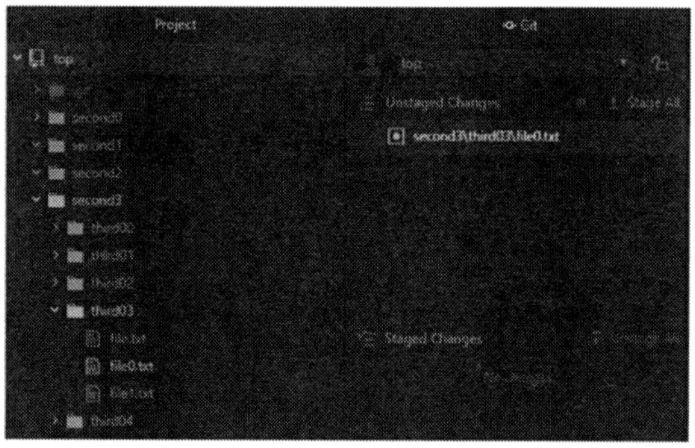

Figure 8. *Atom* text editor with open tree view. The orange marked items can be followed along to the changed item.

tagged because it was changed. The root cause of the tag can however be different as a later example will show. The tagged object can also be viewed as a list (see right side of Figure 7). If the top node is opened the full tree view is shown, which is depicted in Figure 8. The tag of one file is passed along each directory until it reaches the root node which in turn can then be used as a top-level indicator of all objects below.

V. Discussion, Conclusion, and Future Work

We were able to address RQ1 with the requirements identified in Section III-C, and begin to address RQ2 with the draft patterns in Section IV. We found reliability-relevant information in the BIM context to encompass a wide range of aspects, of which we could highlight three with varying degrees of context-specificity. While hierarchical rights management with different user roles has a wide application, the same cannot be said about penalty indicators. While the former can be re-applied in any context, where expertise levels can be defined (and are assumed to be reliability-relevant), the latter can only be used when penalties are part of the project *and* are captured in the system. Recency indicators can be expected to be used in a larger number of contexts, as timely fulfillment is usually a factor in most projects or undertakings. However, that factor can only be applied to data items to which dates can be assigned (invoices, protocols, etc.), which might cover only a fraction of the data a user is interacting with through a management system.

One additional question that is relevant for how to design reliability indicators, is how or if reliability-relevant data should be highlighted or hidden. It would seem obvious that relevant information should be highlighted, this might not necessarily be the default for reliability indicators. Taking the penalty-indicators as an example, these indicators would highlight any item that has a penalty attached to it. However, as we learned from the experts, the presence of a penalty reduces the likelihood of that data being incorrect and increases reliability as a result. If the user is looking for potential errors, then he/she would need to look at the exact opposite, viz. data without attached penalties. Depending on how many penalties are present, switching the behaviour to highlighting all data without penalties by default, might not be a good solution either. If most data items are without penalty, then such a solution would quickly cause visual overload and be ineffective as a result. In the end, it will be difficult to impossible do define a default that works for all contexts and the behaviour will need to be toggleable on the user's end.

In general, a higher level of detail and more solutions are required to solidify the basis for reliability displays in process management and for the BIM context. In future work, we intend to generate full patterns from the drafts laid out in this paper and extend the quantity of patterns to cover additional expert requirements. In particular, the expertise-influencing factors for defining the user roles need to be identified more clearly, data types and how recency can be established needs to be clarified, and we want to further look into penalties and whether a more precise metric (one that includes the penalty amount) is required.

In this paper, we presented an approach towards designing reliability indicators for process management in the BIM context. We generated three draft design patterns, which serve as a basis for continued efforts to introduce reliability indicators into interfaces, where information reliability is paramount. By using a pattern approach, the pool of available knowledge can be continually extended as new working solutions are developed and discovered. Thus, we also want to encourage the community to contribute to the growing field of reliability displays not just within BIM but across application areas and contexts as well.

ACKNOWLEDGMENT

The financial support by the Austrian Research Promotion Agency (FFG) under grant number 878796 (Project: CALIBRaiTE) is gratefully acknowledged. The authors thank Christian Bechinie for his support in preparing this publication.

REFERENCES

[1] B. E. Holthausen and B. N. Walker, "Trust calibration through reliability displays in automated vehicles," in Proceedings of the Companion of the 2017 ACM/IEEE International Conference on Human-Robot Interaction, ser. HRI '17. New York, NY, USA: Association for Computing Machinery, 2017, p. 361–362. [Online]. Available: https://doi.org/10.1145/3029798.3034802

[2] A. Mirnig et al., "Automotive user experience design patterns: An approach and pattern examples," International Journal On Advances in Intelligent Systems, vol. 9, 2016, pp. 275–286.

[3] "EU BIM Task Group," 2020, URL: http://www.eubim.eu/ [retrieved: July 2020].

[4] R. Berger, "Digitization in the construction industry," Roland Berger GmbH, Competence Center Civil Economics, 2016.

[5] B. B. P. I. Europe, "Renovation in practice: Best practice examples of voluntary and mandatory initiatives across europe," Tech. Rep., 2015.

[6] R. Woitsch et al., "Adaptive renovation process and workflow models 1. deliverable d6.2 of the eu h2020 project bimerr," Tech. Rep., 2020.

[7] A. Ghaffarianhoseini et al., "Building information modelling (bim) uptake: Clear benefits, understanding its implementation, risks and challenges," Renewable and Sustainable Energy Reviews, vol. 75, 2017, pp. 1046 – 1053. [Online]. Available: http://www.sciencedirect.com/science/article/pii/S1364032116308413

[8] F. Ekman, M. Johansson, and J. Sochor, "Creating appropriate trust for autonomous vehicle systems: A framework for hmi design," Tech. Rep., 2016.

[9] A. G. Mirnig, P. Wintersberger, C. Sutter, and J. Ziegler, "A framework for analyzing and calibrating trust in automated vehicles," 2016, p. 33–38.

[10] E. J. de Visser, M. Cohen, A. Freedy, and R. Parasuraman, "A design methodology for trust cue calibration in cognitive agents," in International conference on virtual, augmented and mixed reality. Springer, 2014, pp. 251–262.

[11] J. Schrammel et al., " Investigating Communication Techniques to Support Trust Calibration for Automated Systems ," in Proceedings of the 4th Workshop proceedings Automation Experience across Domains In conjunction with CHI'20, Honolulu, HI, USA. Website: http://everyday-automation.tech-experience.at, 2020. [Online]. Available: http://everyday-automation.tech-experience.at

[12] B. E. Holthausen, T. M. Gable, S.-Y. Chen, S. Singh, and B. N. Walker, "Development and preliminary evaluation of reliability displays for automated lane keeping," in Proceedings of the 9th International Conference on Automotive User Interfaces and Interactive Vehicular Applications, 2017, pp. 202–208.

[13] A. G. Mirnig et al., "User experience patterns from scientific and industry knowledge: An inclusive pattern approach," International Journal On Advances in Life Sciences, vol. 7, no. 3 and 4, 2015, pp. 200–215. [Online]. Available: https://www.thinkmind.org/index.php?view=article&articleid=patterns_2015_2_30_70011

[14] C. Alexander, The Timeless Way of Building. New York, USA: Oxford University Press, 1979.

[15] C. Alexander, S. Ishikawa, and M. Silverstein, A Pattern Language: Towns, Buildings, Construction. New York, USA: Oxford University Press, 1997.

[16] E. Gamma, R. Helm, R. Johnson, and J. Vlissides, Design Patterns: Elements of Reusable Object-Oriented Software. Pearson, 1994.

[17] J. O. Borchers, "A pattern approach to interaction design," AI & SOCIETY, vol. 15, no. 4, 2001, pp. 359–376.

[18] J. Vlissides, Pattern Hatching: Design Patterns Applied. Addison-Wesley, 1998.

[19] U. Isikdag and J. Underwood, "Two design patterns for facilitating building information model-based synchronous collaboration," Automation in Construction, vol. 19, no. 5, 2010, pp. 544 – 553, building Information Modeling and Collaborative Working Environments. [Online]. Available: http://www.sciencedirect.com/science/article/pii/S0926580509001769

[20] "SOLIBRI," 2020, URL: https://www.solibri.com/de/ [retrieved: July 2020].

[21] Q. Wang, Y. Ming, Z. Jin, Q. Shen, D. Liu, M. Smith, K. Veeramachaneni, and H. Qu, "Atmseer: Increasing transparency and controllability in automated machine learning," 02 2019.

[22] "GIT," 2020, URL: https://git-scm.com/ [retrieved: July 2020].

[23] "WebStorm," 2020, URL: https://www.jetbrains.com/webstorm/ [retrieved: July 2020].

[24] "Atom," 2020, URL: https://atom.io/ [retrieved: July 2020].